How Did Sex Begin?

How Did Sex Begin?

THE SENSE AND NONSENSE OF THE CUSTOMS AND TRADITIONS

THAT HAVE SEPARATED MEN AND WOMEN

SINCE ADAM AND EVE

BY

R. Brasch

DAVID McKAY COMPANY, INC. NEW YORK

To my
WIFE

my "resident editor-in-chief"
who constantly aids and abets me and who
in this—as in all my books—
has actively shared with me in every phase
of its preparation.

SECOND PRINTING, APRIL 1973

HOW DID SEX BEGIN?

LIBRARY OF CONGRESS CATALOG CARD NUMBER: 72–92655
MANUFACTURED IN THE UNITED STATES OF AMERICA
Designed by Jacques Chazaud

Foreword

I t all started as a joke—which I took seriously.

First intrigued and then enthralled by origins (of every type), my wife and I had given birth to *How Did It Begin?* and *How Did Sports Begin?*

And these two children of ours were well and truly launched and traveling the world. From their original Australian home, they had spread to the American continent, the United Kingdom, Japan and Germany—to mention just a few of their new domiciles.

We were now wondering what next in *How*'s we should explore and were considering various spheres, when a letter suddenly arrived from my American publisher. Why not make your next book, he asked, a research-in-depth of that ever-new, all-important, never-flagging-in-interest universal subject—SEX— and tell us HOW SEX BEGAN?

And like a flash we fell in love with SEX at first sight (of the New York letter). By return air mail we accepted the proposal.

All that remained for us to do was settle the day that "it" should see the light of the (publishing) world, which, naturally, would depend on the period that would elapse between the remote-controlled conception of the book and its safe delivery— on the publisher's desk.

Our enthusiastic acceptance of the fertile thought was acknowledged by a further note from New York in which our publisher confessed that what he had written in his first letter about my tackling Sex, really had been meant merely in good fun!

Meanwhile, however, my wife and I had started our research, and the discoveries we were making were remarkable. What a book *How Did Sex Begin?* would make! And that in brief (and in truth) is the story of how *How Did Sex Begin?* actually began.

Of course, there was one stumbling block and a note of hesitancy in our minds. How could I, a man of the cloth, as it were, remove all covers from a subject that others still regarded as being taboo, in spite of all we say, read, view and do in our permissive age?

However, in effect, religion and sex have never been divorced. They have not only co-existed but lived together from Genesis—the very beginning. Does not Holy Scripture itself praise God as the supreme creator who enriched man with the precious gift of sex?

The Bible abounds in sex. Almost everything appertaining to it is told and dealt with frankly, openly and without shame. Later generations, however, to whom sex had become something unclean, felt compelled, if not to excise the passages they regarded as "sinful," at least to camouflage them. They did so either by using euphemisms, or by purposely rendering the term or passage in so innocuous or obscure a way that the unsuspecting reader would never guess the original meaning, or at any rate would be greatly puzzled by the text. Only the expert scholar is able to dis-cover the original revealing parts.

Thus, throughout this book, whether speaking of virginity, abortion, deviations or prostitution, again and again we shall have to quote the Bible as a most comprehensive sex "manual"—containing many an indication of "how sex began."

Truth has been called "the seal of God." And all I want to relate to the questing mind are the real facts of how sex began. This includes the scores of functions, fictions, aspirations and accessories that have always belonged to or were adopted as rightful (or illegitimate) heirs of sex—in its "protoplasmic hunger" and "nostalgia for lost continuity."

R.B.

Contents

Foreword   v

1. HOW DID SEX BEGIN?   1
   *A Bone of Contention · A Greek Myth · A Question of Sur-
   vival · A Duty That Became a Pleasure · The Magic of
   Intercourse*

2. COURTING   7
   *The Kiss · The Magic of Kissing · Kissing under the Mistle-
   toe · The Religious Kiss · X—The Kiss Symbol · Necking
   · Bundling—A Test of Strength · The Paradox of Virginity · The Hymen—Before and After · The Dangers of Virginity · The Ideal of Chastity · The Chastity Belt · The
   Virgin Birth · The Immaculate Conception · Columbus and
   the Eleven Thousand Virgins*

3. SUPERSTITIONS IN SEX   28
   *"Touching" for Luck · The Spilling of Salt · Bees and a
   Virgin · Selecting the "Right Day" · The Separation Taboo
   of Bride and Groom · The Origin of the Buttonhole · The
   Red Carpet · Kissing the Bride · The Noise Factor at Wed-
   dings · Wedding Songs and All That · Threshold Obsessions
   · Devilish Consummation Hazards · Focus on the Baby*

4. CLOTHING SEX   37

*The Fig Leaf and (False) Modesty · The Grass Roots of
Shame · From "Topless" to Bust Confiners—and Back ·
How the Chinese Invented the Bra · The Revealing Sex Glove
· The Disappearance of the Nightshirt · Sex Deception—
Transvestism · Top-Dressing—Hair in Sex*

5. PUBERTY   53

*The First Change of Life—and Puberty Rites · Only for Girls
· Female Circumcision · A Bloody Curse or "Her Relations
Have Come" · How Woman Became the Inferior Sex · Mas-
turbation*

6. MARRIAGE CUSTOMS   69

*Marriage Is a Private Affair · The Importance of Sex in
Marriage · The Right of the First Night · Tobias Nights ·
Sex Food and the Magic Mandrake · Love Fixation*

7. THE CHILD   80

*The Birth of the Midwife and the Obstetrician · The Cesar-
ean · Navel   Affairs · Abortion · Contraception · The
Story of the Condom · The Battle for Birth Control*

8. FAMILY RELATIONS   102

*Polygamy · Polygyny · Auxiliary Wives · The Harem ·
Multiple Mates Among Mormons · Polyandry · The Green-
Eyed Monster · Mother-in-Law Aversion · Divorce*

9. ILLICIT RELATIONS   122

*Rape · Adultery · Adultery Tests · The Adulterous Birth
of the Lapdog · Sexual Hospitality and Wife-Swapping*

10. THE MALE ORGAN   134

*Phallic Worship · The Magic Penis · Circumcision · The
Fate of the Foreskin · Semen · Swearing by the Genitals ·
Castration*

11. PROSTITUTION   158

*Sacred Prostitution · Sex for Sale—How to Call a Prostitute
· Trade Methods—Ancient and Modern · The Red-Light
District · The Brothel · VD · Gonorrhea · Syphilis*

12. TALKING SEX   178
*All About Intercourse · The Sex Organs · Four-Letter
Words—Sacred and Profane · The Uterus in Hysteria ·
The Testicles in the Orchid · Full of Beans · A Sexual Per-
version of Architecture · The Compleat Bugger · The Bas-
tard · The Genesis of Gender*

13. THE OBSCENE   190
The Writing on the Wall · Pornography and the Obscene

14. OUT OF THE ORDINARY   202
*From Sodomy to Homosexuality · The Legacy of an Island—
Lesbianism · Sadism—the Pleasure of Cruelty · The Lust
for Pain—Masochism · Voyeurism—a Spectator Sport ·
Incest · Indecent Exposure*

15. THE END OF SEX   234
Celibacy

Index   239

1.

How Did Sex Begin?

S tarting with its most literal aspect—etymologically—sex is pure Latin. Sex is a clean "cut"—originally. It (that is to say, the word) goes back to the Latin *secare* and is a "division"—of man into two complementary parts: the male and the female. And all that was to follow is derived from this first operation by God, nature and semantics.

Myths show that all religions and cultures have understandably wondered how this first division of male and female took place, and numerous stories, legends and doctrines have tried to solve the problem or give the definitive answer. Some are delightful yet most improbable; others quite uncouth yet more realistic.

A Bone of Contention

The Bible relates that God created woman out of one of man's ribs. It has been said that ever since that first surgical operation every man has been looking (if necessary, all over the world) for his "missing rib." Some never find it and, in rationalization for their unsuccessful search, they are the so-called confirmed bachelors. Others get hold of "a rib" but, as it is really not theirs, it does not fit properly and causes only hurt and agony. Complete happiness belongs to that man who luckily finds "his" rib!

Even this myth recognizes man's constant yearning for a partner of the opposite sex. Without her, he would be incomplete

—an anatomical and psychological cripple as it were. Only by rejoining man and woman will they become the original "one flesh."

The choice of Adam's rib as the skeleton on which to build Eve has given much food for thought. Naturally, those believing in man's supremacy have quoted chapter and verse to justify their claim. But on the other hand, and approaching the story from a feminist viewpoint—almost two thousand years ago—a woman boldly accused God to her rabbi. The Almighty had acted just like a thief, she declared, by stealing one of Adam's ribs while he was asleep! But the rabbi was not lost for an answer and refuted her statement with a simile. "If someone took a silver ornament from you and returned to you in exchange one of gold, would you call this stealing?" he asked.

Preachers have, in fact, repeatedly pointed to the wisdom of the choice. Taken out of man's side, they said, woman would always be at his side—as his helpmate.

However, cynics acquainted with the original Hebrew have suggested that the selection of the rib was influenced by a hidden pun: the Hebrew for rib—*tsela*—sounded very like the Hebrew for "bad luck" and "stumbling"!

Those who consider the stories at the beginning of the Bible as early man's attempt at explaining the facts of life as he saw them with his limited world view, regarded the choice of the rib as an example of his primitive reasoning. Observing the human body, ancient man pondered why ribs surrounded only the upper part of the torso and not its entirety. The most obvious explanation that offered itself was that it was for the sake of the sexual reunion of man and woman.

A Greek Myth

At the beginning, so Plato relates, "man" was created a hermaphrodite, a "he-she," male-female unit.

Its perfection was symbolized by its spherical shape. Man was then endowed with four arms, four legs as well as two faces. But his very power led him to rebel against his creator. Zeus was determined, once and for all, to put man in his place. In punishment, therefore, he cut man into halves so that each part owned only two legs, two arms and one face. That is how man and woman came to exist as separate beings. But, ever since, they passionately longed to be reunited and, once again, thereby to become complete.

A Question of Survival

The prime purpose of sex is survival. Life would be senseless without (re)production. The sex urge leading to copulation meant population. That is how sex began.

This earth, however small in comparison with other planets, is man's habitat. But it could remain so only if the number of his births at the very least equaled that of his deaths. That, too, is the meaning of sex.

In fact, the story of reproduction is the story of life itself. Without sex it just could not last and the earth would become a dying planet. Two instincts have remained with man without which he could not exist: one is hunger and the other is—sex. From the very beginning, they have been part of his life—for his life's sake.

Greatly simplified, this is the story of how sex began. It all started with the single-celled body. In the earliest fission, this divided and out of one came two. The process could have gone on endlessly. But then each new individual would have been not really new but merely an exact copy of the other. All it would have meant was an ever-greater number of identical cells. And this would never have done. Multiplication of sameness is not enough.

What the world needed was a wealth of change and the richness of variety. Thus genes were not only mixed up but, in mixing, found new partners, and by their unique combination introduced ever more novel features in what was to lead—in far distant days—to the evolution of man.

At the very moment when two cells came together, sex had entered the universe. This fusion (even if only temporary) created a completely new form of life. It was the first link in that long chain of growth from the unicellular body to the separate existence of the sperm and the egg, produced and carried by the strictly divided male and female who were both possessed by the overriding endeavor to "mate."

Sex was needed to ensure an ever-greater variation in the building up of the universe, presenting it with "offsprings" of every type.

The role of the male was often a pitiable one. Once he had done his (sexual) duty and fertilized the ovum, he had outlived his usefulness. Either he simply died or he was devoured by his female partner.

A Duty That Became a Pleasure

Sex, fundamentally, thus ensured the perpetuation of life—for man "to multiply and be fruitful." But, somehow, God (or nature) had to sugar the pill (a rather dangerous metaphor now and subject to misunderstanding) to make certain that the species continued. Therefore pleasure was added to the fulfillment of a strict command which, not accidentally, was the very first in the Bible (Gen. 1:28). That is why the sexual act, physically and psychologically, became the most rewarding and exciting performance of a duty. It roused man to the veritable climax of out-of-this-world worldliness.

Primitive man had very little to break his monotonous existence, to ease his hard battle for life, to give him relaxation and, for a short while at least, to take his mind off the fears and dreads that haunted him. Most of all, he needed some outlet for his tensions.

Therefore sex began also as man's earliest form of "built-in" entertainment. All in one, it played the part of our rich complex of amusement. It combined our commercialized world of art, drink, gambling, sport and rousing novels. Not just to conceive children but to enjoy and lessen the strain of life, was yet another, though supplementary, purpose of sex at the very beginning.

Sex, there is no doubt, is at the root of all fascination. But this statement is not meant in the way it might be (mis)understood. It is used in its most basic and literal sense. Few people, indeed, realize that the very word "fascination" is derived from the Latin *fascinum,* which described the male organ! Fascination, in fact, originally pointed to the enchantment of witchcraft and sorcery. Mothers used to hang the replica of the penis (the *fascinum*) round their children's neck to ward off the evil eye!

And, certainly, fascinating is the exploration of the origin of customs, taboos and phrases of sex. To know them and gain an insight into HOW SEX BEGAN—with all its manifestations and ramifications—can make life all the richer and give much food for thought. But simultaneously, it is hoped, such information can act as a forceful antidote, too, to unfounded fears, outlived prejudices and noxious bigotry.

The Magic of Intercourse

At first, of course (and still among some primitive tribes), no one guessed that there was a definite chain between coitus and pregnancy.

The oddest beliefs, in fact, existed as to what caused a child to be conceived. Credit was given to diverse factors and agencies. Some said that the rays of the sun fathered a child. After all, people knew that the warmth of the sun made things grow. Others assumed that the moon, personified as a male, impregnated the woman.

The intervention of a spirit (good or evil) or a specific food eaten by the mother were additional explanations of the cause of pregnancy. The story is told of an Australian aborigine who was convinced that the pale color of his wife's child was due to her having visited the white man's settlement and eaten white bread.

The Trobriand islanders came nearest the truth in their view that pregnancy was due to the rupture of the hymen. However, they went awry when they further claimed that this could be done by any available means. They believed that having opened up the vagina, a spirit could enter the womb to create a child.

Intercourse in itself was regarded as an experience of rapture, simply there for its intense pleasure, as it were, linking heaven and earth. But eventually, through observation (of both beast and woman), it was realized that coitus apart from its joys was fraught with meaning for the future, the birth of a new being.

To the savage mind the act itself was highly potent and effective far beyond man's "home." Practiced at the right place and time, it would not only beget children but help in the course of nature. That is how intercourse was given magic qualities.

Men and women "bedded" down in the fields at the time of sowing. Their sleeping together there and then, so they firmly believed, by sympathetic magic would also fructify the soil and bring forth a bumper harvest, not of children alone, but of grain. In some cases, it is known, special care was given to synchronize almost with split-second precision the orgasm with the very moment that the seeds were placed into the ground.

2.

Courting

The Kiss

The mystery of the kiss is its very paradox. To the Western mind so fundamentally erotic, expressive of affection and "natural," other races have never known it. A Japanese mother will fondle her child but never kiss it. Nevertheless, kissing—of one kind or another—has its prominent place even in nature.

The origin of the kiss has been explored from almost every angle, and views still differ as to how it all started.

Fish kiss—mouth to mouth. Some races kiss—by rubbing noses. No matter what the technique, every kiss, though in varied proportions, involves several senses. In the majority of cases they are touch, smell and taste. And this fact leads straight back to some of the very roots of kissing.

First of all, there is the sense of touch. We must feel the object of our affection. That is why a cat rubs itself against people to whom it has taken a fancy. Insects make contact with their antennae and birds with their bills or beaks: all just to tell how much they love each other. This tactile pleasure may well go back to the conjugation of the earliest unicellular organisms. These linked their mouths—temporarily—to exchange their hereditary nuclei. Then, enriched, they separated again. Possibly, kissing is a vestige of this initial sexual union and its sublimation.

From very early days onward, smell has also played a role in kissing, at times significantly so.

It has been suggested that when blind Isaac asked Jacob to kiss him, before bestowing his divine blessing actually meant for Esau, his secret intention was to smell him, to make quite sure who he really was. Only Jacob's deception by having donned Esau's clothes made Isaac proceed: "And he smelled the smell of his garments" (Gen. 27:27).

Eskimos and Maoris still "rub noses." A number of primitive races, completely unfamiliar with the mouth kiss, "rub noses" instead. But in their case this is an inaccurate description. What they actually do is to place the mouth and nose against the cheek of the other person and inhale! In some of their languages, tellingly, the very word for kissing really means "smelling," and Borneans do not "greet" but "smell" a visitor.

A beautiful fable tries to explain what it was that gave the sense of smell such importance in loving. A mother sheep had lost one of her baby lambs. Greatly distressed, she started searching for it. She went about sniffing everywhere. Then, at long last, she recognized her missing lamb by its special odor. From that moment onward, to smell each other gave extra satisfaction and a feeling of happiness. A dog still sniffs its master.

No doubt scent has its sexual appeal and is erotically exciting. This, of course, accounts for the creation of a whole industry of perfume.

"I could eat you" is a well-known phrase in ardent lovers' vocabulary, though, naturally, not meant literally. And yet, it is a fact that in nature many a lover has been devoured by his female partner, once he has done all he was meant to do: to beget an offspring. Among certain spiders, for instance, the female will eat the male the moment they have mated.

Though no humans, not even cannibals, have ever gone quite that far, nevertheless they relished getting some taste of each other. Herbert Spencer, indeed, believed that the kiss evolved chiefly from "the instinct tied to the sense of taste." Dogs still love to lick their master or each other. Cows lick their calves. They do so not to wash them, but to show affection.

Kissing with the lips produces also, however softly, some (explosive) sound, of which it has been said that though it was not as loud as that of a cannon, its echo might last a great deal longer.

Of all parts of the body, the mouth alone can taste and feel at the same time. Its proximity to the nose and the labial contact serve equally well the senses of smell and sound. Above all, the combination of mucous membranes and a complex network of nerves have rendered the lips supremely sensitive. With such focus of love, the mouth was bound to become one of man's prominent erogenous zones that could easily activate the very fires of passion.

That kissing is really an atavism is a widespread conviction. Subconsciously it recalls in the grown-up man and woman, so psychoanalysts claim, the earliest days of their babyhood when they were suckled at their mother's breast. And thus, in man's fervent passion survived memories of infantile drinking habits and their supreme bliss. In his *Mémoires* Casanova tells how, when, with voluptuous pleasure, he sucked one of his lover's breasts, he admitted to her how delightful it was "to play the part of the infant." (Psychoanalysts similarly explain that man's enjoyment of smoking is due not merely to the inhalation of tobacco but the pleasure of sucking—the cigarette, cigar or pipe.)

Another theory of the birth of kissing also links it with early nourishment, though detached from the nipples. Just as in nature, among birds for instance, the mother premasticates the food in her mouth then to transfer it by means of a kiss into the mouth of her little one, so did humans in the remote past. And it is the ancestral memory of that early stage that made kissing so wonderful.

Cesare Lombroso, who was not only a great Italian criminologist but one-time professor of psychiatry, held a similar view. He based it on observations made in Tierra del Fuego, at the southern tip of Latin America. Primitive tribes there did not know drinking vessels, not even the traditional gourd. But man cannot live without drink. Therefore they did the next best thing they could think of: either, like an animal, they lapped up the water from its source, or they sucked it through straws. But as young children were unable to do so by themselves, their mothers did it for them and then, with a kiss, transferred the precious liquid from mouth to mouth. That is how, according to Lombroso, modern man adapted a life-preserving technique to become the initial stage of quenching a different thirst, whose ultimate aim was life-producing.

Another early belief, if not accounting for the mouth kiss, well added to its importance. The dead do not breathe. No wonder, therefore, that breath was identified with the life force, man's spirit or soul. It was so easy to escape through that largest of man's orifices—his mouth. This is why yawning was regarded so dangerous and children were taught to cover the gaping mouth with their hand. It was to keep in their soul and thereby stay alive.

People used to kiss the mouth of the dying. They did so not out of affection but to catch the departing spirit and preserve it for the generations to come. Thus, in Virgil's *Aeneid,* Anna addresses her sister Dido when, after her suicide, her body had been placed on the funeral pyre:

> If the last breath yet lingers on thy lips,
> Suffer me with my mouth to gather it.

Hence, lovers felt that to kiss one another—mouth to mouth— would commingle their spirits:

> And when my lips meet thine,
> Thy very soul is wedded unto mine.

Dr. Henry Gibbons scientifically defined a kiss as "the anatomical juxtaposition of two orbicularis oris muscles in a state of contraction." Simply put, even from its very beginning and whatever its origin, the kiss served both to express and to excite love.

The Magic of Kissing

The magic of kissing has played its part in various spheres of life.

Fairy tales keep alive the ancient belief that the kiss could undo spells and remove taboos. It is the recurring motif of the prince who, with his liberating kiss, awakens the sleeping princess.

Little children are still taught the magic of kissing—and not just in those fairy tales. When injured, they are told to "kiss the place and make it well." This custom, too, is a relic of the ancient magic. However, a modern rationalization offered a different explanation. The original kiss, it claimed, was not really a kiss at all but a person sucking out poison from a wound.

Kissing under the Mistletoe

Kissing under the mistletoe is a vestige of former sex orgies which took place during the festival of the Saturnalia, held at what is now Christmastime. At that period, the winter solstice in the northern hemisphere, sexual license was thought—by sympathetic magic—to ensure the rebirth of nature, further promoted by the presence of the mistletoe.

Divine power was attributed to the mistletoe and ancient myths record its many sacred associations. Jupiter was said, on his descent to earth, to have made his home in a mistletoe bush. The god Baldur, though invulnerable in every other way, was slain by an arrow of mistletoe. Whoever carried its "golden bough" was assured safe conduct even in the realm of Hades.

No doubt, because of its divine link and its greenness in winter, the mistletoe was seen as the potent giver of sexual power. From earliest times it was thought to produce fertility in plants, animals and humans.

In his *Natural History* Pliny recorded how the Druids, who "hold nothing more sacred than the mistletoe and the tree that bears it," after their sacrificial service used its potion as a sterility preventative. The old Britons fed mistletoe to their cattle to make them more prolific, and the Japanese mixed it with the seed to ensure the fertility of the ground.

To kiss under the mistletoe thus combined two sex stimulants. Indubitably, it was "the surest way to prove prolific."

An old superstition believed that a girl who had not been kissed under the mistletoe would be barren. In modern days an excuse to take innocuous liberties, it began as part of sexual arousal in honor of Saturn and concern for fruitfulness. No wonder that early Christians, though unsuccessfully, tried their utmost to abolish the custom.

The Religious Kiss

Kissing as a gesture of homage and deference is far removed from its erotic roots. Yet, at times, this reverential symbol was endangered to enter forbidden realms and to be not as passionless as a monk's kiss on the head of a dead man's skull.

The origin of the custom to kiss the Pope's toe (or rather the cross on his right shoe) is thus explained. To start with, the faithful used to kiss his right hand. But when (in the eighth century, as legend has it) a passionate woman not only kissed but squeezed it, the Pope—horrified—cut it off. It was its loss (and the circumstances that accompanied it) that made him, on all future occasions, offer his foot instead, which has been the tradition ever since.

Disregarding this legend, it has been suggested that, in fact, the custom is a continuation of an old form of salutation in pagan worship.

Some rabbis in the East, more than a thousand years ago, used to wear thick gloves, both in summer and winter. They did so as a protection against lust. It prevented them from feeling a woman's kiss on their hand, then customary to be given on Sabbaths and holy days as a token of respect.

X—The Kiss Symbol

That X—a mere cross—came to represent a kiss has its own story to tell. Some have seen in the choice of that figure—from mathematics—a most appropriate symbol. It may signify nothing at all, a mere "zero," or stand for (an) infinity (of delight). On the other hand, it can "multiply" joy and love.

However, the prosaic explanation of this romantic sign may be twofold. Originally it represented the formalized, stylized picture of two mouths > < touching each other X . But then, a little more complicated, the kiss entered the cross by a chain of events and really owes everything to men's lack of education.

Early illiterates signed documents with a cross. They did so for an obvious reason. A cross was so simple to draw and yet, being also a sacred symbol, implied the promise of truth. But to solemnly confirm further the veracity of what had been endorsed thus, the writer kissed his "signature," as he was accustomed to do with the holy book. And that is how, finally, by its very association, the cross came to be identified with a kiss.

Necking

Necking, in its courting sense, certainly is only a comparatively recent acquisition of our vocabulary. It stems from the late 1920s and obviously refers to two people hugging each other around the neck.

Oddly enough, the original meaning of the word is far removed from amorous pursuits. It was either deadly or restraining. To neck, at first, described the stunning blow into the neck, aimed to kill! Alternately, necking was an early method applied in the taming of an unruly cow. She was tied "neck to neck" to another, but docile, bovine creature, thereby learning to "go steady."

Bundling—A Test of Strength

At one period of our civilization "sex" began in somewhat an agonizing manner. It was courting done under fetters—with a safety device built in. And yet, however remote in manner, it definitely is the precursor of modern petting, so freely and easily done.

The young man and woman were put to bed (or rather, did so themselves)—nestling closely to each other but remaining fully dressed. In fact, to ensure the morality of the situation and to protect the girl's virginity, her mother in later years used to tie her legs securely together both at their ankles and, most important, higher up.

This unusual form of courtship was known as "bundling" and, without doubt, presented a delicious bundle of human flesh —well and truly trussed up for the roast. The history of the custom goes back to early days and was known in many parts of the world. Red Indians and New Englanders practiced it. So did families on the continent of Europe and in the Outer Hebrides. The marvel is: how did people in distant lands who had never heard of one another work out the same maiden protection?

The origin of bundling may be traced to primitive society. It introduced the custom out of fear: not of society's censure or parents' wrath but of supernatural powers. By this devious

method the young couple learned to outwit and neutralize the
dangers of sex on their first approach, which then were most
acute.

Certainly bundling continued to play a role in periods of
hypocritical Puritanism. However, everyone knows where there
is a will there is a way and even the best-tied knot can become
ineffective. But to keep up the pretense, the practice of bundling
was still carried on without the susceptibilities of the prudes or
Puritans being hurt, because what actually went on was well
covered up.

Some regions and periods made use of the practice of bundling as some kind of—rushed—trial marriage. Thus a vicar, the
Reverend Andrew Burnaby, recorded how bundling in the state
of Massachusetts in 1759 was known as a very apt means of
finding out just how suitable lovers were for each other.

They did so, by the girl's parents' permission, in her home.
The "old folk" wisely and kindly withdrew early at night, leaving
the young couple on their own.

After the courting pair had spent what they considered a
respectable time in polite conversation, they "retired," lying
down together in the ready-made bed, however without discard-
ing their underwear "to prevent scandal."

If "agreeable" (the text in the choice of this word is vague
and leaves it to the reader's imagination which way it is meant),
the night would be followed by the publication of the banns.
Otherwise, the boy and girl would part next morning—forever.

The Paradox of Virginity

The paradox and ambiguities that abound in sex are most apparent in the way chastity and virginity were viewed.

On the one hand, for a girl to have premarital "sex" was a
common custom. It was not frowned upon. On the contrary, some
primitive groups even fostered it. They saw nothing wrong or evil
in it and no one actually cared one way or another. It was accepted
as natural a function to satisfy one's sex hunger as eating and
drinking. Even trial marriage was a sanctioned institution in some
tribes.

For a girl to have given birth to a child prior to marriage, in fact, was a high recommendation. After all, it was evidence of her fertility. Often the husband-to-be who adopted her child was regarded as most fortunate.

On the other hand and likewise universally, there was almost a cult of chastity. For a girl to have lost her virginity was indeed the worst that could happen to her. Proof of virginity was demanded at marriage. Its lack greatly reduced a girl's value (and, consequently, her bride-price) or led to her execution!

The Hymen—Before and After

The hymen (a Greek word) describes the fold of mucous "membrane" (or "skin") which partially seals up a virgin's vagina. Some have suggested an earlier Sanskrit root of the word, meaning "suture." Few realize the wealth of tradition—both romantic and mythological—behind this simple word and its legacy, which is far removed from its modern concept.

Hymen was a Greek god of marriage, and possibly because of it his name was bestowed on that very part of a woman's body. It has also been claimed that it was the other way round: that it was the god who derived his name from the membrane.

How the figure of Hymen assumed its position in the constellation of love has been related in several versions. Some of them say that it was because of his illustrious parentage. A myth thus tells that the great god Apollo was his father and a nymph his mother. Another makes him the offspring of Dionysus and Aphrodite. A third legend is even more romantic. It tells of a ravishing youth who fell in love with a maiden. Disguising himself as a girl, he followed her on a pilgrimage to Eleusis. When bandits attacked her party, he came to the rescue. Subsequently he married her and they lived happily ever after. Remembering the fervor of his love, ever since, men sang "hymeneal" songs to him, especially so on their wedding day, asking for his blessing. "Already it is night, already the glow of torches flames from afar, and already is heard the sound of the old and yet eternal young song: 'Hymen, O Hymenaeus.' "

It has been suggested that the songs actually evolved out of the "wedding cry" uttered at the very moment of defloration, invoking the god's help. There is no doubt that the "hymn," if not actually derived from, is closely linked with, those original *hymeneal* wedding songs!

For centuries, the only function of the hymen has been social and moral. Its unruptured presence was thought to prove a girl's chastity. This is now known to be incorrect. It is not an infallible sign of virginity.

The real reason for the hymen is still a conjecture. The membrane has been compared with the appendix, an early organ that has outlived its usefulness.

Its original purpose, some have said, goes back to an age when some rudimentary sort of intercourse was practiced in childhood. To grip a boy's immature penis, the opening of the vagina had to be constricted, a condition achieved by the hymen.

Other authorities (and among them was Havelock Ellis) explained the existence of the hymen as a precautionary obstacle to avoid coitus with the immature, the weak and the old. Only the sexually strong could penetrate this "barrier." All others were wisely excluded. It was thus principally a eugenic measure, ensuring healthy offspring. Ellis, in fact, asserted that women preferred powerful men and that the hymen helped them in their choice. It acted as an instrument of natural selection.

Many animals have some rudimentary type of hymen which, significantly, bursts by itself just before the advent of puberty. Its obvious function is therefore to protect the female until she is ready to conceive. It may well be that this was the original and only purpose of a woman's hymen. A girl should not run the risk of pregnancy until she has reached a certain degree of maturity.

The Dangers of Virginity

Several primitive concepts were responsible for the custom of having a virgin deflopered prior to her marriage, by a man not her future husband. There was the superstitious fear of coming into contact with the magically dangerous hymeneal blood. To save the husband from such exposure and its possible harmful effects on his very manhood, he received his young bride, as it were, safely "discharged" of the elemental force.

Defloration, like any other "first step," was implicitly fraught with peril. Therefore the task was left to religiously fortified persons, men of renown, to people of low esteem specially employed (and paid) for this duty, or even to entire strangers. The very fact that they were either of high standing, paid or completely disinterested, made them invulnerable to demonic agencies and the contamination linked with defloration. The wide range of those entitled, compelled or invited to perform the sacred (and dangerous) act extended from the witch doctor and the headman of a tribe to the male guests attending the nuptial feast.

Some societies employed women who undertook the operation by artificial means: either with their fingers or a primitive tool. The "right of the first night" was the final development of this tradition to achieve defloration by proxy.

Apart from protecting the future husband, considerations of fertility once again played their part. Without the god's blessing, it was thought, the woman might never bear children. And to buy his good will, so to speak, she offered him (or a priest, acting as his delegate) her "maidenhead" (which is the telling English term for the hymen).

Priests did not always perform the ritual of defloration personally. There were symbolic copulations with the divine image. Records tell of girls' defloration in shrines by means of an artificial phallus—made of metal, stone or ivory and frequently decorated with the god's image. In classical times some young girls of the aristocratic class had their hymen pierced by the erect penis of a huge statue of the god Priapus.

The choice of time when a girl was deflowered also varied in the different groups. Some preferred early childhood, others puberty with its initiation rite. The rest left it to the advent of marriage.

Almost anticipating modern customs of a permissive society, some races looked upon a virgin with disdain. She held no attraction to their men. After all, so they reasoned, something must be lacking in a girl whom no one had desired so far.

The Ideal of Chastity

A virgin was believed to have extra powers. Her "sealed up" sex imbued her with mystical, magical force, the effect of which could be manifold.

Ancient superstition assumed that a virgin could rejuvenate an aging man. They were bedded down together but frequently warned to avoid actual intercourse. Old King David, it was hoped, would thus regain his vanished strength. He was provided with "a young virgin" who would "cherish him," so "that my lord, the king, may get heat" (I Kings 1:2).

Virginity, too, was imagined to act as a strong devil repellent. It was needed particularly at a wedding, when demonic powers were out "in force" to harm the bride. This most probably created the custom of the flower girl and the unmarried bridesmaid. Both were meant to be virgins. The very purpose of their presence at the wedding originally was not, as it is now understood, to act as an aid to and an embellishment of the bride and the happy occasion. They were there as a vital, supernatural defense against evil forces.

A young girl's pent-up sexual energy at the age of puberty is even thought to have "psychical" effects. It has been suggested that this might explain the phenomenon of the poltergeist which has been observed to occur frequently in her vicinity.

Primitive society employed virgins—dead or alive—to ensure the fertility of the fields, the falling of rain and the shining of the sun.

Virgins were thus specially chosen as a sacrifice to the gods. Typical of such offerings was the service performed at the Sacred Well of Sacrifice at Chichen Itza, Yucatan, Mexico. After a solemn ceremony, beautiful virgins in their late teens were cast into the well. They accepted their fate gratefully—indeed, they regarded it a high honor. At the bottom of the deep well, so they imagined, they would marry the rain god and live in his palace happily ever after.

Young Roman virgins were solemnly carried across fields, magically to fructify them.

Most of all, in ancient days, the virgin was deemed to be the only one worthy and capable of attending to the sacred fire, so essential to life. Only her purity and mystical power could keep it blazing and with it—the sun. That is, no doubt, the reason why, independently in separate parts of the world, virgins were appointed to serve the fire, which was regarded either the direct gift of the god or a godhead itself. The practice existed among the Druids, the ancient Romans and the Incas.

In Rome, out of twenty virgins, six priestesses were selected by lot to serve at the temple of Vesta for a minimum of thirty years. As the custodians of the sacred fire, it was their duty to keep it burning. Their very virginity ensured this. (No wonder that the word "vestal" became a designation of chastity.)

In far-off Cuzco and Machu Picchu, Peru, the "Virgins of the Sun" were actually wedded to the solar god. After a novitiate of three years, they were given the final choice between marriage to a man or their consecration to the service of the sun. Once having taken the step, it was irrevocable and only death could terminate their office.

The virgins' responsibility for the life of man and the existence of the world was so supreme that any lapse on their part carried the death penalty.

Plutarch has left a detailed account of the punishment of a Vestal Virgin who had broken her vow and lost her chastity. He recalled that "no spectacle [was] more horrible . . . nor any day which Rome spends in deeper gloom."

The guilty Vestal was put into a litter which was covered up and securely fastened "so that not a sound could be heard from within." Thus she was carried through the Forum. The crowd stood by silently and then followed the litter to the site of the girl's live entombment. This was known as Agger and was a great mound of earth near the Colline Gate and part of the Servian Wall.

The tomb was an underground chamber, reached by means of a ladder. It was furnished with a bed, a lit lamp and a small amount of provisions.

When the solemn and mournful procession had reached its destination, the ropes fastening the cover of the litter were removed and the Vestal led to the top of the ladder. The high priest offered a silent prayer and, stretching his hands toward heaven, called the gods to witness that the execution about to take place was necessary. While the girl was descending the ladder, the priest and his associates turned away.

When she had reached the bottom of the steps, the ladder was drawn up, and the chamber covered with earth "until the spot was level with the rest of the mound . . ."

The Incas of Peru meted out an even more severe punishment. A Virgin of the Sun who had violated her vow of chastity was not only buried alive, but her guilty partner was hanged and both their communities razed to the ground.

The close association of virgins with the life-giving force of fire has been responsible, too, for a virginity test. A girl under suspicion was asked to blow into a smoldering fire. If it flared up, she had proved her chastity. But if, no matter how hard she tried, the fire died out, this was taken as irrefutable evidence of her impurity.

There were supernatural tests of virginity as well. A Greek myth (related in the fifth century) told how, to establish young girls' purity, the god Pan had used the mystical qualities of his flute. He suspended it in a grotto at Ephesus. The maiden to be tested was shut up in the cave. If she was innocent, the flute was heard playing loud and clear, and the cave opened up on its own volition for the girl to emerge radiantly. But if she was no longer a virgin, the flute remained silent. Instead, a wailing sound emanated from the grotto. When this eventually was opened up, it was found to be—empty.

Perhaps one of the oddest reasons for preference of a virgin-bride was yet another gross superstition. In medieval times it was believed that venereal disease could be cured by intercourse with a virgin (without infecting the girl). And thus some men who had contracted the "pox" restricted their choice of wife—for therapeutic reasons—to a virgin.

Vestiges of the belief in the "saving power" of a virgin can also be found in fairy tales. A frequently used motif is that of a fearsome dragon (or some other abominable creature) that demanded an annual sacrifice of a virgin. If denied, it would bring havoc and annihilation. Usually the king's own daughter was offered, to be saved in the last moment by a disguised "prince charming" slaying the monster.

*   *   *

Primitive man was convinced that on certain occasions and during crises of tribal life the suppression of sex was essential for the well-being of the group or its very survival. Continence was strictly observed prior to hunting and fishing expeditions, before battles and during the making of idols. It was believed that the stored-up sexual energy was vital to ensure the success of the mission and task. And, no doubt, it was the early belief in the magical, supernatural power of a virgin that led to an almost fanatical preservation of her chastity. Its loss prior to marriage could endanger the entire group.

Other factors reinforced the taboo. In early tribal life, the "old men" often regarded the young girls as their property. To safeguard their monopoly rights, as it were, the group was made to ostracize any girl who gave up her virginity to someone else.

Later on, other justifications for and rationalizations of the value of virginity came into being. It certainly avoided unwanted pregnancies and was therefore yet another type of birth control, regulating the economy and population growth.

And it was a combination of those various considerations that led to the condemnation of unchastity and the consequent devaluation of nonvirgins on the marriage market.

Public proof of a bride's virginity was often demanded. Women of the tribe examined the girl internally. Common as well (and certainly practiced in biblical times) was the custom, immediately after the consummation of marriage, publicly to display (to the elders of the tribe or close relatives) the blood-stained garments or "sheet." It was known as "the token of virginity." Elsewhere, women of the tribe inspected the nuptial bed on the morning after. Leaving nothing to chance, other groups insisted on actually witnessing the act of defloration. In some societies the girl carefully preserved the blood-stained garment she had worn on the wedding night. One day it might serve her as a piece of valuable evidence.

A bride discovered to have deceived her groom and found not to have been a virgin, biblical law ordained (Deut. 22: 20–21), was to be stoned to death. On the other hand, a man who had falsely thus accused his bride, was not only fined but could never divorce her (Deut. 22: 13–19). In this connection it must be remembered that early on and for many centuries betrothal was regarded almost as binding as marriage itself and took place at puberty—if not earlier.

And the very tradition of the primitive and crude bloodstained proof of a bride's virginity still lingers on in the custom of a "white bride." In fact, it is its modern equivalent. Its primary purpose was to serve as a public display of her purity! Originally only virgin brides were clothed in white.

Early Christianity prized virginity so highly that it came to worship it. St. Ambrose, one of the Church Fathers, lauded anyone who did not marry at all. "Naturally," he wrote, "I do not condemn marriage, only I consider chastity higher. The former is permissible, the latter I admire."

Man must have considered temptation too great (or perhaps the will power of his women too weak) to enable them to preserve their virginity without aid. That is how he enlisted mechanical or supernatural help. Some natives, in fact, daubed their virgins with paint. They believed that the color would magically protect their chastity and keep them "untouchable."

But not trusting mere magic, others ingeniously and cruelly employed different means. They sewed up part of the vagina, thereby rendering coitus impossible. Or, more barbarously still, they applied the male custom of infibulation to the female organ. They "secured" it against any possibility of intercourse by fixing a clasp, a ring or a needle (the Latin *fibula*) through the labia majora. But the acme of perversion was the chastity belt.

The Chastity Belt

Perhaps nothing speaks worse of man's lack of trust in his wife— and in the moral strength of a woman—than the existence of the chastity belt. Among all inventions of the world it is one of the most incredible. It was meant to ensure a virgin's chastity and a wife's fidelity. Incidentally it also avoided the unwelcome birth of illegitimate children which would have created additional problems.

Did a wife "outfitted" in this manner by her husband whenever he had to leave her for some time never resent the implications of such a farewell gesture? There are also many stories of astute blacksmiths who, out of pity or rapacity, provided (the woman with) an extra key . . . On the other hand, legends and myths tell of saintly maidens who, to be put beyond any temptation, thus protected themselves. And, after the belt had been duly locked, to keep it permanently so, the key was destroyed or safely put out of the way.

Such is the story, for instance, told in Lima, Peru, of Santa Rosa, the city's patron saint. She became a nun in 1606 and was renowned for her virtue. To this day the church and sanctuary dedicated to her memory is a place of pilgrimage. It treasures the very well into which, so it is told, she herself threw the key of her chastity belt, never to be retrieved.

Much advance in civilization is owed to anonymous benefactors. It is no wonder therefore that, all the more, in the case of the chastity belt the identity of its inventor is unknown. Yet its prototype—rightly or wrongly—has been traced to most ancient days.

Already the Bible, it has thus been suggested, recorded the existence of some sort of chastity belt. It did so in connection with the building of the Tabernacle during the Israelites' wandering through the desert on their way from Egypt to the Holy Land.

Moses had called on all the people to donate whatever their heart urged them to give, to raise "funds" for the construction of the Tent of Meeting, to be worthy of God.

And the women gladly offered their precious ornaments, such as their bracelets, earrings and signet rings—"all jewels of gold." But also mentioned in this very verse (Ex. 35: 22) is an object called in Hebrew *koomaz*, which is traditionally translated as "girdle" or "tablet." Rashi, Jewry's most renowned and scholarly commentator of the Bible who—significantly—lived in eleventh-century France, explained the word as actually describing "a golden object (or vessel) fixed on a woman's private part." In support of his interpretation he quotes the rabbis of the Talmud (a work completed in A.D. 500). They had seen in the word an abbreviation of the telling phrase "here is the place of shameful deeds."

To the wearing apparel of ancient Greek women certainly belonged a girdle which was associated with chastity. It encircled their hips and was used to hold up their dress. Its very position, however, rendered it a symbol of virginity. No one could misunderstand the meaning of a phrase in Homer's writings which spoke of "loosening a maiden's girdle."

It is now generally assumed that the first actual chastity belts were introduced into Europe only in the twelfth century. Possibly the Crusaders brought the idea back from the East. Italians produced the first models. They did so, it has been said, because at that time their country witnessed countless love affairs which had made suspicion and jealousy a conspicuous feature of daily life. The girdle was then adopted all over Europe.

Generally, the chastity belt consisted of two parts. A metal belt was locked around the waist, and irremovably attached to its center both in front and the back was a band also of metal, or of bone. This tightly covered the vagina. An opening was left, just large enough to enable a woman to perform her natural function. On the other hand, the aperture was so small that not even a finger could penetrate it. To make doubly sure, it was fortified with sharp teeth. Sometimes only the vagina was thus "protected." But to prevent anal coitus (perhaps as a substitute when the natural way was barred), many belts equally "guarded" the rectal opening.

The chastity belt became known by a variety of names. Early on, people called it a Florentine girdle, no doubt giving credit to one of its places of manufacture and of frequent usage. Much more appropriately it was named the "girdle of Venus" the "padlock of chastity," or "drawers of iron."

Its earliest description extant is found in an A.D. 1405 manuscript of a military encyclopedia published by Konrad Kyeser von Eichstadt under the title *Bellifortis*. It referred to the girdle as a "Florentine."

A legend attributes one of the oldest models in existence to an infamous and cruel despot, Francesco II, the "tyrant of Padua" whom the Venetians strangled in 1406.

Some of the instruments of torture he is said to have designed or employed are displayed in the armory collection of the Ducal Palace in Venice. And among them is a chastity belt. This, it was claimed, Francesco—also known as Novello Carrara—had specially made (if not invented) for his wife. In perfect condition, it is the type which secures both the front and the back, and its flexible iron plates are lined with leather. The opening covering the vagina is fortified by thirty-six spikes, while the small orifice giving outlet to the anus has fifteen sharp teeth!

A modern discovery mixes the abstruse with the morbid. In 1889 a skeleton of a woman was exhumed in a fifteenth-century Austrian churchyard. Unmistakably, her waist was still encircled by a chastity belt.

The Virgin Birth

A fundamental tenet of orthodox Christian theology is that of the virgin birth. It claims that when Mary became the mother of Jesus, her virginity was unimpaired. As support and actual prophecy of this miraculous birth, the Gospel (Matt. 1: 23) quotes a passage from the prophet Isaiah (7: 14) as saying: "Behold, a *virgin* will conceive and bear a son . . ."

The original Hebrew text, however, never said so. The word which the New Testament renders as "virgin" *(almah)*, in fact, describes a "young woman" of marriageable age. (The Hebrew term for a virgin is *betullah.*) But it was the Greek translation of the Bible—the Septuagint—which first erroneously translated the Hebrew "young woman" by "virgin." And it was this mistake which the Gospel adopted.

The philological error which thus came to be so closely linked with a theological concept might very well not have been the result of a faulty vocabulary or ignorance of the Hebrew tongue. It may have been influenced by a tradition found all over the world.

Universally, stories had been told of famous figures who were conceived supernaturally. People felt that such eminent and illustrious persons could not have been born like other, ordinary mortals. Therefore many myths spoke of a supernatural father, such as a god.

Examples abound in the folklore and mythology of man. The Egyptian kings thus traced their birth to a divine father. So did Chinese emperors. The Olympian god Apollo, and not Priam, it was told, was the father of Hector and Troilus. Buddha's mother is said to have dreamed prior to her son's birth that he had entered her womb in the shape of a white elephant.

It must be remembered that early society was not fully aware of the part a man played in conception.

Irrespective of such myths, it has been proved that for a woman to conceive, penetration of the hymen is not always necessary. Semen spilled around the vagina has been known to make its way to and fertilize the ovum.

Nature itself provides examples of fertilization without copulation. Scientifically this is termed (from a combination of the Greek words *parthenos*—for "virgin"—and *genesis*—for "birth") as *parthenogenesis*. It has been found to occur, for instance, among some species of insects. The discovery of this fact, indeed, was welcomed by certain theologians who quoted it to support their suggestion that the virgin birth was a natural phenomenon.

The Immaculate Conception

For well over a millennium the Immaculate Conception of Mary had been a topic of heated controversy. Then, in 1854, Pope Pius IX declared it to be a doctrine which "must be believed firmly and constantly by all the faithful" of the Roman Catholic Church. Its very idea, however, has been misunderstood and confused by many people with the virgin birth. The two are completely unrelated.

The claim of "immaculate conception" has nothing to do with the physical birth of either Jesus or Mary. Mary, all authorities agreed, was born in the usual, natural way. And yet, so the Church taught, as the future mother of Jesus she differed in one significant aspect.

This concerned another doctrine, that of "original sin." It taught that, ever since Adam's disregard of God's command not to eat of the forbidden fruit (the Bible never mentions an apple), all men—until the coming of Christ—were born with sin in their soul. The only exception was Mary. Her soul, at the moment of its creation and infusion into her body, "was clothed in sanctifying grace." The stain of original sin was not removed but had been excluded from her, so that she would be worthy to give birth to the Saviour. And this is what is meant by her immaculate conception.

Columbus and the Eleven Thousand Virgins

The Roman Catholic Church calendar dedicates October 21 to St. Ursula.

Tradition tells that this fourth-century legendary British princess of Cornwall had been chosen by a Scottish nobleman to be his wife. With his proposal of marriage he had combined a request that she should bring with her eleven thousand virgins as brides for his soldiers.

They set sail in three boats. But luck was against them. Strong winds changed the course of their ships which, eventually driven up the river Rhine, reached Cologne. There the Huns captured the virgins and tried to ravish them. The young girls defended their virtue and preferred to die as martyrs (and virgins).

It is rather an extraordinary tale with its astronomical figures. A twelfth-century discovery of a vast number of bones in the burial ground near the church of St. Ursula at Cologne possibly gave rise to the exaggeration.

Other sources suggest, much more feasibly, that not eleven thousand but eleven virgins had accompanied Ursula. One theory actually spoke of only one virgin companion. However, her name, Undecimilla (as it appeared in the Latin text of an ancient inscription), had been misunderstood and interpreted as the Latin numeral for eleven thousand *(undecim millia)*.

Christopher Columbus was steeped in the Roman Catholic faith. And when, in 1493, he discovered a group of islands in the West Indies, he well remembered the story of the "eleven thousand virgins." Like himself, after a long voyage, they had reached "unknown territory." Therefore he called the isles after them, (in Spanish) Las Once Mil Virgines. The Virgin Islands thus, to this very day, perpetuate Columbus's credulity and a legend.

3.

Superstitions in Sex

Man is most superstitious when he feels insecure and faces uncertainty. That is why sailors who have to cross dangerous seas and actors who never know whether the play in which they are to appear will turn out to be a success or a failure are so superstitious. But to everyone's life belong situations in which he feels most vulnerable to outside forces. This applies particularly to the times when he passes from one state of existence to another, such as at birth, puberty, marriage and death. They are the crises of life when man becomes most prone to superstition. Nothing, however, surpasses the mystery linked with sex. The tremendous hold it had over men and life inevitably created its own numerous superstitions, many of which—in one way or another—still persist.

"Touching" for Luck

Gamblers—innately superstitious in their worship of Lady Luck —believed in the magic power of their genitals! After all, they existed for the purpose of (re)production. To touch them with the dice would bestow extra procreative power on those "stones of chance" and thereby multiply their good fortune as well.

The Spilling of Salt

The commonly held superstition that the spilling of salt would bring bad luck, in addition to its various other explanations (associated with immortality and incorruptibility), has a sexual interpretation as well. According to some psychoanalysts, the salt symbolized man's semen. Spilling it presaged premature ejaculation (*ejaculatio praecox*). The very superstition, in fact, revealed man's unconscious apprehension of such incomplete intercourse.

Bees and a Virgin

Bees have been credited as being wise and endowed with foreknowledge. Their association with the home was taken to be so close that British custom considered it essential to inform them of the master's death. Bees, it was claimed, shunned swearing and blasphemy and would not stay near a home in which there was anger and hatred.

It was also believed that a virgin who passed through a swarm of bees would not be stung by them. However, no instance exists of this tradition being utilized as a virginity test!

Selecting the "Right Day"

Right timing has always been considered an essential for success —not least in love. In reverse, it was believed that the choice of the wrong day or hour could precipitate misfortune. Therefore avoidance of, or preference for, certain times and seasons for marriage has been an age-old phenomenon.

Already Plutarch dealt with the question of why Roman men, for instance, shunned the month of May for marriage. He explained that this month was reserved for offerings to the dead and the wearing of mourning. Hence to utilize it for the opposite mood would invite disaster, as joy and sorrow could never commingle.

No wonder that, likewise, in Synagogue and Church a wedding held during a prohibited marriage season was not only regarded as a sin but as an ill omen for the future, tempting providence.

The origin of the selected date has mostly been long forgotten, though frequently it was the association of that day (or period) with some other happy occurrence or misfortune. Friday, for example, as the day of crucifixion, was unlucky among Christians. Pagans, on the other hand, had dedicated this very day to their goddess Freya (hence its name), and to them, therefore, it was most auspicious for lovers.

The Separation Taboo of Bride and Groom

A still widely practiced custom (and superstition) regards it unlucky for bride and groom to see each other on the day of their wedding prior to the actual ceremony. Even for a groom to catch a casual glimpse of his bride-to-be is carefully avoided, as it might endanger their future happiness!

Such isolation and complete severance of all communication are not a modern phenomenon. It existed (and is still carried on) among primitive tribes all over the world. In some parts, girls were not even permitted to speak to the men they had been promised in marriage. (An interesting reflection is what they would have done had they known the telephone.) Betrothed Malayan girls were so obsessed by the danger of their fiancé setting eyes on them that they walked about "as watchful as a tiger." Bedouin brides fled into the hills, where their groom had to find them (no doubt, one of the most thrilling games of "hide-and-seek")!

In New Guinea, the very moment engaged girls saw their future husband approaching they would withdraw behind a tree, and stay hidden there till he had passed by. In yet another region, girls before walking out shrouded their entire body with a king-sized cloak, lest even a small part of them could be seen.

This ominous fear is not the result of mere phobias but the survival of a primitive sex taboo.

For bride and groom to come into contact with each other so near to the very consummation of their marriage might lead to premature intercourse. This had to be avoided at all costs. It was not a moral concept but a dread deeply embedded in man's remote past. Originally, the separation of bride and groom was not restricted to the one day alone but extended to the entire period from betrothal to marriage, no matter how long. And the reason is the very basis of the modern custom.

The marriage ritual, to begin with, was not just a solemnization, a binding of man and woman "till death part thee and me." Much more so and significantly, it was a powerful (magic) measure against mischievous forces ready to pounce on the couple and do them harm. Without the rite they were unprotected and could become easy victims to the curses of incompatibility, if not impotence.

That, in early days, girls became brides at puberty, that most critical period in a woman's life, multiplied the inherent danger.

The joining of two, so far unrelated, groups by the marriage of the man and the woman brought additional hazards. To render ineffective all possible contagion, the two parties were kept apart. In the mind of primitive man, only the ritual of the wedding made both groom and bride mutually invulnerable. This explains, for instance, why the ancient Sumerians called a bride "house-confined." This term is still recalled by the Hebrew word *kallah* (for "bride"), literally also meaning "one who is shut in."

Naturally, it was firmly believed that the nearer the wedding day came, the more anxious the nefarious spirits were to wreak their evil. After all, time was getting very short. Hence the final restriction of the "seeing" taboo to that very last day, which is still adhered to so conscientiously.

Modern psychologists could present a wealth of material in their explanation of this phenomenon. They could see in the so-called avoidance of evil spirits and careful seclusion a young bride's rationalization of her apprehensions and phobias. Not least, the enforced separation of bride and groom increases their anticipatory excitement and burning desire for each other.

The Origin of the Buttonhole

In Anglo-Saxon times, men accompanying the groom fastened their, then still buttonless, jackets with a ribbon which they pulled through holes in the lapels. The knot they tied, they were convinced, not only secured their garment around the neck but, much more significantly, would act as a love charm: tying magically together the groom and the bride.

Modern jackets have buttons and therefore no longer need ribbons. But, although redundant, the buttonhole is retained. The white flower now pinned into it by the male members of the bridal party takes the place of the original love-knot, adding to it its own fertility spell.

The Red Carpet

Bridal couples (like VIP's) get "red-carpet treatment." From the car they step on to this conspicuous runner leading into the sanctuary (whether church or synagogue). And when the knot has been duly tied and their future fate has been signed and sealed, they return the same way to their car as newlyweds.

So decorative, festive and simple a custom, it started, like so much in sex, not as an adornment but as a significant precautionary measure; not for beauty's sake but out of fear.

On their wedding day, primitive society was convinced, bride and groom were specially exposed to malevolent, supernatural forces, jealous agencies and the "evil eye." These threatened them from all directions. Hence the couple had to guard themselves, as it were, from every possible angle.

Not the least of the danger zones was the very ground they trod on. Beneath them, so superstitious belief assumed, there lived and lurked some of the most malicious spirits. Therefore to touch the very ground itself would imperil their future welfare. The contact would bring them within the power of the nefarious forces, which were only waiting to assault them, and by inflicting on both bride and groom irreparable damage, turn an occasion of joy and happiness into gloom.

This dread created numerous precautionary customs which

were linked with the arrival and departure of the couple. All had the same aim and objective: to insulate them from the dangerous ground. It made some tribes actually carry the bride to the nuptials: in a litter, on an animal, or even pickaback.

Another type of protection was to cover the path the bride had to take from her home to the site of the "ceremony" with sand, rushes or (magic) herbs or flowers. These were thought not only to act as a countercharm but to avoid any fatal contact with the demonic forces.

And it is this background of superstitious, haunting fears that survives to our day in the red carpet.

Even the choice of red was purposeful. It is a color which can be clearly seen, so that the young bridal couple in their nervousness could not mistake it and, by stepping off their well-secured path, become vulnerable. One slight slip would make all the difference between a marriage well consummated and its dismal failure.

Kissing the Bride

So lovely a custom nowadays, and so appropriate and full of good wishes and sharing in the joy, is that of "kissing the bride"—by the guests and even the clergy.

Who—in his right senses—would suspect that this innocent practice of "pure" love is a vestige of down-to-earth sex?

Kissing the bride, in fact, belongs to the category of the rights of prenuptial prostitution. These, too, are closely linked with the right of the first night. In some early civilizations, in Babylonia for instance, a stranger took the place of the god or the priest. As in other myths, he was regarded merely as the god come in disguise.

Out of this earliest sacred practice, an even cruder form evolved. Only when all male wedding guests had taken their turn with the bride, could the groom assume his conjugal rights. And all that is now left of such early legalized and sanctified mass rape, most fortunately, is our inherited right of "kissing the bride."

Is it any wonder that the York Missal and other ecclesiastical manuals laid down the strictly enforced religious law which ruled that the nuptial kiss had to be bestowed in church, and immediately following the bridal benediction. It was a precautionary measure, lest some ardent kisser might revert to the ancient custom. So shortly after the holy prayer and while still present on hallowed ground, the circumstances served as a safe means of restraint.

The Noise Factor at Weddings

Apparently jocular wedding customs were far from funny at the beginning. This even applies to and explains the tying of a tin can to the rear of a wedding car.

That the devil was allergic to noise has been an age-old belief, responsible for the introduction of church bells, bells in a ship and the clinking of glasses.

That is, too, why the couple's best friends made a special effort to add noise to the happy occasion. They gathered outside their bedroom window to create a veritable pandemonium and did so by every possible means—bangings, stamping of feet, breaking of crockery and raucous chanting. This was not an exuberant celebration of the final climax but a solemn ritual as well: to drive away the evil forces that might lie in wait and interfere with the consummation.

It all began with sex, or rather the wish to see it work. It still survives in several customs and institutions. The noisy rumpus of the German *Polterabend* is a typical example. The very term *polter* (meaning "mischievous noise") recalls the original bombardment of the devil with a rowdy din to make him beat his retreat. The tin can tied to the back of the wedding car also echoes this remote superstition.

Wedding Songs and All That

Wedding songs, still popular in some parts of the world, to begin with, were not an innocuous way to add to the entertainment of the guests and the hilarity of the celebration.

Not mere sing-songs, their true source was the anxiety of the young couple (and their friends) that some hostile, jealous power or even the evil eye (of perhaps a guest) would harm them. It was for that reason that the earliest songs contained some obscenity believed to be of special efficacy as an antidote. It would frighten off or annul any evil emanation threatening the ensuing first night.

This, in fact, is the background as well of the crude jokes, telegrams of similar vein and suggestive allusions included in the "funny speeches" delivered at wedding breakfasts. Their now imagined humor was originally a most serious matter which could "spell" out disaster or fruitfulness of the union.

Threshold Obsessions

The custom of carrying the bride across the threshold also has a superstitious, sexual basis. Once the threshold was sacred to Vesta, the goddess of virginity. On the very way to her defloration, for the young bride to touch it would be tantamount to sacrilege, adding, as it were, insult to injury. A memorial to virginity would thus be blatantly profaned and thereby invite the hostile reaction of the goddess. As punishment she might curse the union from its inception.

Consequently—mixing the metaphor—it was wise not to start it on the wrong foot. So the groom, anxious to avoid any inadvertent contact between step and bride—lifted her across.

Devilish Consummation Hazards

Even a sacred tradition—like a priestly benediction—may have its source in gross superstition.

A young couple about to retire for their wedding night were haunted by apprehensions of being unable to consummate their marriage. But such failure they never blamed on themselves, some psychological barrier or physiological defect. They looked for a scapegoat and, once again, found it in jealous, nefarious forces, perhaps the devil himself, who were out to destroy their happiness.

Witches, likewise, it was believed, used spells and, by tying a knot in a cord or a thread, could—by sympathetic magic—stop the flow of the man's semen. The "evil one" was lurking around the home, if not occupying the very bed of the newlyweds, to prevent them from fulfilling their conjugal duties.

Therefore, every precautionary measure had to be taken to chase away those malevolent entities, whoever they were. Counterspells were introduced and eventually taken up by the Church which could not ignore human fears.

That is why the priest once not only blessed the bridal couple at the altar in church but accompanied them to their bridal chamber. It was there that he bestowed his final benediction on them when they had "bedded down." The divine words he spoke, however, were not really meant for the bride and groom. They were directed at the devil. On hearing them, he would turn tail at once and decamp from the nuptial chamber!

Focus on the Baby

Pendulums were used to ascertain the sex of a still unborn child. The side of her body on which the mother felt the kicks of the foetus was taken as another "sure" indication whether it was going to be a boy or a girl.

Any boast has dangerous implications, it was assumed. Jealous forces were only too ready to destroy one's happiness. That is why people "cross fingers," "touch wood" or feel that the less said about their good fortune the better it is. This accounts for men's reticence to voice their joy and reveal their good luck.

Mothers, proud of their baby, could tell the infant's progress by its increase in weight. But to speak of it might invite disaster: evil forces might bring sickness, if not death, to the child. To forestall this, it became a superstitious custom not to weigh a baby at all till its first birthday. It was a wise precaution indeed. At a moment of forgetfulness and overflowing bliss a mother might give away the secret.

4.

Clothing
Sex

The Fig Leaf and (False) Modesty

T he story of man's fall and his expulsion from Paradise gave us the sex-loaded fig leaf.

When Adam and Eve, so the Bible tells, had become conscious (and ashamed) of their nakedness, they plucked fig leaves and sewed for themselves garments to cover up their genitals.

Translators vary in the rendering of the Hebrew term for this mini-mini skirt. Among the variety of words suggested are the apron, the loin cloth and the girdle. The choice of the odd "breeches" (in the Geneva edition of Holy Scripture, published in 1560) led to this Bible being known ever since as "the Breeches Bible."

The use of the fig leaf for the purpose claimed has been traditionally explained by its suitability and size. Yet from ancient times it has aroused controversy. People wanted to know from which type and species of fig tree the first couple on earth chose their raw material.

In his *Paradise Lost* John Milton assumed that it was the banyan tree. John Smith (in 1877) maintained that there was no evidence to substantiate the general opinion that the common fig tree had supplied the leaves. Its kind was much too rough for a cover and too thin to be sewn up into a garment of such minute size. Thus myths were built up around a myth.

Once again sex proved the stronger and the "fig," meant to turn away man's attention from sex (and conceal its organ), became its very symbol. No doubt, in the beginning, this was brought about by the similarity of the fruit of the fig to the male genital. However, the fecundity of the tree was responsible for it becoming in antiquity the very emblem of fertility. The tree was sacred to Priapus who himself, in Greek mythology, was worshiped as the promoter of procreation and was often depicted with his enormous penis erect.

The sexual significance of the fig tree also explains why the phallus carried in the processions of the Dionysian fertility feasts and displayed at their orgies was carved out of its wood.

The very word "fig" (and a rude gesture associated with it) has been used for the identical reason in many parts of the world —throughout the Mediterranean area, in India, in Latin American countries and particularly in Brazil—as an abusive and obscene provocation. The likeness of the fig to the male genital was the cause.

No person could mistake the actual gesture: the vulgar sticking out of the thumb between the index and middle fingers of the clenched fist. And yet, in another of the paradoxes and contradictions of life, this symbol was originally not used as an insult or sign of defiance but as a magic guard against the evil eye, as a devil repellent. That is how eventually the "fig" returned to its primary meaning and became a most sought-after good-luck charm. However, to be effective, its wooden reproduction must be received as a free, unsolicited gift. To ask for one or, worse still, buy one is no good.

Various views have been given as to the invention of clothes. The most traditional opinion, of course, goes back to the literal interpretation of biblical writings. Quoting chapter and verse, it said that Adam and Eve designed the first "dress."

When man no longer took the Bible as gospel truth, he changed his belief and now assumed that not feelings of shame but climatic conditions had led to the introduction of garments. Man, it was claimed, felt cold and therefore made himself some kind of wrap from material nearest at hand.

Such a "common sense" answer no longer made sense when anthropologists discovered the facts. These showed that early civilizations—complete with clothes—were established not in lands of cold climate but in warm zones! Primitive man, experiencing cold, never thought of warming his body by means of dress (of whichever type). He just took shelter in a cave or greased his body with fat.

More confusion was created in the minds of those seeking for the true origin of clothing when it was realized that the first "covers" man used really covered nothing! They were G-strings or mere belts around the waist. In part, they were of very practical purpose: to help still pangs of hunger by literally "tightening the belt." And yet the final aim and true explanation was, once again, sex.

After all, the story of Adam and Eve and all it tells of the fig leaf in reality implies the strongest motive of all. Why should the first man and woman have felt ashamed of their nakedness? What was wrong with sex, a God-given instinct?

The explanation of modesty is a comparatively recent idea and certainly almost hypocritical camouflage. It conceals (or rationalizes) an all-consuming, selfish fear.

Man, in those times, felt himself surrounded by hostile forces. More dangerous even than the wild beasts and his human foes to his reasoning were the malevolent magic powers, like witchcraft and the evil eye. They threatened not merely his life but his precious manhood. And it was to guard against them and against their imagined power to make him (or her) impotent and sterile that man began to "dress."

The most potent countermagic was needed: a shield that rendered the darts aimed at his (or her) fertility ineffective. The object chosen as armor was the cowrie shell and, oddly enough, it was adopted almost universally and independently.

Its selection was due to a simple factor: its likeness in appearance to the female sexual organ. This was the very portal through which the child entered the world. But primitive man saw in it not only a passage but a gateway; to him it was the very giver of life. In fact, eventually the pudenda was regarded to be life itself.

And as the cowrie shell so much resembled this, it was imagined that it, too, not only possessed that vital power but did so in its most intensive form. Therefore it was used not merely as a shield and protection against attack. By its very touch of the "private parts" it fortified their life-giving force beyond measure. (In some regions of the world shells were buried with the dead or used to "decorate" their graves, to give the deceased eternal life.)

No wonder, then, that cowrie shells became the most favored means of sex protection and promotion. Only much later, when man had forgotten its initial purpose, did this amulet change into an ornament. It is a metamorphosis equally experienced by (modern) jewelry which likewise evolved from magic.

The Grass Roots of Shame

The feeling of shame is a powerful force to make man conform. To "lose face" is not a deep worry only in the Eastern mind. To be scorned and derided by those around has always frightened and intimidated people.

The idea of shame, however, is relative. It depends on current mores, the dominant pattern of behavior at a given place and time. Women have felt ashamed for being childless, widowed, divorced or "old maids." On the other hand, for centuries people saw nothing wrong (nor felt guilty) in sending children down mines, looking upon (and treating) as inferior men of different color and caste, or persecuting those who belonged to another faith.

To feel shame was originally not an expression of propriety, morality and modesty. It was conditioned by an instinct of self-preservation. Fear caused man to hide himself, or part of his body, or his practice of certain functions. They were not wicked, evil or disgusting. But they were vital to survival and therefore potentially dangerous if exposed to, or appropriated by, hostile forces.

Man was at all times surrounded, at least so he imagined, by nefarious powers, ready to pounce on and injure him. Sorcery and magic could do him untold harm. He was vulnerable to them in so many ways. His spittle was part of his soul essence. Food nourished him. Anything connected with it—in preparation, intake and elimination—concerned him deeply. To yawn opened up not only his mouth but his entire being to evil spirits which could enter and take possession of him. But, above all, his genitals were the seat of supernatural forces, almost beyond his control, inspiring holy awe.

Taking all these factors into consideration, primitive man was not only haunted by fears but took numerous precautions which meant to him the difference between life and death. That is why he retired to perform his bodily functions. He covered his mouth when yawning, buried his spittle and often ate in complete privacy. The Bavairi, for instance, took their meals in individual isolation and, if they could not do so, shamefully averted their heads from one another.

It was for this very reason that man kept his "private parts" hidden or protected, as it were, by a fence of shame. This, in fact, led to the description of the pudenda (more commonly used than its more properly singular form, *pudendum*), which from the Latin —*pudere*—refers to "being ashamed." This linguistic derivation caused St. Augustine to reflect that the name had actually been chosen because the genitals exposed the shame of men who were master of everything but slaves of sex. "Although able to control all things to their obedience, they cannot control these parts," he declared. He, of course, adopted the Christian rationalization of shame in its condemnation of all that was of "the flesh."

Eventually, with the passage of time, the original reasons and causes were forgotten. Man had become emancipated from those early superstitions and fears.Yet the emotions that once had accompanied these "dangerous" actions and displays remained. A new explanation, however, was given. The Greeks said that to break "the rules" would offend the gods. Aristotle regarded shame "an apprehension of dishonor." The Hebrews called such disregard of "fundamental" laws "an abomination unto the Lord." And thousands of years later, man continues to feel compunction and shame and to call those who (without really knowing why) break the ancient taboos disrespectful and immodest.

From "Topless" to Bust Confiners—and Back

The brassiere entered our vocabulary as late as 1916. French in tongue (but not so called in France), it was born in the United

States. That in itself is confusing. But even the very word is deceptive, though, more tolerantly, we might call it a euphemism. Obviously applied to a woman's bust, the brassiere literally does not belong there at all. It really means an "arm protector." Its shortened and now popular description as "bra" stems only from 1937. (The French call it, also euphemistically, "the support of the throat"—*soutien-gorge.*)

The brassiere's purpose was once clearly and amusingly advertised by a manufacturer who marketed three types of bra. He called them "The Dictator" (who suppresses the masses), "The Salvation Army" (who lifts them up) and "The Yellow Press" (who makes mountains out of molehills).

When the first "garments" had come into being, women still walked around bare-breasted, or, in the modern jargon, "topless." All they "covered" was their lower region or part of it. In fact, they wore "dresses" so tightly under their bust that it was lifted up and all the more conspicuously displayed. A series of wide metal rings around the waist achieved this purpose admirably. No doubt this was not mere beauty culture but sex provocation. It is not by accident, therefore, that one of the earliest "figures" in existence showing such bust display is that of a Cretan fertility goddess.

The bra, so recently named as such, nevertheless, has an almost six-thousand-year-old past. It goes back to a band or bandage swathed around a woman's breasts in the ancient Mediterranean culture, most likely also first among the Minoans of early Crete.

One of the earliest types of bra was known as *apodesme.* It was a (mostly woolen) band, narrow at times and at others broad. This was wound either around or below the breasts, to support them or protect them against sudden changes of temperature. Women in ancient Greece wore it. A similar kind had been known to the Egyptians.

But history "progressed" and the pendulum of fashion swung from one extreme to the other. Suddenly women preferred to suppress their female characteristics, and especially so the distinguishing bust. Young girls were made to wear a soft type of bandage around their breasts, but the moment they reached puberty, this was replaced by a leather one. This "restrictor" aimed at arresting the growth, and then flattening, what was meant to protrude. (After all, a cynic remarked, Copernicus was still far off and all the world was as yet flat and not round.)

Then women again became conscious of their sex (and its power) and proud of their bust, and they were no longer prepared to suppress it. All they now wanted was the right type of support. The new kind of bra became known as the *strophium.*

Thus, through the centuries, a woman's breasts really never rested. Something was being done to them all the time: to disguise, hide, display, contain, minimize or expand them. Eventually, with the invention of the corset, they were encased in an iron cage. This was also used to keep them well raised by means of a framework of steel! Some "refinements" were added, such as a great deal of padding and "pneumatic bust forms," promoted in 1901 as "bust distenders."

However, during the First World War woman was truly emancipated. She began to undertake manly tasks and the constrictions of the corset would no longer do. It was duly cut down in size and restricted to a woman's "lower half." This liberated a woman's breasts. (Social historians may well say that this liberated women as well. The tightly laced corset still in fashion in the early years of this century has been described as man's last—but abortive—"stand" to keep women under control. It fettered them, bound them to the home and made them incapable of competing with him.)

Once again a woman's bust came into its own. But it needed some visible means of support. Necessity was the father of invention and led to the birth of the modern bra, completely divorced from the corset.

Earlier attempts to create a bra had already been made in 1902. A patented "bust improver" of flesh-colored material then promised to give every woman "a bust modeled on that of the famous Venus de Milo." Four years later a new, cup-shaped model of perforated metal disks was recommended for its light weight of only three-quarter ounces. But these were all only "forerunners" of the real bra.

The story is told that the American Charles R. DeBevoise first saw a similar garment in France, and he immediately realized its tremendous potential. Back in the United States, he began to manufacture an adapted version, at first for stout women. This he widely advertised and (re)named brassiere. Its popularity soon made every woman wear it, now freed of the straitjacket of cloth and whalebone.

The elimination of the bra in the late 1960s and with it the starting of a "topless" fashion, is merely a return to antiquity, of the last and the latest to its very beginning . . .

How the Chinese Invented the Bra

The Eastern world has its own story to tell as to how the first bra came into being and, unashamedly, traces it back to "sex."

A famous concubine of the eighth-century Chinese emperor Hsuan Tsung of T'ang had an affair "on the side" with one of his generals. She was able to keep the duplicity of her amours so discreet that her royal lover was none the wiser.

Then, one day, a crisis occurred. In a burst of passionate ardor the general scratched and bit one of her breasts. The scars of battle would inevitably give away the show that very night when she was expected to report on duty to her king.

Desperately seeking some way out, she found it in—camouflage! And when, that same night, she appeared in the emperor's bedchamber, she wore around her bust, most decoratively, a red silk apron—the first Chinese bra.

Little guessing the true purpose, the emperor admired her ingenuity. Did it not show his lover's constant endeavor to offer him something completely novel? He liked the new "garment" so much that he asked his mistress to wear it always.

So much indeed did he take to the cloth curtain that an "ad hoc" improvisation was elevated to a foundation garment. And as all the other ladies at court inevitably adopted it, the women outside the palace soon imitated the bra: the gift of a desperate courtesan, born out of infidelity and deceitfulness.

Invented on the spur of the moment for the purpose of deception, the Chinese bra was a real "falsie." For more than a thousand years Chinese women have cherished it, not so much as a foundation garment but as an adornment for sexual stimulation. To add further to the allure and to rouse the men, some Chinese women also learned to embroider their bra with pornographic scenes. It was a true game of hide-and-seek.

The Revealing Sex Glove

No man likes to see his virility impaired. It is therefore not surprising that he went out of his way to protect it, particularly so in combat. To safeguard his genitals he enclosed them securely in a protective sheath. Soon his artistic bent made him decorate the utilitarian phallic appendage with suitable ornamentation.

Sex wants to have its own way. And that is how this original penis protector evolved into an instrument of sexual boast and provocation. When, through new forms of armor, the sex shield had become obsolete, it was not discarded.

Sex, no doubt, is a prime mover in all fashion. In the majority of cases garments have been designed not so much to cover up but to reveal (by whatever means) certain parts of the body.

Times changed and with it man's desire proudly to display or modestly to hide what there is of the "man" or "woman" in each of us. A period came in which it was the male who wished most to draw attention to his sex and to point blatantly to his virile manhood. He did so by a queer kind of exhibitionism (not in the technical sense of the term).

He made his tailor adapt the invention of warfare—his "sex glove"—to serve the new purpose. The breeches he wore then did not cover his genitals inconspicuously by means of a "fly" but enclosed them most pronouncedly in an outsized pocket, a "sex purse" which by its voluminous appearance seemed to promise lots of change. Almost like a male "falsie," though on a different part of the anatomy, men vied with each other in their genital display.

The popular sex pocket came to be known by various other names. From the Latin *barca* for "breeches," it was called *brayette* or *graguette* by the French, and from the Old English *cod* for a "bag," it was referred to as a cod-piece.

This bagged appendage became so popular between the fifteenth and seventeenth centuries that ever new versions were developed. To increase its size even more, men had it specially padded and embroidered. A pocket was added to its front in which the noble liked to keep his purse, handkerchief and pieces of fruit which, with little-concealed suggestiveness, straight from there, he offered to young ladies.

The sex glove, indeed, is an odd piece of male accessory in man's hazardous journey from generation to generation. It is rather strange to think that in our sex-mad world it has so far not experienced a revival.

The Disappearance of the Nightshirt

Originally and for over a thousand years, from Greek days onward, "civilized" men and women went to bed identically clothed. They retired the way they had walked about, fully dressed: wrapped in their (one) toga, that flowing garment.

When—luxuriously—they started wearing two togas, one on top of the other, they merely discarded the outer shell, and their nightshirt was the toga beneath.

The obvious next step, particularly among Romans who loved cleanliness, was to keep a separate toga for night use only. Nevertheless, it was the same type of garment, and there was no differentiation between male and female.

But then, by the end of the eleventh century, it suddenly happened that men and women began to go to bed stark naked. Why they did so has mystified many writers, and several reasons proffered have been discarded like the nightshirt. Certainly it was not scarcity of material, the cost of the apparel or a change of temperature in medieval Europe which made the bed too hot. The only plausible explanation was once again the intrusion of the erotic.

For too long man and woman had tried to hide or forget their "otherness." Now they had become very conscious of how different they were in every respect, and they no longer wished to conceal this fact. Thus they even "sexed" their dress. Tight trousers fitted the man and the ever-larger robe enveloped the woman. That in the East the styles were reversed, did not really matter. The main intention—sexual distinction—was maintained.

Unisex certainly was out. But to show their diversity of sex during the day and to do so with all the emphasis at their disposal and then to forget about it (costume-wise) when going to bed was out of the question. Someone, of course, could have then invented a "sexed" nightdress. But the art of love was very suggestive and a helpful aid. Much more telling and cheaper for the purpose was the ready-made natural state of man and woman. Had not nature equipped them so splendidly? Their naked bodies could leave no doubt as to what sex they were. That is how man and woman took off the thousand-year-old shirt and went to bed naked.

The disappearance of the nightshirt thus revealed the medieval emphasis on sex. And never again (at least in bed) did men and women forget to display their differences, one way or another. And even when—four hundred years later—nightclothes were reintroduced, these, too, were always fully "sexed," if not in shape, at least in color and, whenever possible, in texture.

Sex Deception—Transvestism

Transvestism—a term derived from the Latin and meaning "cross-clothing"—is a practice that can be traced far back into antiquity. It is found among primitive races as well.

The primary cause for a man to dress like a woman and for a woman like a man, no doubt, is sex. It increased erotic excitement and did so through various factors. These included the soft touch of a woman's dress, its very tightness, and the mere fact of looking "different" and thereby conspicuous. Frequently, its ultimate aim is masturbation. The custom was never confined, as is often wrongly assumed, to the homosexual.

It must be remembered that every human still carries in his or her body vestiges of the opposite sex. Typical examples are the woman's breasts in a man and the man's penis in a woman's clitoris.

There was, indubitably, from the very beginning, at least some awareness in man of his original bisexuality. The Greeks thus spoke of the androgynous nature of humans and linked it with the custom of "dressing up" as the other sex. Best known is the story of Hermaphroditus. (This introduced the "hermaphrodite" into our vocabulary as the description of an individual who has both male and female sex organs.)

Hermaphroditus was the son of Hermes and Aphrodite. As a youth of fifteen he traveled to Caria. There he visited the spring which was the abode (and bore the name) of Salmacis, a nymph. She was so struck by his ravishing beauty that, instantaneously, her passion was roused. But he rejected her impetuous desires.

Undaunted, the nymph did not give up her pursuit. She lured him into the spring and, attaching herself to the youth, implored the gods to unite them so firmly that he could never leave her. Her prayers were answered. They became one being, endowed with both sexes.

Early on, because of its sexual arousal, exchange of clothes played a prominent part in the sex orgies of fertility rites, in the cult of Astarte for instance. People went beyond donning the dress of the other sex. Women thus carried a spear and a lance like a man, or put on false beards. Men, on the other hand, wore earrings or performed female duties.

That the Bible condemns transvestism, calling it (Deut. 22:5) "an abomination," was closely linked with the Hebrews' vehement opposition to those fertility cults. Moses Maimonides, Jewry's greatest philosopher, living in the twelfth century, rightly pointed out that the antagonism was caused as much by the sexual aspect as its very association with paganism.

No wonder that in some early cultures even at wedding feasts and in marital life, men and women appeared in the others' dress. A Spartan bride, for instance, received her husband garbed as a male, while on the island of Cos the young married man dressed up for the benefit of his wife as a female. Havelock Ellis went to the extreme by suggesting that the entire phenomenon of transvestism was based on the exaggeration of the normal desire to identify oneself with the person one loved.

But sex was not the sole factor responsible for the exchange of clothes. Another important motive was, once again, that of life preservation: man's fear of evil, supernatural forces and his con- tinuous battle to ward them off.

Man (meaning the male) has always regarded himself as superior to the woman. She was so weak and, hence, no one really envied her existence! Therefore she could not be "attractive" either to evil forces who would just ignore her. Man was their special target. And to fool the devil (and thereby protect himself), he did the obvious thing. He disguised himself as a woman and did so, of course, first of all, by his dress.

Such camouflage of sex was particularly practiced in the case of children. The mere fact that they were so young made them least resistant and most prone to attack. Hence, to avert from them the evil eye (or whichever agency took its place), they were made to look as someone they were not—the other sex. And as, once again, boys were the chief victim, they were dressed like girls. Surely, the devil would ignore them. At times their disguise, too, went beyond clothing. In some parts of the coastal region of India, in the Konkan, for example, a boy's nose was pierced like that of a girl, to carry a ring.

Yet another cause of transvestism was the belief that change of clothes meant change of luck. That is why Zulu men donned female girdles when drought threatened their land. Their own transformation into someone else, they imagined, would induce (magically) nature to change as well and for rain to descend.

Contact with the clothes of the other sex, it was also assumed, would transmit a man's characteristics to a woman, and vice versa. A wife would thus put on her husband's clothes, confident thereby of making him experience her pains.

Naturally, in his fight for survival man also adopted woman's garb as an effective camouflage during military operations. Josephus, first-century soldier-historian, recorded this custom as part of the strategy of a band of guerrillas led by John of Gischala. In the general's mind, it was not "playing the game." In his chronicle of *The Wars of the Jews* (Book 4, Chapter 9), he wrote of those fighters: "While they decked their hair, and put on women's garments, and were besmeared with ointments: and that they might appear very comely, they had paint under their eyes, and imitated not only the ornaments, but also the lusts of women . . . while their faces looked like the faces of women, they killed with their right hands; and when their gait was effeminate, they presently attacked men and became warriors . . . and drew their swords from under their finely dyed cloaks, and killed everybody whom they came upon."

Age-old as a practice and manifold in its causes, transvestism survives with some of its earliest motives. It plays a part in modern pantomimes in which certain roles are enacted by the other sex. Likewise, it is still the custom in many countries to dress up little boys as girls.

Top-Dressing—Hair in Sex

Hair has been endowed by man with supernatural qualities as well as those of sex! One of the most likely reasons was the fact that hair continues to grow on the dead. It is one of the most indestructible parts of the body. The head altogether was regarded as the seat of a vital spirit, and the hair was a conspicuous part of it.

Is it any wonder that it was equally thought that the more there was of hair, the greater would be a man's power and his virile strength? The Samson type of legend testifies to this ancient belief, which also prompted the introduction of men's wigs. It may be that the identical notion (perhaps unconsciously) motivated the 1970s men to let their hair grow long.

Hair, thus early on, played the role of a sexual stimulant and a fetish. The mere sight of a woman's hair (her "glory," in the words of St. Paul) aroused a man's passion. To display it to anyone but her husband was regarded as indecent exposure.

Therefore it became a strict Oriental rule (first decreed in the ancient Assyrian code) for women to cover their head with a veil. This, in fact, is the background of the once strictly enforced custom for women to wear hats in church! By doing so, no lustful thoughts would arise (it was hoped) in the minds of their male co-worshipers. The same tradition led many artists to depict Mary Magdalene, "the woman which was a sinner," with hair so long that it almost touched the ground.

Some cultures went to the very extreme and demanded that a married woman had to shave off her hair. This deprived her of a forceful means, it was thought, to seduce men.

A Jewish orthodox woman, certainly no longer knowing why, considered it a pious duty at marriage to shave off her hair and start wearing a *sheitel,* which is the Yiddish term for a "wig." Originally this was not meant as an ornament but an ugly "disguise" to render her unattractive to the other sex. She would have hardly believed that its introduction was due to lack of trust . . .

And what applied to women was true for men as well. Obviously, hair viewed as an expression or excitant of sexuality could have no place in the realm of asceticism and world denial. As a sign of renunciation the Nazarite of the Bible was asked (Num. 6:18) to "shave his consecrated head." Members of holy orders (Buddhist, Taoist and Christian) either kept their hair exceedingly short or shaved it off. This is the origin of the monk's tonsure (a word of Latin derivation, meaning "sheared"). The very absence of hair became the symbol of chastity and the outward sign of celibate priesthood. (Several types of tonsure developed. In the sixth century Christians introduced the kind in which a rim of hair was left round the shaven head. This was explained to represent either the crown of Christ's priesthood or his crown of thorns.)

Psychoanalysts (such as Charles Berg) even claimed a deep, "unconscious significance of hair." Hair, they said, was a symbol of the genitals. Consequently, to cut or to shave it off constituted symbolic castration and an attempt to control primary aggressive impulses.

It goes without saying that pubic hair has its indigenous sexual meaning. The prophet Isaiah (7:20) referred to it euphemistically as "the hair of the feet." It is interesting to note that among the ancient Greeks, men—for hygienic or aesthetic reasons—preferred their women to remove it. These did so by either singeing it off or pulling it out. An Arab legend attributes a similar attitude to the ancient Hebrews. It tells that when the queen of Sheba visited King Solomon, he refused to go to bed with her till she had shaved off her pubic hair.

Hair, playing such a significant role in the life of man, as part of his very essence and sexuality, led to numerous customs, superstitions and, at times, to a sexual aberration.

Parents dedicated their children's hair to the gods. So did warriors after successful campaigns.

People made sure that no clippings of their hair would fall into the hands of others. These, they imagined, could use the hair to cast an evil spell on, or totally dominate, their lives. Therefore they disposed of it (mostly by burning it) the moment it had been cut off.

On the other hand, to give a locket of one's hair to the person one loved was not merely a beautiful gesture. It really meant that one delivered oneself, body and soul as it were, to the recipient.

This tradition of hair, especially its erotic roots, surely accounts for the fact that hair, too, took such a prominent place in the life of a fetishist. To cut it off women gave him sexual arousal. There are psychologists who even suggest that this very desire is what causes some people to take up the occupation of hairdresser.

With all this background of hair, is it any wonder that we say of people who give free vent to their feelings that they "let down their hair"?

5.

Puberty

The First Change of Life—and Puberty Rites

Man is born—in the natural course of things—either as a male or a female. But this differentiation of sex would mean very little without the maturing of the real man and woman. This we call puberty.

The word "puberty" itself comes from the Latin for "adult." This in turn, however, has its root in the description of one of the distinctive features apparent in man and woman at the time of their sexual maturity. *Pubes* in Latin refers specifically to the pelvic hair whose growth most marks the arrival of the period of reproduction, with the enlargement of the breasts and menstrual flow in the woman and the breaking of the voice and sprouting of facial hair in the man.

No wonder that primitive man (lacking the inhibitions of later generations) highlighted this time of change with rites that have no equal at any other phase of human existence—from womb to tomb. But that he did so was not for the sake of celebration. It was to him a matter of good or evil, of life or death—for both the child and its group.

To grow from childhood to manhood was, in his eyes and mind, not a mere physical and natural change but a complete metamorphosis. It was a death and a resurrection. As it were, a child died for a man (or woman) to be born.

Savages thus regarded this monumental human crisis with

fear and awe. They did everything within their power to help the "new man" to be strong and to become a worthy member of his tribe.

The fact of his becoming a new being they expressed by the bestowal on him of a new name. This was not a mere symbol. A name was not just an outward label and designation but a most intimate part of a person and his soul.

All new beginnings are dangerous. But none is potentially more so than the advent of manhood. Therefore every precaution had to be taken to neutralize all possible ill effects.

To become a full member of a tribe necessitated the transference of extra strength on the novice and his being guarded against weakness and harm.

Other factors suggested as the source of initiation rites cover a vast area. They were intended, once and for all, to separate a youth from his mother. Until puberty he had depended on her so much that eventually he almost replaced (and rivaled) his father. The right balance had to be established now. The young man had to realize his independent existence and his responsibility toward the tribe. Indeed, to rivet the individual to his group, according to yet another authority, was the chief object of the ritual. British anthropologist Sir James Frazer believed that one of its prime motivations was the wish to assimilate the candidate to his totem.

Whichever of these considerations is adopted as the principal factor in the creation of puberty rites, all share the one aim: the identification of the novice with the adult members of his group.

Procedures, of course, differed in the various parts of the world. But no matter what they were, because of their supreme importance they were intricately devised and executed, often in secrecy, with utmost care.

They were not pleasant celebrations of an important date but solemn manhood tests and initiation rites. The young boy (or girl) had to endure severe ordeals and, at times, suffer terrible pains. Among the tribulations were all kinds of mutilations, lacerations and beatings.

Almost universally observed—and most significant—was the rite of circumcision. Frequently, too, the filing or knocking out of teeth, the perforation of lips and ears, and tattooing belonged to the "statutory" initiation.

Victims had to withstand the ferocious bites of venomous ants without wincing. In some regions the novices were anointed with human blood or actually had to drink it. The importance of food and its influence on man made dietary regulations a prominent part of initiations. Some tribes demanded prolonged fasts from the candidate. Others forbade him to eat any food that either came from a female beast or had been in possession of a woman. On the other hand, among American Indians, novices were given strongest emetics and sweat baths to purge them of all that belonged to their former being. It was imagined that thus "emptied out," their body was ready for the new birth.

A special feature among certain tribes, particularly Central Australian aborigines, is scientifically known as subincision. This refers to the cutting open of the urethra along the underside of the penis.

The ceremony was most painful. The boy was put on a human "operating table," consisting of squatting men. The medicine man then performed the operation.

Several suggestions have been made as to the reason for this fearsome rite. Some explain it as a crude teaching method. At puberty the boy was told all the secrets, the laws and the lore of his tribe. He was admonished to respect the tradition of his people. It was imperative for him never to forget the lesson nor reveal the secrets imparted to him. As if to burn it into his flesh and to provide him with an indelible aid to memory, the subincision took place. We know of similar yet harmless modern applications of this identical psychological technique. For instance, the story is told of a father who, for the first time, showed his son one of Rembrandt's masterpieces. All of a sudden and without any apparent reason, he smacked the boy. Asked why he had done so, he explained that now his son would never forget seeing the painting!

Another hypothesis, proffered by Freudians, claims that the subincision had to be understood in terms of castration. It expressed "vagina-envy." Man was jealous of woman: her sex organ and its blood flow. The operation itself at least approximated his genitals to a woman's. The flow of blood reminded him of her menstruation, and ever after the initiate could urinate only if (like a woman) he squatted down. (One tribe actually described the incision as "man's menstruation.")

Even the kangaroo has been enlisted for the explanation of the practice. It was imagined that the transformed penis took on a close resemblance to that of the marsupial. But it was not really its visual similarity that was the main object of the plastic surgery. Much more so it was the kangaroo's outstanding virility which, it was hoped, would thus be magically acquired by the boy.

*   *   *

The initiation over, the new member of the tribe was duly recognized. The clay with which his body had been daubed was ceremoniously washed off, and his old clothes were burned. Donning his new garment and having assumed his new name, his rebirth was complete. A feast and a dance celebrated the occasion.

Only for Girls

Puberty rites, of course, differed for girls. Male initiations took place as part of a solemn and communal tribal ceremony. The female's first menstruation (in most cases) was a strictly private and family affair, although it concerned the community, if anything, even more. A male could merely fail in his duty toward his tribe. A woman, however, could do it immeasurable harm.

Menstruation, in itself, was regarded as a period in which a woman was charged with the most dangerous supernatural power. But to experience this phenomenon for the very first time had every aspect of a tremendous crisis—both for the girl and for the tribe. The beginning of the menstrual cycle rendered the girl a source of contamination and of destructive forces against which every possible precaution had to be taken.

The potentiality of her evil effect threatened most of all the very mainsprings of fertility: the earth and the sun. To protect them from the girl was primitive man's primary consideration. Her very touch of the ground would stop things from growing, and for the sun to see her, or to be seen by her, would deprive the solar body of its fertility-producing gifts.

It thus followed that in the puberty rites all over the world the first demand was the complete isolation of the girl from the ground and the sun. Only the way this was done differed from tribe to tribe. Once her strict separation had been assured, other measures were taken further to restrict her possible adverse influence.

Whatever the methods employed by tribal law, tremendous feats of physical and psychological endurance were expected of the girl. She was confined, sometimes for a period of a hundred days, to her first menstrual hut. Often she had to undergo an extended period of fasting (up to four or five days), before or after which her diet was limited. She could eat only vegetarian food and had to avoid cold water.

Some tribes made her stay in a dark hovel, or in a cage raised above the ground, or even in a hammock suspended between trees. Sometimes she was forced to sit motionless, for perhaps three or four days, in the dark. When outside, she had to cover her head so that she could not see, or be touched by, the rays of the sun. To insulate the ground from direct contact, her feet were mounted on platforms—the predecessors of modern heels. Any man who spoke to her would be severely punished, in some regions with death. And, of course, she was never left to her own devices but all the time was strictly guarded.

Among many groups, in preparation for her future sexual life, the rupture of the girl's hymen was also part of the rite. After all, the advent of puberty most of all proclaimed her being ready for marriage.

Girls were warned that should they transgress any of the taboos, they would inflict irreparable damage on themselves. Thus fear reinforced their observance and made the girls willing partners in the ordeal and all it implied.

All the greater was the relief and joy when, eventually, the test was over and the girl was admitted—like the boys—with a feast and a dance into the adult group, with her new status.

The initiation rites are obviously the very origin and basis of the Jewish Bar Mitzvah and the Christian confirmation ceremonies.

Female Circumcision

Even girls were circumcised, though, of course, the application of the term in their case is inexact. The operation took various forms. These ranged from making a mere gash in the vagina to the removal of the labia minora and/or clitoridectomy, the excision of the clitoris, that rudimentary penis in the female genital.

Though less widely practiced than male circumcision, the custom nevertheless was known in many parts of the world, among Peruvian Indians, ancient Egyptians and Malayans, for instance.

A Moslem tradition tells that God commanded Abraham to cut out Sarah's clitoris when he lost his prepuce. Another Arab myth alleges that Sarah introduced female circumcision. While still barren, she was jealous of Hagar, her husband's concubine and her rival. Therefore she had disfigured the young girl's genitals, and then enforced that very same mutilation on all Egyptian women.

Apart from such legends, suggestions as to the original motivation are almost as varied as in the case of man and, at times, contradictory.

Female circumcision possibly evolved in imitation of the male rite, an early example of woman's quest for equal "treatment." She just copied and adapted to her physiology a male institution.

Its purpose much depended on the actual time the rite was performed. If done at a very early age, circumcision tried to protect the girl's chastity. The clitoris was recognized as the center of sexual excitability, and its removal thus eliminated the prime source of sexual arousal.

Just as in male circumcision, in the majority of cases its female counterpart took place at the time of marriage, in preparation for the first coitus, and often coincided with the girl's defloration. It was seen as a means to promote her fertility and to facilitate intercourse. When, through the practice of masturbation or other causes, the female genital was abnormally enlarged, circumcision surgically remedied such hypertrophy.

Psychoanalysis here, too, has presented numerous interpretations and explanations. Female circumcision had its origin, it was said, in the belief that the operation with its shedding of (genital) blood would give man control over the mysterious phenomenon of menstrual bleeding and power over the vagina.

Other authorities claimed that women themselves had

adopted the rite to assert their equal status with men. Envious of the impressive male initiation rites, they had copied them (even at the cost of their own hurt), adapting them to the features of the female anatomy. On the other hand, it was thought that men had forced the painful surgery on women. Why should only the male suffer damage to his genital? Furthermore, being jealous of the woman's ability to bear children, man wished her to suffer for it (even more) by inflicting on her the (additional) discomfort of circumcision.

The social effect of circumcision in primitive society was diverse. In some groups only a circumcised woman was permitted to marry. There were, in fact, some tribes who regarded its absence as grounds for divorce. Circumcision gave a woman the right of intercourse and was, as it were, the admission ticket to full membership in her tribe. The uncircumcised woman was shunned as unclean and a source (and target) of misfortune.

The operation was performed by a priest, a male relative or, most often, by a woman. Frequently it took place (again parallel to the male rite) at a secluded site.

The removed part of the female genital, like the man's foreskin, was treated with caution and reverence, stored away or destroyed in like manner. At times, the blood flowing during the operation was collected and reserved as an invigorating or rejuvenating potion for the feeble, the sick or the injured.

A Bloody Curse or "Her Relations Have Come"

Menstruation is such a clear and objective term. It records the "monthly" (Latin *menses*) recurring discharge from the womb, a woman's "period."

What then caused man (who in this case, as so often, embraces woman as well) to avoid the use of such an innocuous, dignified description, and to choose in its stead a multitude of disguises and euphemisms, such as "she's got a visitor," "her relations have come" or "she is unwell," a most ambiguous phrase which could mean so many different things? An American gynecologist referred to menstruation perhaps most appropriately as "the tears of a disappointed uterus."

Blood is a vital fluid of any creature. Though primitive man was not literate, his powers of observation, if anything, surpassed those of his "civilized" successor. He could not help but notice, whether in warfare or hunting, that loss of blood resulted in a substantial weakening of the injured person or beast, if not its death. He therefore reasoned (in the words of the Bible, though long before it) that "the blood is the life." The Iliad described how both soul and blood issued from a mortal wound.

Blood thus became an object of sacred awe. This very phenomenon, however, produced diametrically opposite effects. Man either avidly used blood to increase his soul power and strength, employing it as a potent remedy against disease and in magic, or fearfully observed every possible measure to protect and guard himself from any contact with it. Whichever way it was, he became obsessed by blood and its power for good and evil.

On the one hand, he drank blood as part of orgiastic rituals or partook of it in sacred communion with the divine. Conquerors inflicted wounds on their captives' bodies for the sole purpose of sucking from them the precious liquid. Natives mixed special drinks with blood, believing that this strange cocktail would render them invincible. Others spilled blood upon the ground to make it fertile. Solemn pacts were confirmed by mixing one party's blood with that of the other, creating a "blood-brotherhood" that could never be broken.

On the other hand and at the other extreme, to shed any blood or swallow even its most minute quantity was regarded as sinful and as foreboding misfortune. It would do the worst possible harm. That is why, for instance, many primitive tribes in various part of the world took great care when slaughtering animals, lest any of their blood be spilled on the ground. The identical awe of blood explains why in medieval law capital punishment was frequently carried out not by the executioner's sword or ax but by burning or stoning the condemned to death.

Jews and subsequently Moslems too evolved their meticulously observed methods of ritual slaughtering. Its (original) purpose was to drain from the beast a maximum amount of blood lest this be eaten. To make doubly sure that no trace of blood should be left, according to Jewish orthodox tradition, the meat had further to be salted and soaked in water before being cooked.

To see a woman exude blood—this mysterious essence of life —not as result of an injury she had suffered but, as it were, through incomprehensible, supernatural causes, filled early man with numinous dread.

People at that time did not take the occurrence of menstruation for granted, and what we would now call a biological fact was far from understood. As there was no obvious natural explanation, the flow of blood could not but mystify and puzzle early man. He was bewildered and wondered how it had all come about.

In myths he spoke of how it was first caused by the bite of a snake or a wild beast. (Among the Chiriguano, in fact, women pounded the floor and walls of the hut where a girl had been isolated during her first menstruation, to drive away "the snake that has wounded the girl" and thus had made her bleed.) Others believed that it was due to an injury inflicted on the woman by a demonic spirit or a supernatural force. All these "explanations," of course, made her menstrual blood all the more perilous and ominous.

Religious thinkers put forward the view (though without actual scriptural evidence) that the woman's period was part of the curse which God had imposed on Eve, as a punishment for her leading Adam on to fornication and sin.

A modern (pseudo)scientific theory is intriguing. It was published in 1920 in a German journal of sexual research and was evolved by Professor A. Gerson. He claimed that at first women did not "bleed." However, when, during moonlit nights, primitive man chased them with but one aim in mind (which needed no explanation), the females became sexually aroused beyond measure. Their eager anticipation of what was to follow, anxiously hoping to be caught, caused a physiological reaction, a phenomenon defined as *uterine hyperemia*.

Their extreme excitement made the lining of the uterus swell so much that it started bleeding intensely. The blood flow eventually became so profuse that the uterus could not contain it. Seeking an outlet, it found the only available channel. And that is how the first menstruation took place . . .

A woman having a period (as this later term actually indicates) at regular intervals and the fact that her blood flowed from the very spot which was also the source of birth, gave her—in the eyes of primitive man—supernatural power, an influence potentially dangerous and destructive not only to others but to herself. Sir James Frazer, in a telling metaphor, compared it to an enormous electric charge which could do the worst possible damage.

A menstruating woman's power over people and things was thought so immense that anything (or anyone) she touched—like herself in her menstrual state—became taboo.

Pliny in his *Natural History* asserted that the mere touch of a menstruating woman would turn wine into vinegar, dim mirrors, blunt razors, rust metal, and if not actually kill bees, would at least drive them from their hives. Others claimed that her pernicious influence would sour cream, spoil wine, cause cakes and bread to sink while being baked and glassware to break. Red Indian mountain women of Ozark believed that for a woman who was "unwell" to kiss or merely to wink at a man would result in the birth of an illegitimate child.

The identical awe of menstrual blood accounts for the custom of extremely orthodox Jewish men of refusing to shake hands with any woman even today. They are afraid that she might just happen to be in her "dangerous" state.

Every possible precaution has been taken by different societies throughout the ages to avoid a menstruating woman or to undo any evil effect she might have had. Uganda natives thus destroyed vessels with which she had come into contact. British Columbian Indians discarded arrows over which she had stepped as they had lost their potency.

Menstruating women were warned off fishing and hunting grounds, as their very presence would impair any success. To exclude the possibility of even an accidental "communication," primitive society confined them in huts, set up at a safe distance and carefully guarded.

Continuing Frazer's simile, the electrically charged female had to be completely "insulated" lest any contact electrocute the trespasser.

Some tribes regarded her as still being dangerous for some time after her period had stopped. For that reason she had to cover her face with a veil, since even to see her at such a time carried untold, mysterious dangers.

It followed almost inevitably that to have the most intimate contact with a woman while she was bleeding, to sleep with her, became a strictly observed taboo. The Bible threatened both parties either with exile or death: "And if a man shall lie with a woman having her sickness [!], and shall uncover her nakedness, he has made naked the fountain, and she has uncovered the fountain of her blood—both of them shall be cut off from among their people" (Lev. 20:18). The reason certainly was not modesty but, once again, the dreaded awe of the blood.

Coitus with a menstruating woman, other superstitions believed, would cause measles or syphilis in the man. Any future children would be weak, sickly, if not insane. They would be disfigured by huge flaming molelike birthmarks on their faces.

The abstention was practiced worldwide, and it is still being observed in many cases though it is now explained by saying that sexual intercourse during a woman's period was unhygienic and unaesthetic. A modern theory has added weight to the taboo, but this time for vital reasons. It suggests that statistics prove that cancer of the uterus occurs less frequently among Jewish women who continue to obey the biblical law.

Superstitions about menstruation abound so much that to list them all is out of the question. Another wrong notion, based on the approximately equal length of a lunar month (roughly twenty-nine and a half days) and the menstrual cycle (twenty-eight days), imagined a causal connection between the moon's phases and the woman's bleeding. It is as farfetched and misleading as the belief that it is harmful for a woman who is "unwell" to bathe or to wash her hair.

Perhaps of all sexual phenomena none has given rise to so many misconceptions, fallacies, strange fantasies, phobias and taboos as menstruation. Yet all of them started with and are based on the original dread of the flowing blood.

How Woman Became the Inferior Sex

In an age of women's liberation, it must be realized that since the beginning of "man" woman has played a secondary role. Some

short-lived or rare examples of matriarchy, Amazons and powerful queens are merely the exceptions that prove the rule.

Theologians quoted the Bible and saw in woman's degradation a divine institution. After all, they said, man came first and
Eve was created only afterward, as a "secondary" being. The
story of Genesis suggested to them that she was made out of a
"supernumerary bone" of Adam—thus adding insult (to the
woman) to the injury (of the man).

"Woman is womb," it was claimed, good only for procreation. And the early teachings of religion were not improved by
the philosophers either. After thanking God for having been
created a free man and not a slave, Plato immediately added his
gratitude for having been made a man and not a woman. And
Aristotle—without compunction—stated that a woman was
female through her lack of certain qualities, being "afflicted with
a natural defectiveness." The "imbecility and instability" of her
sex were quoted by Roman lawyers as reasons to restrict her
rights.

Man's superiority was taken for granted and accepted by
most women quietly. The male certainly affirmed and enforced
his status continually by every possible measure.

Legally a girl belonged to her father and on marriage became
the property of her husband. That is why she is still called by his
name (except in some advanced countries, such as Iceland). Even
language has perpetuated woman's subordination. The term
"man" designates not merely (sexually) the male but *all* human
beings of whom, as it were, woman was only a subdivision.

Such background and history explain why still in modern
times women were restricted to what the Germans called the
three K's—*Kinder, Kirche* and *Kueche,* easily rendered in English
as the three C's—children, church and cooking.

Even if the claim that matriarchy preceded patriarchy were
correct, the fact is that man must have won the battle and that—
apart from a few secluded spots in the world—he has had the
upper hand for thousands of years. What then put woman (and
kept her) in her (inferior) place? How did it all start?

By nature of her very sex woman was at a disadvantage. She
was preoccupied with menstruation, pregnancy and childbirth.
These were her greatest handicap. They confined her activities

and sapped her strength. The general absence of birth control made pregnancies not few and far between but almost as regular as clockwork and therefore fettered woman and gave man all the chance.

However, these biological factors were only minor, if compared with the dread and fear those very situations of her life aroused. To the primitive mind, after all, menstruation, pregnancy and childbirth were not natural phenomena. They were mysterious, mana-laden states when a woman became highly dangerous. She was like a live volcano, ready to burst forth and do tremendous harm. She was contagious, unclean and defiling.

Therefore man had to limit her power, to keep her, as far as he could in dealing with supernatural forces, "under control." And it did not take long for all the fears and dreads associated with those special occasions to taint the entire concept of woman and affect her treatment by man.

Masturbation

Perhaps no other sexual activity has plagued man's mind more as being wicked, sinful and dangerous both to mental and physical health than the phenomenon of masturbation. This simple act of manipulating the genital organ to produce pleasure (and an orgasm) has been described as "self-abuse."

The term "masturbation" itself, from the Latin, is equally loaded with contempt as it (most probably) means to "defile with the hand" *(manu-stuprare)*. And yet, to begin with, masturbation, far from being decried and condemned, was practiced as a religious duty.

Masturbation belonged to pagan worship. It was a sacred practice. To serve the gods, men wildly manipulated their penises, offering the issuing semen as a solemn sacrifice. This they either placed on the altar or fed into the mouth of Moloch.

In vivid description and imagery, ancient myths and statuary —stemming from India, Egypt and Mesopotamia—recall this ritual of holy masturbation.

Through its very act, so Egyptian tradition taught, Aton-Re had created the universe. The large rivers fructifying the earth—

the Nile, Euphrates and Ganges—were depicted, literally and figuratively, as the life-giving liquid gushing from the ever-erect enormous divine lingam.

To maintain the world and its fertility the gods needed ever more semen, and it was man's duty to provide it. Without their gift, the gods would not be able (or willing) to preserve life. Voracious in their semenal appetite, they required a constant supply. Semen indeed was nectar—food for the gods —whether to the Indian Shiva or the Ammonite Moloch. That is how men daily reenacted at pagan shrines the original divine creative act and nourished the ritual fire with the fire of lust.

Masturbation was thus still far removed from its later description as self-abuse and all it implied. In fact, secular primitive society as well accepted its practice as something "normal," at least for certain periods of life, particularly adolescence. It was taken for granted, and no one condemned it as wicked or imagined that it had any deleterious effect on body or mind.

No feelings of guilt accompanied the practice of masturbation among primitive races. At times, boys masturbated in groups. Marquesan youths even held masturbation contests, the winner being the lad who first had an orgasm.

However, a different attitude was generally taken toward adults who continued to masturbate. But even then it was still not a cause for shame but merely for amusement or, at worst, for pity. Obviously, the savage mind reasoned, such people must have a defect in their body or no one wanted them. In other societies men did resort to masturbation, but only if they lacked the opportunity for having natural intercourse. In some rare cases they did so for the purpose of population control.

The change of attitude toward masturbation was due in no small measure to Judeo-Christian tradition. No doubt, the very fact that it was part of pagan cult roused the initial vehement opposition. To eradicate the erotic rites, masturbation had to be eliminated.

The condemnation is actually based on a passage in early biblical writing of which the meaning is not even clear. It tells of Onan who, to fulfill the Hebrew (Levirate) law, was commanded to marry his childless, widowed sister-in-law for the sole purpose of begetting a son and thereby perpetuating his dead brother's name. Though apparently agreeing and about to fulfill his duty, at the last moment he did not sleep with her but spilled his semen on the ground (Gen. 38:1–11). Some authorities saw in his action an example of *coitus interruptus.* Generally, however, it was taken as a typical case of masturbation.

To punish Onan for his neglect (so the Bible says), he was put to death: he had done that which was "evil in the sight of the Lord." And masturbation (also called after him, onanism) consequently became a crime.

An additional factor that added to its condemnation was the general view of both Jew and Christian on the purpose of sex. Man produced semen with the one aim: to beget children. To waste it for mere pleasure was therefore sinful. More so, could not that very ejaculation by sexual contact have fathered a child? Hence, authorities soon declared a masturbator guilty of a capital crime. As it were, by default he had potentially killed a human being. Thomas Aquinas said that masturbation was worse than fornication. The Zohar, Jewry's mystical Bible, decried the "vice" as the most severe sin.

This was not the end of the matter. Everything had to be done to avoid even involuntary loss of semen. Men were made responsible for this as well, as they could have taken some precautionary measures to prevent the "issue." Almost an entire catalogue of prohibitions was thus drawn up by rabbinical authorities. No man should indulge in sexual daydreaming, wear tight trousers or hold his penis when urinating. Any action or thought that was likely to stimulate him should be shunned as a first step toward the desire to masturbate.

Is it any wonder that with this background subsequent rationalizations of the ancient taboo led people to believe in the harmful consequences of masturbation which, in reality, are merely old wives' tales. So-called educationists were possessed with such misconceptions and warned parents and children of the evil effect of self-abuse. One authority advised anxious parents to put a clasp on their boy's organ to prevent him from indulging in the habit. In the early 1800s little cages were introduced to be securely locked over a boy's genitals. Only the father had the key to open it up—when nature called. An ingenious inventor went further and suggested providing the enclosure with inward-pointing spikes. These would set off a bell the moment the boy experienced an erection . . .

A sad tale, indeed, is the story of masturbation!

6.

Marriage Customs

Marriage Is a Private Affair

In biblical times a specific marriage ritual was unknown. Sex itself was the ceremony. There was no additional vow, no formula, officiant or "documentation." The actual sexual union of the man and the woman, making them "one flesh," was all that was needed.

Celebrations came later and were of a secular nature, expressing marital joy. There were no established rules and regulations. We hear in some instances of a marriage feast and a nuptial period at times extending to an entire week. Festive processions, arranged separately for the bridal party and that of the groom, became a further feature. Either they themselves or the friends accompanying them intoned appropriate songs. At night torches illuminated the happy scene. But altogether it was as yet a family affair and not a matter for "state" and/or "church."

Legally, however, the relationship between both parties was already established by their official engagement. This was effected by the groom's payment of a purchase price to the girl's family. This could take the form of a sum of money, property or a personal service, such as working on the land or fighting in battle. After all, in the framework of an agricultural society, his future wife had served her family well as a worker and economic asset. Therefore her marriage implied a considerable loss to them. Thus

69

the earliest bride price (dowry in reverse) was a unique type of "workers' compensation."

A betrothed couple's obligation to one another was so firm and binding that its dissolution required a divorce and any infidelity or violation on the part of the engaged girl (not the man!) was condemned as serious an offense as the adultery of a married woman.

The Importance of Sex in Marriage

That marriage is a gamble may be true or false. But no one can deny that (etymologically) a wedding is a "pledge." It recalls the ancient institution of an official betrothal at which the bridegroom made the formal pledge *(wed)* to marry the girl and no other.

To begin with, marriage had as its sole purpose the begetting of children. It was therefore an institution of tribal (and later national) importance. Organized sex relations were essential for the maintenance of a firm social structure. Is it any wonder that at times every possible means was employed to discourage people from staying single?

Spartans, for instance, deprived the unmarried of civic rights and further punished them by imposing on them the execution of menial tasks. Romans tried to encourage matrimony by levying on bachelors a special tax and denying single men the right of inheritance.

Jewish tradition regarded an unmarried man as being "incomplete." His very state of unmarriedness broke the perpetually valid commandment to "be fruitful and multiply." Religious perfection indeed could be attained only in the married state.

Restrictions in marriage, in ancient Hebrew law, were only rare. Apart from generally forbidden "degrees," they applied to a priest who could not marry a proselyte, a divorcee or a prostitute. The high priest had to choose a virgin for his wife. Unless he was married, his prayers could not be completely efficacious, and therefore he could conduct the worship on the Day of Atonement, the most sacred day of the year, only if he was married. Otherwise God's forgiveness of the people's sins, brought about by his intercession, was in jeopardy!

Christianity, as the child of Judaism, for the first three centuries of its existence, did not generally object to marriage nor demand celibacy of its priests. In spite of ascetic tendencies, it could not deny the necessity of wedlock. The New Testament saw in it a compromise between sensuous indulgence and sexual abstinence. Nevertheless, it viewed as a man's sacred duty his begetting of children.

The Right of the First Night

Virginity was sacred. After all, it was from the divinity that woman had gained her generative power. Therefore it was only right to sacrifice to him what was the very guardian of the gateway to fertility—the hymen. It was the most welcome offering.

The priests, as the god's delegates, arrogated the task to themselves and acted on his behalf. Thus they claimed the "right of the first night," which in legal nomenclature became known by its Latin rendering as *jus primae noctis*. They observed it not as a privilege, a pleasure or in abuse of despotic power. It was their sacred duty for which (to add, as it were, insult to injury) they additionally charged a "fee."

It sometimes happened that impecunious women had to stay spinsters because they could not afford to pay the price. To sleep with a man prior to having the hymen pierced in the temple would offend the god (or his delegate, the priest). In fact, this practice was so important and became so firmly established that no man would dare have intercourse without the piercing having been performed! It is the origin of prenuptial temple prostitution.

The actual reason was far from vested interests on the part of priesthood, as anticlerics might be tempted to suggest. After all, even more fraught with danger than the menstrual blood was the blood of the pierced hymen. For any ordinary man to deflower a girl and thereby to come into contact with the blood would inflict on him irreparable harm. The divinely protected priest therefore undertook the perilous task. A bridegroom, not grudgingly but almost gladly, delegated to him the "right of the first night."

Once the hymen was pierced and the blood had been shed,

the spell was broken and nothing further could threaten the man's virility.

Ecclesiastical rights waned and, secularized, were appropriated by civic power. That is how this significant "right," once sacrosanct as based on potent (though imaginary) fears, eventually became the cherished privilege of royalty and, later on, of feudal lords in medieval Europe.

Girls living within the jurisdiction of the lord of the manor had to appear before him, or rather to share his bed, before the actual wedding night. This *jus primae noctis* now became known by the French *droit du seigneur,* referring to "the lord's privilege" to take the girl's virginity.

Meticulously he observed his "duty." No vassal of his domain would act in defiance of this practice and carry away a girl without "payment." However, it was at the lord's discretion to waive his right. If he did so, he was entitled to a properly assessed monetary compensation.

The system even survived in the American South, where plantation owners practiced it with Negro women. They explained that it was a master's obligation "to pleasure his wenches the first time." Only the abolition of slavery in 1863 did away with this custom.

A psychological interpretation (if not rationalization) of the "right of the first night" claimed that, in reality, it did the future husband a favor. It diverted from him any resentment the woman may have subconsciously felt against the person who took her virginity.

Tobias Nights

It was only natural that both bride and groom longed to consummate their marriage at the earliest possible moment. And yet ancient tradition strongly guarded against the realization of that wish. Almost superhumanly, it demanded and expected of them a completely sexless "first night." Not moral scruples or an assumption of an innate shyness on the part of either party was the reason, but pagan superstition and belief in demonic forces.

A sexual "quarantine" of three days (the sacred trinitarian

number) in fact was eventually introduced. It was felt that this period of abstinence would make ineffective any attempt on the part of the evil powers to ruin the couple's future happiness. Moreover, primitive man believed in the magical power of sex contamination. Immediate coitus would bring disaster. Only a gradual sexual coming together and coupling would minimize this perilous situation, as already encountered in the custom of "bundling."

Sexual contact therefore had to be refrained from for those first three nights, so that the pair's marital life would be secure. And, considered from that angle, the premium to be paid for this unique type of insurance policy was well worthwhile.

Later generations, though cognizant of the cause of this sex taboo, have tried to give it a "reasonable" sort of explanation or some more tangible interpretation.

Most quoted as the source of such contra-natural abstinence from intercourse is the story contained in the apocryphal book of Tobit.

This tells of a certain Sarah who, living in the land of Media, had been widowed seven times. To add to the tragedy, each of her seven husbands had died in the bridal chamber on their very wedding night. Their deaths were due, the book claims, not to an overstrained heart or the excess of excitement but to the nefarious intervention of the demon Asmodeus.

On a mission to collect an outstanding debt in Media, Tobias, son of pious Tobit, so the tale continues, not only encountered the unlucky and misfortune-bringing girl but fell in love with her.

Aware of, and yet not intimidated by the fate of the seven former spouses, he decided to marry her there and then. But he was wise enough to take precautionary measures. To avoid suffering the fate of his predecessors, he followed the advice of his travel companion who, though appearing in human form, in reality was an angel in disguise.

On the possibly ominous first night, he burned in the bridal chamber the heart and liver of a fish he had previously caught. By so doing he had fumigated the bridal room against the lethal demonic force and thus survived that dangerous night—to live with his wife happily ever after.

Obviously the story contains remnants of the great fear associated with the changing of a virgin into a woman, so fraught with danger, particularly through the blood shed by the piercing of the hymen.

To begin with, abstinence was observed only on the first night. Its extension to two and then three nights was almost a foregone conclusion, to make doubly and trebly sure that no harm would be done. Traditionally the "three nights" are traced back to the book of Tobit, not to its original version but its Latin translation, in the Vulgate. The text there links the couple's immunity to their keeping apart not just for one night (as mentioned in the Greek version of the book and the King James translation) but for three. And it is for this reason that ever since these have been known as "Tobias nights."

The Christian Church could certainly not adopt the pagan background, though, of course, it was well aware of it. Hence it spiritualized the explanation. According to it the sexless nights were necessary. To consummate the marriage immediately after the pronouncement of the sacred benediction over holy matrimony would be tantamount to an act of carnal lust!

Sex Food and the Magic Mandrake

Magic, mystery and sex combined in ancient times to make the mandrake a powerful gift to love-starved sterile women. The very word "mandrake" does not conceal the early association of a *man* and a *drake* (here meaning a dragon). It is an obvious allusion to both the manlike, bifurcated shape of the plant's root and its assumed magical properties attributed to its dragon part.

Abundant evidence, from all over the world and from antiquity onward, shows how the mandrake was treasured as a potent aphrodisiac and a cure for sterility in both man and beast. Barren women believed that, by partaking of it, they would be able to bear children. Avidly and trustfully they ate the mandrake root, just as nowadays women take "the pill" (only for the opposite reason).

Myths abound with examples of its magical use. Circe, the enchantress of the legendary island of Aeaea, is said to have mixed it in the charm-producing brews that lured her lovers to their doom.

People, anxiously wishing to see a newlywed girl become a mother, either presented the bride with a "sprig" of the plant or secretly hid its root under the bridal bed. Even as erudite a man as Albertus Magnus, thirteenth-century theologian, philosopher and scientist (!), still believed in the mandrake as a remedy for barrenness.

But best known of all examples of how the mandrake was valued as a sex plant of magic and mystery is the biblical story in the book of Genesis (30: 14–17). Its Hebrew term, rooted in an ancient Ugaritic word for mandrake, literally means "love giver." Its Aramaic rendering stresses its power to "chase away" demons who no doubt were maliciously trying to rob the woman of her gift of fertility. The margin in the Revised English Version of the identical passage appropriately translates the word as "love apple."

Its magic influence was well known even to children in the Bible. That is why young Reuben, when finding a mandrake in a wheat field, brought it home to his mother Leah. But Rachel, her still childless rival, hearing of it, begged Leah to hand it over to her as she needed it so much more. And in her anxiety to own this valuable plant, she was even prepared to strike a costly bargain: in return for this wonder-working aphrodisiac, she would give up one night with Jacob and let Leah sleep with him instead!

And the result of that night's intercourse, brought about not by the mandrake itself but by its sale, was the birth, nine months later, of Issachar. That, in fact, is the explanation of his very name which for all time gave away—to those who know Hebrew—the circumstances of his conception. Issachar is derived from the Hebrew verb *sachar*—"to hire for wages"! Rachel had hired out her husband for the price of a mandrake!

It is only fair to record (and thereby also to indicate the realism and truthfulness of biblical writing) that in spite of all the hope and expectation, the mandrake had not at first the desired result. Rachel remained childless. When eventually she became pregnant (with Joseph, the eleventh of Jacob's twelve sons), it was not on account of the mandrake but because "the Lord remembered."

To find out how sex came to be associated with the mandrake plant offers no difficulty. A mere look at its forked fleshy root does not require much imagination to recognize the reason. Almost twelve inches long, the root roughly resembles a man's body with his two legs. More significantly still, a subsidiary root strikingly suggests his penis. That is how, no doubt, the mandrake entered the pharmacopoeia of aphrodisiacs. Its fruit, of pungent smell and the size of a small apple, probably benefited by its mere association, and soon was accepted as "sex food" as well.

The mandrake's assumed sexual potency (always viewed with awe) and all the magic with which it was surrounded, almost inevitably led people to regard the plant as possessed of dangerous power. Thus, even its mere removal from the soil was fraught with danger, which could prove fatal. Early harvesters imagined that the mandrake fiercely struggled against being pulled out and even asserted that it emitted a cry when disturbed. Therefore, an odd means of breaking its resistance was the douching of the plant with either the urine of a woman or her menstrual blood!

To safeguard himself, man began to employ dogs to gain possession of the precious herb. First he dug a trench around it, leaving only the actual root embedded. He then fastened a cord to it, tying its other end around the dog's neck which, called to from a distance, obeyed its master's command and thereby not only uprooted the plant but simultaneously choked itself to death.

A more humane version of the procedure had the cord tied to the dog's tail. A piece of meat was then enticingly held just out of its reach. By making a dash for it, the dog pulled out the mandrake . . .

Love Fixation

Superstition has ruled the minds of men and women in the entire realm of sex relations and, once again, above all where there was anxiety, worry and doubt. Uncertainty always provided the most propitious field for that fertile weed.

A woman who, in spite of all efforts, could not conceive a child, in her despair and frustration took refuge in every type of magic.

To gain and retain the love of a person opened wide the gates to superstition. Every and any means was employed magically to attract the other sex. Lodestones were a popular feature in this medicine chest of sex "appeal." Their magnetic power, it was firmly believed, would draw near the desired "object" of affection and do so inexorably even against his or her wish. Present-day innocuous habits or ornamentations grew out of these early manipulations and superstitions.

Thus the locket of hair, to start with, did not serve as a constant reminder of and close contact with at least part of the person one loved. Much more subtly, it ensured a man's or woman's permanency of love by remote control.

A gruesome form of love magic led straight to the cemetery. Long before modern usage of certain "strips" to kill pests, in Ireland the lovelorn employed a "deadly" strip to preserve love.

A girl anxious to keep the affection of her man stole to the graveyard in the dead of night. There she exhumed a body buried exactly nine days—a trinity of trinities. This done, she cut from it a strip of skin. Still that same night she tied the macabre token thus acquired, like a magic circle, around either the arm or leg of her sleeping lover. Significantly, however, she carefully removed it before he woke up, as only then the spell would work and "fix" permanently the man's love.

The most frequent and widespread means to ensure love was the use of philters. The word philter is derived from the Greek *philtron,* meaning "love." To speak of a "love philter" therefore is really a pleonasm. However, this duplication of the word "love" might not be the result of lack of (Greek) knowledge. Perhaps it was purposely introduced to act as a verbal charm. To say "love" twice would double its strength.

The institution of the honeymoon owes its very name to a love potion. All through the first month ("moonth") of their marriage, groom and bride used to partake of a drink made from fermented honey. They were convinced that this would act as an amatory stimulant.

Honey, indeed, was one of the favored ingredients of many an aphrodisiac. Arabs thus drank camel's milk laced with honey. The famous sixteenth-century manual of Arabian erotic techniques, the *Perfumed Garden,* advised those anxious to stimulate their sexual powers to take nightly before retiring a glass of honey with twenty almonds.

Philters were infused from almost every type of exotic plant, of animate and inanimate source. The more farfetched they were (in oddity or rarity), the greater their efficacy was assumed to be. Because of some specific association with the erotic—in language, shape or original function—certain parts of an animal or a plant were regarded as particularly helpful in this conquest of love. An obvious example was the choice of semen or testes.

In his *Natural History* Pliny the Elder tells of the popularity of a bracelet which contained the right testis of an ass. It was treasured for its aphrodisiac qualities thought to be specially potent, as the donkey was regarded a particularly lascivious animal.

Even where the original link of the substance of a philter can no longer be traced or guessed, it might just be that through the distance of time it got lost but existed in the mind of man in far-off days. A typical instance is the use of the tongue of the wryneck. Ancient mythology has the key. Legend tells that the bird really was Iynx, the nymph. She had been a very amorous creature causing much heartache to Hera, Zeus's wife. Clandestinely Iynx had acted as a messenger of love between the god Zeus and the priestess Io. One tradition even claimed that Iynx herself "on the side" had a love affair with the great god.

In anger and jealousy Hera had punished the nymph by transforming her into the bird. And always to be reminded of her preoccupation—carrying messages to and fro between Zeus and Io, she—now in the form of a bird—was forced to move the head almost constantly from side to side. This, too, explains the Latin description of the wryneck, a kind of woodpecker, as *Jynx torquilla.* Is it any wonder, therefore, that its tongue was chosen for the concoction of love philters? Pindar records how the bird's entire body—spread on a wheel—was also employed as a love charm.

Another highly prized but gruesome element for love potions was moss from the skull of a murdered man. This time not a myth but a primitive train of thought led to this "fancy."

A murdered person died prematurely, before the completion of his natural term of life. Because of it he must still have had an unused store of vital power. This so-far-untapped life energy was thought to grow into (or to be absorbed by) the fungus. Its use would therefore prove beneficial in a love philter.

Exotic and even nauseating are many of the prescriptions that have survived for the preparation of love potions. One of these was milk of an ass mixed with the blood of a bat. Other ingredients suggested included frog's bones (among the ancient Greeks and Romans), cow's dung (among the Navajos) and human excrement (among the Apaches). Frying, boiling, grinding into powder and brewing were some of the methods used in mixing the drug.

Indians believed in the powerful erotic effect of perfumed fumigation or the rubbing in of the body with certain salves. Well known is the popularity among natives of powdered rhinoceros horn. In fact, it was so much in demand that in certain parts of Africa it almost led to the extinction of the animal.

Thus numerous, indeed, are the potions and ointments that have served from earliest days and in almost every clime as love philters. Some, unknown to the dispenser, really were powerful aphrodisiacs. Others, though physiologically entirely ineffective, nevertheless achieved their aim by firing the imagination of the recipient, showing the power of mind over matter. If nothing else, the marketing of philters and potions has served commercial enterprise and has paid high dividends on the stock market of sex.

* * *

Oddly enough, even the terminology of human anatomy has preserved the "love potion." Philtrum is also the name of that mysterious groove or channel between the septrum of the nose and the center of the upper lip. No one really knows its origin and purpose. Perhaps that is why, situated so closely to an erotic zone, it has been named so "lovingly."

Another possible explanation is that a drop of perspiration, easily caught in this diminutive cup, might be sucked up by a passionate kiss. As an excretion from the lover's own body, it would act like a love charm and exciting sex stimulus. Poetically, indeed, this dimple forms part of the upper lip and its cupid's bow. In fact, it makes it so and thereby perhaps conveys its message of love and gave it its name.

Anatomically, however, the philtrum is part of the juncture between the two halves of the face. The blasphemous might even suggest that a seam left thus showing may reveal bad workmanship.

7.

The Child

The Birth of the Midwife and the Obstetrician

The first midwives were men. This indeed is not surprising, as the term itself (though often misunderstood) does not stipulate for a woman to act this part. Midwife, from Old English, merely means "with [the] wife."

Typical of numerous like legends is the Bornean myth of how midwifery began.

Descended from animals, man continued to learn from them. Kelili, a Bornean father-to-be, went out in search for food, and in the jungle he came across a family of large monkeys. He had seen many of them before but this time he was struck by a scene he had not previously encountered.

One of the animals, obviously very pregnant, was crouching on the ground, shrieking with pain. Nearby sat her mate, looking very concerned.

Kelili was so fascinated that he remained to watch. After a long time of observation, his patience was rewarded. He witnessed the birth of the monkey baby—aided by its father!

What a monkey could do, Kelili reasoned, he could do just as well—if not better. And at the birth of his own child, he likewise assisted his wife and by his example taught all men the new art of midwifery.

To start with, no doubt, a mother gave birth to her child

unaided, all on her own. It was an event in the natural course of things, without much fuss or worry. Instinct or intuition was her sole guide.

She herself severed the umbilical cord by biting it off or cutting through it with a sharp flint. The husband (not necessarily conscious of being the father) completely kept out of the way. He entered the scene only when all was over, displaying his joy and welcoming the infant.

It was almost a foregone conclusion that eventually the man became the first "standby," merely watching or, if need be, assisting his wife. His task was then taken over by women of the family circle, mostly one of the grandmothers or, if none was available, the mother-in-law. But the man still attended the birth, helping in diverse ways. In some communities (as on the island of Engano) he sat on the ground, holding his wife in his lap and periodically massaging her abdomen. At other places (among Caribbean natives) he went to bed during the latter stages of his wife's pregnancy, vocally sharing her birth pangs by moaning and groaning loudly.

This was just a variation of the widespread and very ancient primitive practice referred to by the French term *couvade*. The husband, by dramatically taking to bed, played the role of the pregnant woman. In fact, he made it appear as if he and not his wife was giving birth to the child.

In several regions, indeed, he was "nursed" for an entire week after the delivery. He shammed as if it was he who needed all care while his wife went back to work, only returning home to feed the baby.

Couvade literally describes a "hatching" or "sitting on eggs" and is derived from the Latin *cubare*, to "lie down." Several reasons have been given for this practice. Some see in it a case of early sympathetic magic. The husband, by shamming a birth, helped his wife in her labor.

Others discovered in the custom a surviving, earlier stage of man's evolution when, it was believed, both sexes produced milk to nourish the infant. A feeling of guilt on part of the husband, a third hypothesis says, made him pretend to suffer pain, thus paying the gods for man's sin of sex. Again, it was claimed, his dramatization served the assertion of paternity. He was anxious to proclaim publicly that he was the father and to announce the special bond which existed between the offspring and himself.

Most of all, *couvade* was regarded as an essential precautionary act to guard mother and child. Birth, particularly, was a beginning and therefore fraught with enormous peril. Everyone, of course, knew that the father was merely playacting. But he did so not for fun or out of imagined self-pity. His act of simulation was meant to deceive the devil. Through her pregnancy and the child's birth, his wife was in a state of ritual uncleanness and physical weakness. The baby itself was not only feeble but most vulnerable. The husband and father therefore felt it his obligation to offer himself as the target and, acting as a decoy, to divert all attacks on himself. After all, he was strong and healthy and ritually clean, and his very manhood in itself made him able to resist and ward off all the more every onslaught.

* * *

The earliest (and most natural) position for a woman giving birth was to crouch down. To help her maintain it with ease, the birth stool was invented. Originally this consisted of just two stones, one for each of the woman's buttocks. One of the earliest literary mentions of it is contained in the Bible. The term used there, and usually rendered "stone basin," actually says "two stones" (Ex. 1:16).

Assistance at birth did not remain a family affair. Soon the "wise women" of the tribe assumed this duty. They were the first professional midwives, eventually to become specialists in their task. However, their help and advice went far beyond physical aid. They encouraged the mother in her labor. They used magical means to ease it, to keep away evil spirits and to help the baby.

The number of midwives attending varied in the different cultures and—in Persia, for instance—might amount to eight women. At the height of Greek civilization midwifery had become an honored profession. The mother of Socrates was a midwife, a fact that, no doubt, caused him to compare his search for truth with the art of midwifery and his mental anguish with labor pangs.

Finally, an office which in prehistoric days had started with a concerned husband's administration to his wife was assumed by the male specialist. However, he continues to recall in his name

the "standing by" of the wise women. His title is derived from
a Latin form ending with the female *trix!* He is the obstetrician.
From the Latin *obstetrix* this means "a woman [!] who stands by"
—to receive the child.

The Cesarean

The extraction of a child from its mother's womb by cutting
through the walls of her abdomen is one of the oldest operations.
It was already known among ancient Hindus. So far back indeed
does this type of delivery go, when normal birth was impossible,
that even myths speak of it.

That is how, tradition relates, Asclepius was born. When the
dead body of Coronis, his adulterous mother, had been placed on
the funeral pyre, Hermes had snatched from her womb the still
unborn child!

A less gruesome tale is part of Persian legend. This tells how
the lovely moon-faced wife of King Sal almost died from the
enormous size of the babe she carried within her. A Zoroastrian
priest, however, saved her life. After having given her an anesthetic, he cut open her body and thus delivered the child, Rustan.
Having completed the operation, the priest took great care to sew
up the incision which, in no time, healed. Rustan was to grow into
the Persian Hercules!

At first—and for almost two thousand years—the "cesarean
section" referred to the removal of a child from its dead mother's
womb. The term was first used by Pliny. He, too, originated the
erroneous notion, still encountered from time to time, that it was
by a "cesarean" that Julius Caesar came into the world. The births
of all children attained in like manner have therefore been called
after him. However, the existence of letters Caesar wrote to his
mother refute this claim.

The most likely origin of the term goes back to Scipio
Africanus, the first member of Caesar's family. His mother had
died before he was born. But his own life was saved by "cutting
him out" from his dead mother's body. Everyone was so happy
by his "unnatural" miraculous birth that to celebrate and com-
memorate the occasion the most appropriate name by which to

call the boy was "the cut-out one," from the Latin *caedere*—Caesar. It became so honored that for generations to come all male
members of the dynasty adopted it as a cognomen.

Roman law, indeed, made a "cesarean section" obligatory in
the case of a woman who had died in an advanced stage of
pregnancy. Her body had to be cut open immediately to save the
baby. Numa Pompilus, the first ruler of Rome (elected king in
714 B.C.) is said to have thus decreed. Hence it was *Lex Caesarea*
—the "emperor's law." That is how we continue to speak of a
cesarean birth, though now it describes the excision of a child
from a living mother.

The earliest such recorded case belongs only to the sixteenth
century. The surgery was then performed not by a doctor or a
midwife but by the woman's husband. Jacob Nufer of Sigers-
haufen had watched anxiously the agonies suffered by his pregnant wife. Attempts by thirteen different midwives to end her
pain by helping her to give birth had proved unsuccessful.

Jacob himself was a sow gelder and perhaps his experience
and agility in his profession encouraged him as a last council of
despair to take fate into his own hands. With a sharp razor he cut
out of her womb a lusty boy. His wife not only survived the
operation but (undaunted by her tribulations and undamaged by
his surgery) lived to have six more children. The baby boy delivered by his father reached the ripe old age of seventy-seven!

The first illustration of a cesarean birth does not belong to
a medical work either. It was contained in the printed edition of
second-century Suetonius' *Lives of the [first] Twelve Caesars*. This
appeared in 1506 and the drawing, obviously still picturing a
post-mortem cesarean, was part of the text. It must have been so
popular that in the second printing it was removed from inside
the book to form its frontispiece.

Navel Affairs

No part of man's anatomy has been excluded from speculation
about its origin and purpose. Not least problematic was man's
navel.

A Turkish myth tells how, when God had made the first man,

the devil had seen the divine handiwork. To show his contempt he had spat on man's stomach. Allah immediately realized that the devilish action could do immeasurable harm to his creation. So losing no time and before the malignancy could spread, he grasped the infected spot and removed it from the belly. That is how man has a navel.

Theologians seriously wondered whether Adam was created with or without this important junction, forming the connecting link between mother and child. Controversy raged for centuries as to this "navel affair."

God, one school of thought said, does nothing in vain. Therefore he would never have bestowed on Adam anything superfluous. Hence the navel was only a later addition when birth had become an earthly matter. Others, however, claimed that in his wisdom God always thought of the future and, providing for it in advance, had already equipped the first man with a navel, without which he would have been imperfect.

Some of the great sculptors and painters paid heed to this issue. Consequently, taking sides, they either depicted man with or without his navel, or—being uncertain as to its earliest existence, or afraid to become partisan on the matter—cleverly hid that part of the body, leaving its presence or absence to the beholder's belief or imagination. It was a clever, if not cowardly, camouflage. Eve's long flowing hair particularly lent itself to serve as a "cover."

Michelangelo in the Sistine Chapel came down very definitely in favor of Adam's navel. And yet even his fame did not settle the question permanently. In 1646 Sir Thomas Browne rejected "the authentick draughts of Angelo and others" and showed himself an adamant antinavelist! For Adam to have had a navel would have made God a wastrel by introducing "superfluities or ordained parts without use or office."

That rounded depression in the abdomen became a veritable focus of attention, not least for the Buddhist monks in their meditations. The realization of the vital function of the navel in humans soon caused man to look for a universal navel which therefore assumed cosmic proportions. It was the center of the universe.

New Mexico's Zuñis, for instance, had several legends which

accounted for their people's migration in their search for the navel of the world. Greeks told how it was discovered by Zeus sending out two eagles. They flew at identical speed from the opposite ends of the earth—the east and the west—and met exactly above the central point of the earth. This was marked with a sacred stone of rounded, conical shape and significantly called *omphalos*—the Greek word for "navel."

Mythologies of the various faiths thus sanctified particular spots on earth as its navel, thought to be the focal point of their revelation: the Greeks, the temple of Apollo at Delphi; the Hebrews, Mount Moriah; the Indians, Delhi; and the Moslems, Mecca.

Like the navel, the umbilical cord was regarded as a center of life. Zuñi mythology depicted the god of war with the cord (in the form of a carved stick) protruding at right angles from his body. The cord was viewed with awe by many races. Early man was convinced that even after it had served its initial purpose as a lifeline to the child, it would continue to exert a significant influence on the well-being of its previous beneficiary. Mysteriously it stayed linked with his or her life and was part of the "external soul."

Among primitive people it was mostly the father who severed the cord. He did so by biting or cutting it off with a sharp flake of stone or bamboo knife. Among the Chinese, on the other hand, midwives detached it with a red-hot iron.

The cord was then concealed at a selected site, maybe in the cleft of a rock, on top of or inside a tree (split for that purpose), or buried in the soil. From there, it was thought to be magically effective.

Swahili natives interred the cord under the very hut where the child had been born. This, they believed, would act as a powerful magnet and—like a homing beacon—guide back the child from wherever it went. The Mayas buried the cord on a battlefield. They were sure that this action would make a boy grow into a valiant fighter. The North American Hupa Indians embedded the cord in a young tree, confident that the tree's future fate would reflect what happened to the infant. The Incas of Peru used the umbilical cord as a dummy for sick children. By sucking it, they would be cured. The Teutons even fed the cord to the child that once had been nourished through it, as, according to their tradition, this would endow it with wisdom.

Other traditions linked the positioning of the cord with future qualities of the child that had owned it. To make a boy a good climber, for instance, his cord should be "planted" on top of a tree. A girl would become a good cook if her cord was placed under a grinding stone.

On the other hand, parents carefully guarded the cord lest it fall into the hands of evil forces or be swallowed by a beast, for in either case calamity might befall the child. Nefarious powers could put a spell on the infant or it would grow up inflicted with the worst traits of the animal. Under no circumstances was the cord to be thrown into the sea or a fire. Such disposal, once again by—delayed—sympathetic magic would cause the boy or girl one day to be drowned or be burned to death.

It was believed that no man or woman could really ever completely sever contact with that early lifeline. It continued to influence magically, if not to determine, his or her fate, to the very end.

Abortion

Abortion goes back to earliest days and has been known among most primitive tribes. Therefore its institution is not the result of so-called "sophistication" or civilized women who, anxious to keep their freedom, terminate pregnancy; nor was it due to the wish of unmarried girls to avoid giving birth to an illegitimate child. Likewise, abortion was not practiced in dark back alleys (or their ancient equivalent), or by "professionals" who knowingly broke a solemn oath, or against the law of the land.

On the contrary, in many cases abortion was a duty, socially sanctioned and even enforced by the tribe. It belonged to the warp and woof of the tribal pattern. In fact, to get rid of an unwanted foetus was at times thought to ensure the survival of and to avoid misfortune for, not only the woman, but the entire clan. On the other hand, many of our "modern" reasons that prompt women to seek abortion were known and acted upon thousands of years ago.

And yet, also from the very beginning, the practice of abortion was viewed with contradictory attitudes. Either it was approved of and, indeed, commanded, or it was greatly condemned and severely punished. It all depended on the type of society and the circumstances.

Various motives led early man to abort. These included life-preserving considerations and what we would now term economic factors.

Among nomads, for instance, pregnant women were afraid of being left behind in the wanderings of their tribe and, to save their own lives, they got rid of the foetus.

Periods of famine fostered the practice, sometimes with cruel, cannibalistic features. Women have been known to feed the aborted foetus to their other children who were "meat-hungry."

Primitive communities forced a woman to abort her child if she had conceived it with the "wrong" man. He could be a slave, a member of a hostile tribe, a captive or "demon-possessed." All of these were considered not only an insult to the group but a danger to its welfare, if not very survival. Other rejected paternity included incestuous and adulterous unions and pregnancy which was the result of rape.

Of some women it was said, or they claimed so themselves, that their child had been fathered not by a common mortal but a mischievous spirit. Therefore it would not be a human being but a monster, which to abort was essential lest disaster strike the community.

Superstitious fears thus contributed their share to the incidents of abortion. If the girl had not yet undergone her initiation, she was not permitted either to give birth to a child.

Abortion belonged, too, to some of the earliest (rather painful and dangerous) types of primitive "birth control." This was applied frequently to ensure not only a proper spacing out of the children but equally their economic security. It was an important measure to protect the society against the curse of overpopulation.

Mere vanity on the part of the woman made her seek abortion. She did not want to spoil her body by motherhood.

Prophylactic reasons also played a significant role in early days. Abortion took place if the mother was thought too young or too old. At the height of Greek civilization, Plato advocated abortion of an offspring conceived in the case of a father being above the age of fifty-five and a mother over forty. In some primitive cultures women aborted the foetus because they dreaded childbirth. Their fear of losing their own life was so much stronger than any intimations of mother-love.

A frequent occurrence was the abortion of a first child. This, no doubt, was prompted by having seen other women die during delivery. It was believed that the abortion of the first child would facilitate subsequent pregnancies and thus smooth the way for all future births.

There was the strictest taboo on coitus during the periods of pregnancy and lactation. The mother's attention should focus only on the new baby, and her maternal love should take precedence over any sexual desire and gratification. More so, it was feared that any intercourse that took place during the time she was carrying the child would damage both the body and spirit of the developing foetus. It was no longer any "good" and therefore had to be eliminated.

In the Bible, abortion is mentioned only once and then, as it were, merely incidentally. The passage deals with the bodily assault on a pregnant woman which resulted in the abortion of her unborn child, really a miscarriage (Ex. 21:22-23). If no harm was done to the woman, the attacker got away with a fine. This constituted the payment of a monetary compensation for the lost child. If, however, the attack resulted in the mother's death, he was executed. The attacker now had to pay "life for a life."

It was the—inaccurate—interpretation of this passage which caused abortion to be held as a crime and a pagan abomination. The Church (from Tertullian onward) voiced this condemnation which was then adopted in state legislation. Prevention of birth was tantamount to murder. It made no difference whether one took away a life when actually formed or while forming. "Even every fruit already exists in its seed." The only difference of opinion concerned the time when a foetus was considered a human being, i.e., when the soul joined the body. Tertullian ruled that the soul entered the male embryo forty days after conception. In the case of a girl it was after eighty!

*　　*　　*

As varied as were the causes of abortion, so were the times when it was favored and the methods then employed.

What was regarded as the right moment for abortion differed among the various tribes. It extended to almost any stage of pregnancy. Elimination of the foetus was seen as less dangerous to the tribe than infanticide.

To begin with, the pregnant woman herself attempted the operation. But soon the "old women" of the group and witch doctors were engaged in the occupation which, at times, became a carefully guarded privilege and monopoly. Eventually, mid-wives also looked after this "end" of their trade.

Earliest methods of abortion ranged from magic incantations and procedures to very effective surgical techniques.

Sympathetic magic, of course, was well known. Typical is the recorded instance of a gourd being roasted on a fire. As it burst, it would cause the foetus inside the womb to do likewise.

Women squatted on some magic plant and fancied that, by doing so, they would lose the baby. They possibly did so—psychosomatically.

A common measure of abortion was—by one method or another—to constrict the woman's waist. Friends might squeeze her in an ever-increasing degree, or she might be given a special "constriction belt" which she was obliged to tighten progressively. More cruelly, cases are known in which the pregnant girl was buried up to her waist in the ground—till the growing child, with the belly unable to expand, was choked to death.

Once again, his powers of observation helped primitive man in designing his own techniques. Having seen a woman lose a child by an accident or by carrying too heavy a load, they applied these very measures with varying success.

Other women pummeled her belly, not merely with their hands or fists but with stones. The pregnant woman might throw herself repeatedly against a rock or jump down from great heights.

Another well-known abortion method was medication. All types of drugs, potions and ointments were used.

Mechanical means played their part in the practice of the ancient and primitive abortionist. The simplest instrument used was a pointed stick, inserted into the vagina. The abortionist also manipulated the foetus with his or her hands, grasping or choking the growing child.

* * *

Psychoanalysis and psychiatry have provided some intriguing suggestions as to the subconscious reason for abortion. They claim as its cause a hidden but strongly felt desire on the part of the woman to castrate her husband whom, unknowingly, she hated.

The foetus growing in her womb seemed to her like the presence of a supersized penis which, instead of being removed after a while, stayed inside her "permanently." At first she loved the knowledge of carrying it constantly, and ecstatically relished the feeling of its progressive "swelling." But such sensations were eventually replaced by an even greater satisfaction in ejecting and destroying it—by abortion. This, in fact, represented in her mind and imagination the castration of her husband. Did not the abortion deprive him of his child? As it were, in its final result the abortion rendered the father impotent.

* * *

Certainly, in spite of the widespread approval, its social sanction and even the enforced practice of abortion, other communities strongly condemned, abhorred and punished it. To them it was a heinous crime that threatened the well-being of the group. In ancient India, for instance, abortion was looked upon as evil as the murder of a Brahman. The penal code of the West Goths condemned it as a crime against the welfare of the state.

Much depended on how far (and how soon) the foetus was considered a living being, endowed with a spirit or soul, or whether it was merely taken to be "a piece of wood."

Abortion, it was thought, insulted the gods; it precipitated floods and droughts and numerous other calamities. Most of all, these were caused, so it was asserted, by the ghost of the foetus. Deprived of its abode, it hovered about to haunt the living and to take vengeance. To appease it and to avoid disaster, precautionary actions had to be taken.

The aborted woman herself became taboo. She was not only shunned but also punished. Her husband could divorce her and her tribe could exile her. She could be flogged or, according to ancient Assyrian law and Aztec codes, be put to death by drowning or impalement.

Likewise, those who had assisted her in the act of abortion did not escape scot-free. Their penalty included a heavy fine, the killing of some of their cattle or bodily chastisement.

* * *

The early story of abortion shows how, from the very beginning, man was forced to think about the benefit and the burden of children. He could not escape from facing the problems that confronted him in the clash between his own personal interest and the welfare of his group, parental affection and gross superstition, selfish considerations and religious tradition. Above all, and nothing has changed ever since, he came face to face with the question of what was right and wrong, what was good and what constituted evil.

Contraception

However modern "birth control" is as a slogan, its practice goes back to most ancient days and oldest cultures. Even primitive races knew of it. This is rather intriguing, as they were not fully acquainted with the "facts of life" and did not completely realize the role of the father. Somehow, in spite of their belief in spirits and other outside agencies as being instrumental in the begetting of a child, they must have given the man some credit and guessed, early on, that there was a connection between coitus and birth.

Astonishing indeed is the multiplicity and variety of applied methods and aids. More surprising still is the fact that, although many of the earliest modes of birth control certainly were ineffective superstitions, others anticipated to a striking degree modern methods of contraception. No doubt, they were arrived at by trial and error.

There were several reasons that made earliest man practice birth control. They were magic, religious, hygienic, prophylactic and economic. Some of them, also, forestalled twentieth-century motives and considerations.

Population control, thus, was an original factor. Limited *Lebensraum* and scarcity of resources led already primitive man to seek out ways to limit his offspring. Of course, to start with, he attained this aim much more frequently by abortion and infanticide.

Previous experiences of pain and suffering during pregnancy and at childbirth induced women to take any measure within their power to avoid further pregnancies. Another potent ground for contraception was the fear of death. Women remembered how in the past they had lost young babies and had watched mothers dying while giving birth.

Women who had fallen out with their husbands, and certainly prostitutes, were keen on avoiding pregnancy. In groups which permitted intercourse between young unmarrieds, for a girl to conceive a child was still regarded as being immoral. Among some East African tribes, for instance, youths of both sexes slept together in a common hut, but the boys carefully practiced "withdrawal."

Last, but by no means least, was the influence of religious and ritual motives.

* * *

Far back in antiquity women were taught to place inside their vagina some obstruction or barrier that would prevent the sperm from reaching the ovum. The "experts" (medicine men or physicians) might not have known the physiological facts, but some instinct or partial knowledge put them on the right track.

The first prescriptions for birth control extant are almost four thousand years old. They are contained in papyri discovered at Kahun in Egypt in 1889, dating back to 1850 B.C. The different methods suggested, amazingly, are prototypes of modern techniques. It is recommended that the woman should insert a gumlike substance into her vagina. An alternate method is the application of the first "jelly": a mixture of honey and natron. We also encounter the earliest pessary—made of crocodile dung!

The Ebers papyrus (1500 B.C.) advocated a pessary made of lint saturated with honey and acacia gum. African natives ingeniously produced plugs from every available material: from roots and balls made of finely cut grass to rags. The rabbis of the Talmud were among the first to recommend the sponge as an absorbent.

In addition to using spermicidal substances, thousands of

years ago, women also fumigated their vagina prior and douched it immediately after coitus. And they did all this not for hygienic reasons but to prevent impregnation.

A Sanskrit text advocated certain manipulations of the penis at the moment ejaculation began. This technique eventually became known as *coitus obstructus.*

As was to be expected, many of the earliest methods, side by side with "scientific" techniques, belong to the realm of superstition. Examples from all over the world abound.

They include the drinking of carefully brewed concoctions (apparently the more obnoxious these were, the more they were thought to be efficacious); the eating of certain foods; the swallowing of the foam from a camel's mouth; and the tightening of the waist by ropes.

Chinese women burned on their navel three balls made of leaves of wormwood plants, and the moment these had turned into ashes, they felt "safe." Magic, of course, played an important part: the utterance of spells, the wearing of amulets and, most of all, the tying of knots.

Women, likewise, believed that certain manipulations and jerky movements of their body ejected the semen or that specific positions taken up during coitus avoided conception. According to an ancient Hindu belief strong sunlight favored conception, and therefore it was suggested to those wanting to remain childless to have coitus in the dark.

Breath control was regarded as yet another means of birth control. It was believed if a woman would only hold her breath and remain completely dispassionate, intercourse would have no effect on her whatsoever!

The assumed duration of sterility achieved depended on the various traditons and the frequency of application. In the "tying of knots," for instance, each knot represented one year, and therefore the woman could easily control (so she thought) her periods of fecundity and sterility. Cherokee Indian women, on the other hand, believed that if they partook of the root of a certain plant, chewing and eating it for four days running, they would acquire a lifetime protection against conception.

It is surprising how long such superstitious methods prevailed and how obstinately women believed in their potency.

Early taboos even forestalled the rhythm method. At certain periods of her menstrual cycle a woman was regarded potentially so dangerous that men carefully avoided contact with her. They erroneously imagined that these "dangerous" times (before or immediately after menstruation) coincided with the phases when a woman was most vulnerable to conceive a child.

A matter of controversy was the Australian aboriginal custom of subincision. Certainly, this caused the men to eject their semen externally before it entered the vagina. However, an early opinion that it was actually introduced as a means of birth (and thereby population) control is untenable. Although subincision, in the words of Dr. Norman E. Himes (in his *Medical History of Contraception*), constitutes a deviation from optimum conditions for conception, it is "not an infallible preventative" but "only reduces likelihood of fertilization." Birth control was not its conscious and ultimate purpose.

Universally applied from earliest days was the *coitus interruptus,* the total withdrawal of the penis before orgasm. It is assumed that this form of contraception as a means of family planning is referred to in the Bible's account of Onan, in the very passage also quoted in connection with masturbation (Gen. 38:1–11).

Scripture is rather vague and does not distinctly state how Onan spilled his seed, whether by interrupting the coitus or by masturbating. However, it is this text which Roman Catholic authorities have quoted as the very basis of their stand against birth control of any kind (except by the rhythm method). Man was meant to beget children and that was the only justification for intercourse. Therefore, anything artificially done to frustrate the purpose was a mortal sin.

Protestantism, generally, permits the application of contraceptives for medical reasons and "when there is a clearly felt moral obligation" to limit parenthood. Judaism and Islam, likewise, have not objected to contraception, if it served therapeutic or other compelling reasons, no matter whether these concerned the mother, the child or society; although, of course, through the ages, opinions have varied in the interpretation of the situations.

Of course, the most obvious method of contraception was continence: abstention from coitus altogether. And early man did just that when the occasion required it.

The Story of the Condom

That, to begin with, contraceptive measures most of all, if not exclusively, were taken by the woman, had its reasons. After all, primitive man was not fully aware of his own role in conception. More so, as only the woman experienced pregnancy, it was thought that she alone could prevent it. It may well be, too, that man in his selfishness tried to enjoy intercourse to the fullest and regarded any preventative steps on his part an awkward impediment, a practice he gladly left to the woman.

The male sheath can also be traced to the remote past. Its prototype, thousands of years before the discovery of rubber, was made of seedpods, skin, tortoiseshell and cloth. In fact, any material at hand was used. The Chinese, way back, made sheaths of oiled silk paper.

Those earliest sheaths, however, were not used to avoid conception, a function which, as it were, was only their final "by-product," millennia later. They served as protection for the man's penis, a consideration also instrumental in the creation of the sex glove. They were meant to shield his treasured organ against injury in battle, insect bites or magic attacks by demon forces. Man wore them as a proud badge of rank (each grade had its special color!), a fertility charm or a decoration, not least to draw attention to that important part of his body.

In its penultimate stage the sheath guarded the man only against contracting syphilis and gonorrhea. Gabriello Fallopio mentions it as such in *De morbo gallico,* his famous work on venereal disease. Indeed, he claims to have invented a linen sheath for that very purpose.

The origin of the condom has even been linked with ancient Greek legend, a myth cited in the *Metamorphoses* of second-century Antoninus Liberalis. It tells how Minos, king of Crete, in spite of his power, was unfortunate in his love life. Every time he had intercourse, he ejected with the semen serpents and scorpions which inflicted grievous wounds on his lovers. Greatly concerned with this dreadful affliction, he chose Pasiphaë as his wife. As she was the daughter of Helios, the sun god (her very name meant "shining on all"), she would be safe from any attack.

His plans, however, went awry. Their union proved childless

through the continued presence of those obnoxious reptiles on every occasion of coitus, though they did not actually hurt her.

Help came from most unexpected quarters. Living at the court at the time was Prokris, daughter of the king of Athens and wife of Kephalos. She had been forced to flee from her husband whose jealousy and anger she had roused. Possibly to repay the hospitality she was receiving from the Cretan king, she came forward with an ingenious plan and duly put it into effect.

She inserted a goat's bladder into the vagina of a chosen woman and then invited the king, her benefactor, to cohabit with that woman, emptying all the serpents and scorpions mixed with the semen into the improvised sheath. After this merely preliminary intercourse, none of the reptiles were left in him and he joined his wife in bed.

The scheme worked and, adopting this method, Pasiphaë conceived with Minos eight children, four sons and four daughters!

It has been suggested that the earliest version of this myth, as extant in the *Metamorphoses,* misrepresents one significant fact. In reality, the bladder had not been inserted in a woman's vagina but was used to ensheathe the king's penis. Indeed, it had been the first condom ever.

Another tradition claims a slaughterhouse as the birthplace of the condom. A butcher there, handling animals' guts, had suddenly conceived their new application as a prophylactic against VD.

The description of the sheath as a condom is said to perpetuate the name of a seventeenth-century English physician, also alleged to have been its inventor. Some say that in fact he practiced at the court of King Charles II. One story actually links the invention of the condom to the king himself. He had been greatly worried, it is told, by the many illegitimate children he sired. He discussed the "problem" with his court physician, Dr. Condom, who, to help his majesty, embarked on experimentation and careful research, finally to invent the "instrument," made from the intestine of a lamb. In acknowledgment of his services, the grateful king honored him with a knighthood!

There is another story, however, which claims that his invention made Condom so notorious that people were loath to call

him by his proper name. In fact, this had become so improper that
the good doctor felt obliged to change it.

In reality, hardly anything is known about Condom. Sometimes he is called a colonel. Even the spelling of his name is not
certain. It also appears, for instance, as Condon and Conton.
Perhaps, after all, he was a mere fiction. That the invention of the
condom was attributed to him by a comparatively great number
of "sources" proves nothing. Most of them merely copied the
"fact" from each other!

There are other claims and suggestions as to how the condom
first got its name. Some trace it to Condom, a French village in
the Department of Gers, which was founded in the eighth century
and is also famous for a special brandy. Others derived the word
from Persian, Greek and Latin roots of words that described
concealment, protection and storage.

No matter how the word originated, the sheath was first used
in the eighteenth century for the express purpose of preventing
conception. It was revolutionized by its mass production due to
the modern process of vulcanization of rubber, discovered by
Charles Goodyear (1800–60) in America and developed by
Thomas Hancock (1786–1865) in Britain.

Perhaps only circumstances of sex could account for an odd
phenomenon. Usually, countries vie with each other for the privilege of having been originators and benefactors. But apparently
no country wants to have the credit for the condom. On the
contrary, the English call it the "French letter" and, as it were,
returning the compliment, the French refer to it as the "English
hood"—*capote anglaise*—capote really referring to a (military)
greatcoat.

The Battle for Birth Control

Contraception thus, one way or another, dates back to the remote
past. Though known almost everywhere, however, it was practiced by comparatively few people, who were more the exception
than the rule. It became a worldwide movement only in the
nineteenth century.

But the very agitation for birth control roused strongest

opposition both on religious and ethical grounds and brought about acrimonious controversies and police prosecutions. This battle for contraception, at the beginning, even led to a confusing misconception. It concerned the Reverend Thomas R. Malthus (1766–1834), the famous English clergyman.

Most conservative in his background, Malthus strictly adhered to traditional morality, and any idea of artificial birth control horrified him. In spite of it, he has been regarded, and quoted many times, as its father and pioneer! His very name was adopted to describe its philosophy. "Malthusianism," for many years, was widely used as a term for birth control and preceded as a "war cry" this modern word.

It all began when Malthus strongly disagreed with his father about the future of the world. Malthus, senior, an enthusiastic follower of William Godwin and an innate optimist, took the view that Utopia was not a dream. Man, having advanced so far from savagery, was destined to reach the Golden Age of happiness and equality for everyone.

Young Malthus, a Fellow of Jesus College, Cambridge, could not be convinced. On the contrary, he saw only misery and wretchedness as the future of man because the growth of population completely outstripped food production.

He published his thoughts (at first anonymously, in 1798) in *An Essay on the Principle of Population as It Affects the Future Improvement of Society*. This caused a considerable stir and necessitated new (and revised) editions.

Malthus stressed that the discrepancy between population increase and the increase of food products could only lead to vice and misery. Population, when unchecked, tended to multiply in geometrical proportion, while means of subsistence tended to increase only in arithmetical ratio. The problem was to find some "benevolent remedies," some "prudential check" in births as alternatives to the exclusive operation of such grim factors as overcrowding, epidemics, war, poverty and vice.

The only solution, to his mind (first propounded in the second edition of his book), was to restrict births by "moral restraint." By this he meant postponement of marriage and of all sexual relations till later in life and even then to restrict these. This would ensure small families.

That was all Malthus advocated. Any other type of birth control, specifically to check population increase by contraception, he strongly condemned as vicious and deplorable. Thus he explicitly stated in the 1816 edition of his *Essay* that "Indeed I should always . . . reprobate any artificial and unnatural modes of checking population, both on account of their immorality and their tendency to remove a necessary stimulus to industry."

In spite of Malthus' disavowal, Malthusianism captured the imagination of people as a call to artificial birth control, forgetting all about its original, very limited and completely different meaning and proposition.

*   *   *

Birth control, as a term, is of recent origin. It first appeared in print in (June) 1914. Its author was Margaret Sanger, the famous American fighter for women's rights.

Margaret was the sixth child of a mother who had died at the age of forty-eight after having given birth to eleven children. A nurse by profession, she came into contact with the worst features of slum life in the Lower East Side of New York. But she was, in her early years, also deeply influenced by what were then regarded as radical, revolutionary ideas on life, motherhood and poverty. She was shocked by the many illegal abortions she witnessed, with often fatal results, and the denial to give women information as to how to avoid pregnancy.

In *My Fight for Birth Control* (1931), Margaret recalled how she heard "over and over again" of women's "desperate efforts at bringing themselves 'around.' " Their exotic, futile and most dangerous methods included the drinking of herb teas, taking drops of turpentine on sugar, steaming over a chamber pot of boiling coffee or of turpentine water, rolling down stairs, inserting knitting needles or shoe hooks into the uterus . . .

But however anxious Margaret was to advise the women on how to prevent pregnancy, she herself lacked the necessary knowledge. She tried—in vain—to gain it by reading up on it in medical books and in this endeavor spent many (wasted) hours in libraries. Eventually she went overseas, to Europe, and there at last, particularly in France, she was able to collect all the information she needed.

On her return home she was ready for battle and took it up

ardently. She immediately realized that the choice of the right kind of name for contraception was essential for its promotion. It had to be dignified and stress its importance for both the individual person concerned and the community. Mrs. Sanger herself has given two versions as to how the term "birth control" was adopted.

In her *Fight* she tells how one evening in her apartment she discussed the question with some of her friends. All agreed that the name so far commonly used, Malthusianism, was unsuitable. Many suggestions were made—and at once discarded. These included such ponderous words as conscious generation, voluntary motherhood and preventception. Some further discussion clarified their minds, and much more appropriate terms were proposed, such as family control, race control and, eventually, birth-rate control. And then, "finally," Margaret wrote, "it came to me out of the blue—Birth Control! We all knew at once that we had found the perfect name for the cause."

In her *Autobiography* (1939), however, Mrs. Sanger did not take the credit that birth control was born in her mind by a sudden intuition. She and her friends, she tells, had discussed such expressions as population control, race control and birth-rate control. "Then someone suggested, 'Drop the rate.' Birth control was the answer: we knew we had it."

8.

Family Relations

Polygamy

The term "polygamy" is often misunderstood or erroneously used. People imagine that it refers specifically and exclusively to a man having several wives which, actually, is polygyny. In reality, polygamy may equally apply to a woman having several husbands—polyandry.

Polygamy therefore means for a male or a female to have more than one partner. The term is a combination of the two words, derived from Greek, *polys* ("many") and *gamos* ("marriage").

Polygyny

Polygyny joins *polys* ("many") with *gyne* ("woman"). Etymologically *gyne* goes back to a root meaning a "bearer of children."

For a husband to have more than one wife at a time was so well established and accepted a custom in Old Testament times that the Bible takes it for granted and certainly does not criticize it. Man, any man, could marry as many women as he could gather (and afford). It was all a matter of economics and supply. It was only out of fear of idolatry that the Bible warned kings against hoarding too many wives. Their possible pagan background might lead the monarch astray.

Jacob was the husband of both Leah and Rachel. David, before settling in Jerusalem, already had eight wives. Solomon is claimed to have had seven hundred. Though the figure is a typical Oriental exaggeration, it indicates the admiration held for such wealth and (its implied) virility. The New Testament did not condemn polygyny either, and the Koran merely limits the number of wives to four.

Nevertheless, though permitted, the practice of polygyny very much depended on circumstances.

A very important reason for a plurality of wives, no doubt, was a man's sensuality, his sexual appetite which, at times, he could not satisfy with just one wife. In addition, primitive society greatly restricted coitus. A woman was taboo for considerable periods of her life: during menstruation, pregnancy and even lactation, which sometimes extended up to three years. Marital relations then were completely "out."

Man's innate love of variety and change included sex. He easily got bored with sameness, and to have several wives overcame its frustrations. Again, women getting on in age and thereby becoming less attractive and less able to fulfill their matrimonial duties, were also supplemented by extra, "fresh" wives. But such sexual factors, however prominent, were by no means the only reasons for polygyny.

Wars greatly diminished the number of men, and plurality of wives was a practical method to look after the surplus of (unemployed) women. Increase of population was an important consideration in any group. An essential if not the predominant purpose of marriage was the procreation of offspring. But it took some time to bring a child into the world. Therefore, for one man to make several women pregnant more or less simultaneously was all for the good of the tribe. That, too, is why polygyny was part of early society, always deeply concerned with its survival. Plutarch pointedly compared Spartan marriage with a stud of which the chief aim was the production of the greatest number and the most excellent type of progeny.

The barrenness of the first wife (or her giving birth to only girls) was yet another reason for a man to take a co-wife. She was expected to supply the (so far missing) male children. Offspring assured a man's posterity, and the greater the number of his children, the more influence he wielded in the community.

To own several wives was a matter of prestige. Only the powerful and the rich could afford more than one spouse, who, after all, was a valuable piece of property and an economic asset. A man might not be able to employ extra labor but he could marry—profitably—more wives to work for him.

Surprisingly perhaps, women themselves were proud of the very fact of being one of several spouses. Only a man of distinction, like their husband, could be a polygynist! (It is a case parallel to the modern fashion of owning several cars!)

To some women it was not merely a question of standing. In the pecking order of humans, the primary wife often had preferential rights. She could enjoy her superiority by bossing her "juniors" and delegating arduous "household duties" to them.

Inevitably, the situation carried with it problems. It invited jockeying for position—both in the house and in "bed." It created jealousies and bitterness (a typical example is the quarrel between Rachel and Leah as to which of them should sleep with their husband "this night").

Diverse laws and regulations tried to avoid such complications and unpleasantness, ensuring a more or less smooth running of a polygynous "home." There were several ways of putting a wife into her (right) place. The most obvious one adopted the rule of seniority. Whoever had been chosen (or purchased) first remained the chief wife. Alternate systems bestowed the rank to the spouse whose family had the highest standing in the community, or to whoever had been the first to give birth to a child. Mohammed, on the other hand, stipulated complete equality and a fair division between the several wives.

Conjugal rights, likewise, were carefully allotted: to each wife according to her position in the marriage constellation.

Even more significant was the method of "housing" the multiple mates. This was done either in a commonly shared "apartment" or by assigning to each wife her own, separate domain. The one demanded an intricate organization which, eventually, created the institution of the harem. In the other no co-wife could interfere and her husband would visit her whenever he so desired.

*   *   *

Whether, at the beginning, polygyny preceded or followed monogamy has been a controversial subject. Certainly at times, both systems co-existed. (A third type of marital union, early on, was "group marriage," when several men lived with several women.)

Many animal species are strictly monogamous. Therefore to have only one spouse is not just a matter of a higher civilization or a more advanced morality but also of nature. Pressure of circumstances often caused the adoption of polygamous or monogamous unions. The enforced, sanctioned or traditional number of partners in marriage depended on many factors. They included essential needs of sex and economics, power politics and the question of supply and demand.

It must be realized that, no matter when, polygyny was restricted in scope. However often a new supply of women was added by warfare or theft, there was never an inexhaustible surplus. More so, only the rich and powerful had the privilege and ability of owning several wives. And, whether enforced by law or the inevitable result of circumstance, sooner or later monogamous marriage became the rule. Though, of course, its sexual restrictions were greatly alleviated, if not completely side-stepped, by the keeping of concubines.

Auxiliary Wives

The taking of a concubine into marriage was an early-established custom. It was one that belonged to the ordinary way of life, and was regarded almost as a necessity. The peaceful co-existence of wives and concubines was invariably taken for granted.

In an agricultural society especially, children were wealth, and constituted a valuable, unpaid labor force. And a woman who had shown herself unable to supply them by proving barren had failed in her duty as a wife. Therefore it was in her own interest to employ, as it were, on her behalf someone more capable to provide children. This was the actual birth of the concubine, a term which literally and very appropriately points to the "lying together."

The famous code of Hammurabi dealt in detailed form with her rights, privileges and duties. It actually distinguished between two types of concubines: the "lesser wife" and the concubine "proper."

The husband either himself chose this auxiliary wife or was —wisely—presented with her by his childless spouse. Her rights were almost the same as that of the wife. The concubine, on the other hand, was then mostly a maidservant with whom the "boss" slept to beget a son, which (happy) event effected her release— without any further obligations on either side.

It was, no doubt, this Babylonian background that influenced biblical married life. The early Hebrews, in fact, accepted without qualms or scruples the taking into the home of a concubine. Her rights were completely equal to that of the wife. But her purpose, to begin with, was not the enjoyment of sex but procreation. A wife that was barren was so ashamed of her inability to bear a child that, if she could help it, she herself provided her husband with the secondary wife—of her choice. The child(ren) born of the union certainly had no inferior standing.

Sarah thus introduced Hagar to Abraham, while Jacob's two concubines enjoyed almost a childbearing competition with their two mistresses. But such consideration of population growth soon gave way to more (and, eventually, mere) hedonic wishes.

Concubines became luxury items in the household of the wealthy and mighty. Biblical statistics do not disguise the fact and record that King David employed ten concubines. He did so not only for "home" work but house work as well, in a rather stingy sort of manner. His son Solomon surpassed all (biblical) records by having in his harem three hundred concubines. Rehoboam, his son, in a kingdom very reduced in territory, wealth and power, could afford—only—sixty!

The concubine who came into existence as an auxiliary force and a child provider finally came to occupy (in not a few cases, to monopolize) the marital bed—as the (new type of) mistress, a supplier of sex.

The Harem

The word "harem" (from the Arabic *harim*) originally referred to any area that was "out of bounds" or anything that was "forbidden" or "sacred." Only in its ultimate development was the term specifically applied to a woman's quarters in a Moslem household, established to ensure her complete privacy and seclusion.

This was merely the final stage of the old and Oriental tradition to protect and isolate a woman. The ancient Greeks had seen in the tortoise a symbol of her existence: to be shut up within the narrow confines of the house.

From the moment a girl matured sexually, she had to be watched over and was forbidden to display herself, or any part of her body, to anyone but her husband, closest relatives, eunuchs, children or women. It was for this reason that, early on, some tribes made her cover the face with a veil, a custom which was not introduced but merely adopted and sanctified by Mohammed.

The first harems were a simple division of a home, a particular portion allotted to the women. In the course of time, this developed into a separate quarter, which was securely enclosed and carefully guarded from the outside. In the Ottoman Empire it grew into a unique institution. The most famous harem, no doubt, was part of the seraglio of Constantinople. (The word "seraglio" itself has been used both for a Turkish palace and a harem. It is derived from a combination of the Italian *serraglio,* "a cage for wild animals," and the Persian *serāi,* a "building.")

The seraglio's harem was a world of its own. Its administration was unsurpassed. Every aspect of its life was highly organized. Not a man but a woman (the sultan's mother) was in supreme charge of it, and only death could end her term of office. An entire "cabinet" assisted her in the running of the establishment, with a specialized and well-trained bureaucracy in control.

A vast army of women and (black) eunuchs were responsible for the various and numerous tasks. Their duties and responsibilities were clearly defined, indicated by the very titles they bore: the mistress of the robes, the custodian of the jewels, the reciter of the Koran and the supervisor of baths, etc.

No one knew in advance which of his many women the sultan would choose on each occasion. But the moment his eyes had rested on a girl for more than a fleeting moment or he had discussed her with his attendants, it was assumed that her turn had come. There was an even more telling invitation in his vocabulary of love. This was expressed neither in words nor by the casting of an eye but by the throwing of a handkerchief. It was a gesture that, unmistakably, revealed the sultan's desire.

The moment a girl had been selected, no matter which way, as the sultan's (momentary) favorite, she was immediately isolated from the other girls and given her own suite. This was fully staffed with eunuchs and slaves. She was bathed, shampooed, her body hair shaved, anointed, perfumed, beautifully clad and adorned—all ready for the "call."

When the expected summons arrived, she was led into the sultan's bedchamber which was a significant part, of course, of the harem. There, too, she had to follow a definite set of rules. The sultan had preceded her into bed. This she had to approach from the foot end. Then she had to lift the bed cover, touch it with her lips and forehead and, from that end, to slip upward into the bed, till both the sultan and she were side by side . . .

All night long, two female slaves stayed in the chamber. They were quietly replaced at regular intervals. It was a peculiar version of a "changing of the guard." Their chief duty, however, was to look after two torches which were kept burning throughout: one at the bed's end and the other at the door.

Next morning the sultan was first to leave. He dressed in a new suit and left his discarded garment as a special gift to his "sleeping partner." All the money it contained which, at times, amounted to a considerable sum, was hers as well.

The girl then returned to her quarters. If she became pregnant, she was declared a sultana of the year. If the child born was a son, her pleasure and honors were supreme.

Harems, however, were not a pure paradise and a "Turkish delight." They also became a hotbed of jealousies, quarrels and intrigues. Nevertheless, they survived for many centuries and were outlawed in Turkey as late as 1926, when Kemal Atatürk banned polygyny. A count made in 1909 at the deposition of Sultan Abdul Hamed II revealed a harem population of 370 women and 127 eunuchs.

Multiple Mates Among Mormons

Polygyny experienced an unexpected revival in Western society soon after 1830. The then newly created Church of Jesus Christ of Latter-day Saints, commonly known as Mormons, adopted it as a divinely sanctioned way of life. Joseph Smith, the founder of the Church, based the institution of plural marriage on its practice in biblical times which, he stressed, was approved by God. In fact, he referred to polygyny frequently as "Jacob's blessing." As for its being immoral and degrading, Mormons maintained that experience had proved the opposite. Multiple marriage raised mankind from a condition that was "a corrupt and hypocritical system of enforced monogamy."

It has been suggested (and very unkindly so) that Joseph Smith's personal love of women and extra-marital affairs were the real cause of his "revelation" and theological reasoning. "Whenever I see a pretty woman," he once confessed to a friend, "I have to pray for grace." Though he himself denied the actual figure, he is said to have married fifty wives.

At first, Mormons did not openly teach their practice of plural marriage. They knew only too well that undue publicity of that type would damage their young Church. But with the growing of the movement, they felt that time had come to promulgate their new way of life.

A pamphlet by Udney H. Jacob, published by Smith's authority in 1842, thus advocated polygamy as a divinely inspired institution which would prove itself a marital benefactor. A divorced man, it claimed, was unknown in the entire canon of Holy Scripture. This made incompatibility in marriage a veritable curse. A man, unhappily married, was still forced to "hug the serpent to his bosom." It was a situation which was not only impossible, degrading to the nature of man, but "a gross sin" and "a fornication in the wife." But a plurality of wives would end such a dismal existence.

Inevitably, the news roused strongest opposition and ridicule among non-Mormons, dubbed Gentiles. A thirteen-stanza poem entitled "Buckeye's Lamentation for Want of more Wives," made fun of the new doctrine and revelation. Typical was the verse:

> I once thought I had knowledge great,
>   But now I find 'tis small.
> I once thought I'd religion too,
>   But now I find I've none at all—
> For I have but ONE LONE WIFE,

And can obtain no more;
And the doctrine is I can't be saved,
Unless I've HALF A SCORE.

On September 14, 1852, a special edition of the *Deseret News* announced that Joseph Smith had received his "final revelation" on plural marriage. Thenceforth it was to be an official doctrine of the Mormon Church that "if any man aspouse a virgin, and desire to aspouse another, and the first give her consent, and if he aspoused the second, and they are virgins, and have vowed to no other man, then he is justified; he cannot commit adultery. . . . and if he have ten virgins given unto him by this law, he cannot commit adultery, for they belong to him. . . ."

It is only fair to state that the Mormon Church stipulated that any husband about to enter into a polygamous union had first to prove his moral character and his economic ability to support a plurality of wives.

Nevertheless, as was only to be expected, the new polygamy, now so openly avowed, roused fierce protest. A bitter controversy and protracted struggle ensued. In 1856, at a meeting in Philadelphia, the Republican Party adopted as its platform the resolution that it was "both the right and imperative duty of Congress to prohibit in the territories those twin relics of barbarism— polygamy and slavery. . . ."

A federal law condemned and prohibited the practice. The Church, however, refused to conform and declared the legislation an unconstitutional infringement of religious liberty. But when, finally, in 1890, the Supreme Court of the United States upheld the government ruling, the Mormons were forced to capitulate. Wilford Woodruff, the then president of the Church, promulgated a new law which, as a new divine command, outlawed polygamy.

Polyandry

Polygyny is a well-known practice. For a husband to have several wives (concurrently) is taken for granted as part of the history of man. However, there existed also a custom which permitted a woman to have more than one husband at a time. (After all, it should be equally true that "what's sauce for the gander is sauce for the goose"!) This phenomenon is appropriately termed "polyandry," from the Greek *polys* ("many") and *andros* ("man"): "many men."

Though much less frequently than polygyny, polyandry was already practiced in ancient times and has been found all over the world: in Alaska (among Eskimos), in Malabar, in the Himalayan area (by the Todas), in Africa (among Bantus) and in South American regions.

The institution of polyandry was not accidental but the result of several factors.

Its most obvious reason (and even necessity) was a situation in which men outnumbered women. This, of course, was a phenomenon among races which extensively practiced female infanticide. But it could also be found in zones where the climate was too harsh for women.

Poverty on the part of the man was, if not another reason, a very significant contributory cause. One man on his own just could not afford to acquire and keep a full-time wife. Therefore economic considerations were responsible for the next-best arrangement, a joint partnership. Men got together to share the cost and the upkeep of one common wife.

A third factor was an odd kind of birth control, when limited space and scant provisions outruled an abundance of children and abortion or infanticide were unknown or shunned by the group.

Yet a further case for polyandry arose when a husband proved impotent or was too old to father children. To give birth to an heir and that most treasured unpaid labor force of children, the wife gladly entertained a second and, if need be, a third spouse. Her first husband, in the circumstances, could hardly afford to object.

Even deep concern for one's wife was an excuse for polyandry. This, however, happened only in exceptional cases. Husbands who had to absent themselves for extended periods of time, as in the case of warfare, hunting expeditions and pastural duties, were only too happy to leave an "associate" husband at home to protect their wives.

Of course, the institution of polyandry necessitated much

thought and strict rules. First of all, there was the question of how to select one's joint husbands. Two systems prevailed: the fraternal and the nonfraternal. In the first case all the husbands were brothers, usually the eldest son of a family being the first and his brothers joining the "home" the moment they reached puberty. In the second case, obviously, the choice was much more complicated.

It was also important to know who came first in standing and could be looked upon as the chief husband. This problem was mostly solved chronologically. In the fraternal system, inevitably the eldest brother took precedent. Equal regulations determined the position of children within the family. At times the husband-in-chief was acknowledged as the father of all, no matter who had sired them. All other "fathers" were looked upon (and addressed) as "uncle." A different custom assigned the various children to different husbands. However, it did so not according to physiological facts. Whoever had performed a certain ceremony during the mother's seventh month of pregnancy was designated the father.

To avoid jealousies and fights, it was essential as well to fix the time and place of cohabitation. Strict timetables were thus followed. In the fraternal type of polyandry the brother-husbands shared one home and their common wife went to live with them. All were one happy family. In most other cases the wife had her own "residence," where she received, in turn, her various husbands.

Polyandry, certainly, presented a complex system, which required superb organization.

The Green-Eyed Monster

Jealousy has always been a mighty force—at times "a tyrant of the mind"—in the realm of love. The biblical Song of Songs calls it as cruel as the grave and compares it to flashes of a vehemently burning fire.

La Rochefoucauld analyzed the emotion and discovered in it more self-love than real love. Yet early society already recognized in jealousy a potent sexual stimulant as well, which therefore could be listed among mental aphrodisiacs. Thus the second-century Greek satirist Lucian, in one of his *Dialogues of Courtesans*, pictures how a "girl of easy virtue" cunningly rouses her young client's passion by psychologically playing on his feelings of jealousy.

The description of jealousy as the "green-eyed monster" was popularized by Shakespeare, in whose writings the Bard thus refers to it in *Othello*. The origin of the metaphor was due to several factors. There was a time when people assumed that jealousy caused a greenish complexion (hence "green with envy"). Tigers, cats and other feline creatures were observed playing with their victims before killing them, meanwhile hypnotically staring at them with their green eyes. Jealousy itself—devouring, as it were, the beloved one—appeared as a mixture of hatred and passion, of loathing and loving. Is it any wonder that the relentless green-eyed stare with which the feline species mocked the meat it fed on came to be applied to human jealousy, even before Shakespeare's era?

Another tradition may well have further contributed to the adoption of this colorful figure of speech. When dark-green jade was first imported into Europe from the East, superstition believed in its occult power. Ground into fine powder, jealous men mixed it into love potions to ensure the faithfulness of their lovers.

Mother-in-Law Aversion

The story is told how a veterinarian was asked to cut off a dog's tail. The family was expecting a visit from the mother-in-law and no one and nothing (not even the wagging of the dog's tail) should suggest a welcome!

No relative has been the butt of more jokes than the mother-in-law. Volumes could be compiled of what has been said about and against her.

Adam has been called the luckiest man, as he had no mother-in-law. Her calumniation ranges from the Roman satirist Juvenal's view to "give up all hope of peace so long as your mother-in-law is alive" to the morbid and horrid proverb extant in several languages (among them German and English), claiming that "there is but one good mother-in-law, and she is dead." In the Rumanian tongue, by a play on sound *(soacra—poama acra)*, she is compared to "bitter grapes."

This almost worldwide dislike of the mother-in-law cannot be accidental. The late George Ade, famous American humorous author and playwright, rightly observed that in reality the mother-in-law joke was not a joke at all but a very serious question.

It all started long ago and is a survival of the untutored savage's awe and dread with which he regarded his mother-in-law. Sir James Frazer described this apprehensive and ominous attitude as one of the most familiar facts of anthropology. And he has no lack in quoting telling examples.

In primitive society, mother-in-law avoidance was practiced almost universally and only the degree of its manifestation varied.

It existed among Australian aborigines, African natives, American Indians and Mexican Mayas. Its diversity extended from the prohibition for a mother-in-law and a son-in-law to look at one another (or even merely in each other's direction) to the total ban of conversation. If any communication became necessary, the offices of a "go-between" had to be employed.

A mother-in-law covered her face in the presence of her son-in-law. Should she inadvertently come across the path of her son-in-law, the latter had immediately to take evasive action by going into hiding. Other laws forbade the two parties even to share the same abode, a taboo in some parts of the world mitigated by the provision of a partition.

To see the bare breasts of a mother-in-law was specially dangerous and could cause sickness. The only possible remedy in such case was for the unfortunate son-in-law to send her at once a cloth made of bark which, used like the modern brassiere, would act as a protective screen against the perilous "radiation."

Frequently mere warnings were regarded as insufficient and the harshest punishment was threatened to anyone violating the mother-in-law taboo. The penalties included the exiling of the guilty party from camp for a fixed period of time, obligatory divorce, enforced suicide and public execution!

Thus the mother-in-law complex is deeply rooted in antiquity and in the recesses of the mind, man's ancestral memory. It related, as these few telling examples show, to every type of contact—a casual glance as much as a mere word.

Sigmund Freud rightly reasoned that the multiplicity and ubiquity of such stringent and meticulously observed restrictions suggested the presence of a powerful impulse which needed severest countermeasures to prevent its consummation.

Of all the theories offered, the most likely is that at the very basis of mother-in-law avoidance was the fear of the most intimate contact of all: sexual intercourse. This was incest, viewed with almost the horror reserved for the supernatural. Not only would it offend the godhead but such sacrilege would bring disaster to the entire group, tribe or clan.

Had there perhaps existed also early on, in the tradition of "as mother so daughter," a subconscious attraction with the ambivalence of a love-hatred relationship that contributed to the inclusion of the mother-in-law in the category of forbidden "degrees"? Could this at least partially account for a precautionary psychological measure to keep both parties away from each other by picturing any mother-in-law as an ogre?

That is how, out of the early mother-in-law avoidance (according to primitive society for vital reasons) evolved our present-day mother-in-law aversion. To explain it by a mother's wish to continue being "useful" in her "need to be needed" and thereby her potential meddling with the young couple's lives (plus the threat of breaking up their home) is merely a modern rationalization of a now psycho-pathological attitude born in the mind of the savage.

All the more intriguing is the fact that in the early days of the human race, in the Bible itself, though it cursed "him who lieth with his mother-in-law," the mother-in-law herself stands supreme.

Moabite Ruth addressed to her (and not to her lover as is often erroneously assumed) the immortal words: "Intreat me not to leave thee, and to return from following after thee: for whither thou goest, I will go; and where thou lodgest, I will lodge . . ."

Divorce

Though divorce has nothing to do with "how sex began," from the very beginning sex has served as a most potent reason for divorce. And, surprisingly, divorce was part of the most primitive pattern of life, often regulated very carefully.

Possibilities of divorce (or its complete absence), of course, depend on the view taken of marriage. And as this has differed in the various regions of the world, divorce, likewise, has been regarded in many ways.

To some isolated, primitive races, in fact, wedlock meant almost a fleeting affair, hardly meriting to be called marriage. Hence both parties, without qualms, tribal interference or mutual obligation, could go their separate ways (again) the moment they felt like it.

Some South American tribes, for instance, terminated wedlock as freely as they had contracted it. A similar short-term marriage was not uncommon with Ungava Eskimos. And, if "grounds for divorce" were demanded, these could be of the most trivial nature. Divorce among Mayas consisted of little more than a simple repudiation, and these ancient dwellers on Mexican soil could abandon their spouses for the most trifling reasons. An early Spanish document thus relates how "there were men who married ten and twelve times, and the women had the same liberty to leave their husbands." In quite a different part of the world, Marquesan couples could equally easily "untie the knot." Without hesitation, one or the other party took his or her leave, never to return. Occasionally, they did so in the company of a lover or mistress. Maoris, too, did not know divorce as an institution. In case of a disagreement, the man and woman just separated, the woman going back home. The ancient Greeks permitted divorce, if husband or wife felt that they could do better and find a more congenial companion.

But these were the exceptions. Much more often the opinion prevailed that a man owned his wife, having duly purchased or captured her. Therefore, as with all his chattel, his decision alone determined what would happen to her, and he had to give no account for his action. To begin with, no doubt, he could discard her without any explanation. Indeed, divorce then was tantamount to an expulsion.

But it did not take long for certain conditions to be made and grounds for divorce to be demanded. These, most prominently, featured sex: its abuse or absence, adultery or sterility.

Sex was all-important. For a wife to give it elsewhere was the worst possible crime. On the other hand, as marriage was meant for procreation, a wife forfeited all her rights and could be sent away if she failed in this task. Different cultures merely varied the period of time allowed till childlessness took effect as grounds for divorce.

Of course, the various native groups established many other reasons that entitled a man to rid himself of his spouse, though none equaled in importance and frequency those of sex. Such additional grounds for divorce included a wife's laziness, her bad temper, disobedience, her lack of cooking ability or just that he had become tired of her.

Ancient Chinese law (as related in *Li Chin*) gave a husband seven causes for divorce. He could dismiss his wife if she did not heed the words of her parents-in-law; had borne no children; had committed adultery; had proved herself of a jealous disposition; was inflicted by an obnoxious disease; talked too much; or had been caught stealing. However, three circumstances could invalidate all these reasons. A husband had to keep his wife permanently, no matter what she was, did or neglected to do, if for three years she had mourned her parents-in-law; if his family who, at the time of their marriage, had been poor, had become rich; or if she could find no home to take her in.

Romulus, as recorded by Plutarch, in a severe law forbade a wife to leave her husband, but permitted a husband to divorce his wife "for poisoning her children, for making duplicates of his keys and for adultery."

* * *

In some regions of the world the opposite was the case. The wife was accorded the right of initiative, and it was she who could end the marriage unilaterally and even arbitrarily.

Among certain African tribes, for instance, if a wife—for the flimsiest pretext or no reason at all—wished to break up her marriage, all she had to do was to move away. Other (Central African) groups gave a wife sufficient grounds for divorce, if her husband did not sew her clothes, refused to pull his weight in work or stayed away from home too long.

In *The Sexual Life of Savages in North-western Melanesia* Bronislaw Malinowski tells of Melanesian women who abandoned their husbands without compunction when they fell in love with another man. On one of his visits to the Trobriands, he encountered the case of a young wife, "bubbling over with health, vitality and temperament," who deserted her spouse and went back home to live as a single girl, "simply because she was tired of her husband."

The next category of divorce was the (advanced) stage when man and woman were given equal rights and dissolution of marriage was possible only by their mutual consent or with a just cause.

The law of the Aztecs, for example, specified that a husband could divorce his wife for her barrenness, prolonged bad temper or neglect of home duties. A wife, on the other hand, could dismiss her husband if he ill-treated her, did not look adequately after their children's education or her economic security.

Lastly, there was the other extreme which did not permit (or even know) divorce. This situation was typical of orthodox Hindus, and could be found in Ceylon, New Guinea and the Malay peninsula. Marriage was an indissoluble bond, a sacrament. You married your spouse till death parted you, or even beyond—forever. Some groups, however, to alleviate such hardship, under certain conditions allowed a husband, without actually divorcing his wife, to acquire an additional, second one.

*   *   *

The procedure of divorce, too, varied greatly. It extended from a mere walking out (and return to one's original home) to the obligatory attendance of both parties at a specially summoned council of elders and a solemn ritual. Every intermediate stage existed. A wife had to leave her husband (in ancient Chaldea) if he presented her with an appropriate letter to her father or (in some parts of Africa) with a piece of reed! Other measures effecting a divorce included the repayment of her bride-price or similar monetary compensation (already decreed in the code of Hammurabi). A marriage was dissolved by the utterance of a fixed formula (such as, "you are not my wife"), the writing of a special document (the earliest "decree") and its transference to the other party in a solemn, prescribed manner.

In some societies a divorce could not be final without attempts at a reconciliation first being made. Thus special "ambassadors" moved between the two families. They gave up their endeavor only if they found that neither party could be persuaded to resume marital relations. Deserted Maori wives underwent a special ritual at a river, assumed to cool down their ardor and to extinguish the fire of their love.

The Hebrew Bible takes divorce for granted. It contains no passage specifically ordaining its institution. However, this is implied in several regulations. These take divorce still as the sole right of the man. A wife is seen as his property. The Decalogue, in its prohibition of desired objects, included the wife in a catalogue of private possessions. It put her on the same level as the neighbor's house, his servants and animals, whom "you shall not covet."

One reference (Deut. 24:1–4) deals with the instance of a divorced woman who remarried. But, for the second time unlucky, she lost her—new—husband: either through death or another divorce. In such case, the Bible rules, her first husband could not marry her again.

The text, though comparatively short, contains some significant information. First of all, it demanded at least some grounds for divorce. The wife must have "lost favor in her husband's eyes" and this because he had discovered in her "some unseemly thing" or, as other translations render the phrase, "some indecency," something "obnoxious."

No doubt, at the time, people knew what this meant. But to later generations the very vagueness of the passage unfortunately left much room for interpretation and dispute. One (first-century) school of thought—that of Shammai—felt that the only "unseemly thing" was a wife's unchastity, her adultery. The other extreme—represented by the school of Hillel—considered almost any trivial reason sufficient grounds for a wife to displease her husband and effect her divorce. He could send her away, for instance, if she had burnt his food!

Such almost frivolous excuses to terminate a marriage were nevertheless made difficult to apply by the second stipulation contained in that passage of just four verses. This required the presentation of a "decree": a "bill of divorcement." Already at that early stage, the Hebrew Bible demanded legal authorization of a divorce. This in itself acted as a brake. A husband could not dismiss his wife straight away and the preparation of the official document gave him time to reconsider his possibly rash decision in a more balanced frame of mind.

Judaism continued to permit divorce but, if inevitable, greatly deplored it. One of the rabbis of the Talmud expressed the typical opinion that, as it were, "the very altar shed tears when a man divorced the wife of his youth." "I hate divorce, says the Lord" was an often-quoted verse from the prophet Malachi (2:16). Every possible safeguard was introduced to protect the wife who, nonetheless, remained at the receiving end.

Diversity in the statements of the New Testament has led to various attitudes toward divorce in the Christian Church. According to Mark (10:1–12), Jesus denounced and condemned divorce absolutely, in any circumstance. From the beginning of creation God had made humans male and female and the two were meant to be "one flesh": "What therefore God has joined together, let not man put asunder." In Matthew (19:1–9), however, the parallel passage makes Jesus prohibit divorce—"except for unchastity." Finally, St. Paul (in I Cor. 7:12–16) ruled that, in the case of disharmony, a Christian married to an unbeliever could attain a divorce at the express wish of the non-Christian party. He could even remarry but then only if he did so in his faith—"in the Lord."

Islam, following the ancient Oriental example, reaffirmed a husband's "privilege" to repudiate his marriage at will—without any reason or decree. All he had to do was to pronounce a short formula. This, most commonly, was the threefold repetition of the Arab phrase for "you are dismissed!"

With the passing of time, attitudes toward divorce changed and often reflected the special climate of thought of the age. During the decadence of Roman civilization, for instance, there were no grounds for despair for a dissatisfied husband or wife. Either party fully enjoyed the liberty to pursue happiness elsewhere, as to get a divorce was the simplest and easiest matter. The records survive of a husband who dismissed his wife because she had gone to the games without his permission. It was said that some women counted their years not according to consuls but according to their marriages. Juvenal mentions the case of a woman who had wedded eight husbands within a period of five years. People were known to have been married more than a score of times.

Eventually the pendulum swung back and divorce, if allowed, was made more difficult in the various cultures. Ever more restrictions and regulations were added. And what once perhaps could be obtained quite capriciously and without any further obligations or blame on either side, as long as the children were cared for, became a strictly controlled procedure with safeguards, decrees, witnesses, guilty parties, "stigmas" and alimonies.

In modern days the wheel has come full circle. Almost any ground (or no grounds at all) can effect a divorce. Just as in the oldest days and among some of the savage societies, it is sufficient for either party to feel tired of his or her partner. Paraphrasing words used by Oscar Wilde, it can be said that people no longer think of breaking the bond of marriage but its bondage. Indeed, though they might still get together "for better or worse," many no longer do so for good.

9.

Illicit Relations

Rape

Rape, now regarded as one of the ugliest sex crimes, originated, it has been suggested, in one of man's very early
methods of acquiring a wife. This was not by peaceful but
violent means. He simply stole (that is captured) her
from his own or a neighbor's tribe. He raped and then carried her
(to his) home. This ancient tradition, in fact, also accounts for the
now beautiful custom of carrying one's bride across the threshold.
It is the last remnant of the final steps of the (successful) raping
expedition.

Etymologically it is not accidental, therefore, that the word
"rape"—like "rapture"—is derived from the Latin *rapere,* meaning to "seize," to "carry away."

This original institution of "marriage by rape" is recalled in
the well-known legend of the Sabine women. During a festival
they were carried away—to be raped—by Romulus' men, it is
told. And when, their anger roused, the Sabine fathers and husbands marched against the ravishers of their women to take due
vengeance and recapture their daughters and wives, these would
not have it. They placed themselves between the opposing lines,
thereby stopping the men from killing each other. And instead of
the expected bloodshed, peace was established and Sabines and
Romans joined to become one people. . . . Rape of another tribe's
females was an early form of enforced intermarriage.

Several theories have been advanced why men, to begin with, raped women to make them their wives. One viewpoint (expressed by D. McLennan, for instance) had it that the entire idea of wife-stealing was the result of a short supply of girls at home. On the other hand, it was thought (by H. Spencer) that it all started—as so many "innovations"—in war. A captured woman had double value. She served not only as a slave but also as a trophy of victory. Therefore she came to be treasured more than any girl of the tribe. The raped captive was a status symbol for the young ambitious warrior, for he had proved his power. And as there were others like him, they came to a mutual understanding. They condoned the successful violence and endorsed their individual "booty." The might (to rape) became the right (to own). Marriage, based on the original rape, had become a sanctioned tribal institution.

Eventually the arrangement of marriage, of course, took friendlier forms and, instead of stealing a wife, one purchased her. It is therefore not surprising that rape became an offense to be severely punished. The crime now concerned not the girl alone but the tribe and often precipitated cruel retaliation.

Roman legend contains a vivid illustration in the story of the rape of Lucretia by Sextus. This led not only to her suicide (after telling her husband of what had happened), but to an uprising that brought about the bloody end of the Roman monarchy and the establishment of the republic. Not even a king could take the liberty to ravish a woman without consequences.

The dramatic (and unembellished) story of the violation of Dinah, Jacob's daughter, and its fearsome aftereffects, is a telling biblical example (Gen. 34).

We are told how Shechem, "a prince of the land," possibly because of his power considering himself "beyond morality," raped Dinah. He "saw her, seized her, lay with her, and humbled her . . ."

To those early Israelites it was not merely a heinous crime that debased and degraded the victim but the most serious kind of sexual evil, involving the whole community.

Worse still is the mass rape of a Levite's concubine as related in the book of Judges (chapters 19–21). We hear how Benjaminite men, after having violated and abused her "all the night until the morning," then left her in her agony. Exhausted, she collapsed, ultimately to die as the result of the rape. The incident led to a punitive expedition that (even if the biblical figures are highly exaggerated) ended with a frightful massacre, the annihilation of almost an entire tribe (and more rapings).

It is therefore no wonder that early legislators made an attempt to outlaw such outrageous, wild retribution and to restrict punishment for rape. The Assyrian code of law thus forced the ravisher either to marry the girl or to pay her family three times the amount of her bride-price, in compensation for the irremediable damage suffered by her defloration. However, it also gave the injured family the right, in fact the duty, of retaliation "in kind," as it were, "a rape for a rape." The girl's father had to seize the raper's wife (or daughter) and have her raped in turn and "he shall not return her to her husband."

Biblical law further humanized and restricted the penalty (Deut. 22:28–29). Only the guilty party was to be punished. The man who had raped a virgin had to marry her, if her family so agreed. Additionally, he had to pay to her father the customary bride-price. But he could never divorce her.

The Bible also specifically dealt with the rape of a girl already engaged to be married. (It must be realized that a biblical "betrothal" was regarded as much more binding than people in later centuries took it to be.) A careful distinction was made as to where the rape was actually committed. If it had taken place in a city, both parties were considered guilty and accordingly punished—by stoning. However, if the crime was perpetrated in the country ("in the field"), only the man was sentenced—to death —and the girl went free. The Bible itself gives the reason for this differentiation in treatment. It assumed that surely any cry for help on the girl's part would have been heard within a populated area like that of a town. Therefore she must have been a consenting party. Outside the city, however, she was given the benefit of the doubt and presumed to have tried to summon help but "there was none to save her."

It is of interest to note how differently the rape was still looked upon (and consequently punished): whether it concerned an—unattached—virgin or an engaged one. The loss of value to the girl's owner (whether he was her father or her fiancé) counted more than the personal feelings of and hurt suffered by the girl. In the one case, merely the rapist's enforced marriage to the victim was the penalty. In the other, his death. There was still a long way to go to the modern concept of rape.

The history of rape thus leads from a sanctified institution (to capture one's wife) to a severely punished sex aggression. Yet its very basis never changed. It has always been—for one reason or another—"to take the favor of love without loving consent."

Adultery

Through the ages and almost from earliest times, adultery has been a major if not the chief reason for divorce everywhere. And yet there are conspicuous instances where it does not feature at all in the dissolution of a marriage. But this apparent omission was not the result of viewing infidelity (if committed by the wife) lightly. On the contrary, "to betake oneself to another" (Latin: *ad alterum se conferre*) was so grave a crime that, to punish it, divorce was regarded insufficient. Both parties were put to death.

It is a striking phenomenon that, from the outset and universally, adultery caused such repugnance and carried with it the most ruthless retaliation. In fact, to start with, the injured husband himself took the law into his hands and—without trial—killed both his wife and the corespondent. And all of the tribe not only approved of, but expected, his action.

At times a husband might prefer the whole community to participate in the punishment of his wife and her paramour. Stark naked the adulteress was driven out of her home, and her ears and her nose were cut off. She was then further humiliated, outraged and eventually—like the man—killed. It was all unbelievably cruel and inhuman. In ancient Rome an adulteress, if lucky, was merely expelled with disgrace. However, she also could be put to death by a family council, acting in conjunction with her husband.

On the other hand, a wife whose husband had made love to another woman had no rights at all. A man, so long as he did not involve another man's wife, was given full (sexual) freedom. He could do what he liked with impunity, as for him adultery just did not exist. This situation was clearly expressed by Cato who wrote: "If you take your wife in adultery you may freely kill her without a trial. But if you commit adultery, or if another commit adultery with you, she has no right to raise a finger against you."

The attitude toward adultery, originally, was not interested in the feelings and happiness of the woman. It concerned the property rights of the man which he guarded most jealously. It was not a case of immorality, but of theft—stealing another man's goods. After all, a husband had acquired his wife at great cost. He might have captured her, endangering his own life, or paid a considerable amount of money or cattle as her purchase price.

Why then should he share his property with an interloper who, by his very action, greatly devalued and degraded his estate? It is no wonder, therefore, that natives in the Torres Strait used one word to describe both "adultery" and "theft." They referred to an illicit love affair as "stealing a woman." Likewise, African tribes used to punish adultery like thieving, by cutting off the adulterer's hands!

The proprietary rights of the man, however, were not the only factor that rendered adultery so grave an offense. At its very roots were already then the germ of later moral condemnation and the question of impurity. As sex was a mysterious, magical power, full of potential danger, even a legitimate husband had carefully to watch and observe sex taboos and take countless precautions. Was it not obvious, then, that an interloper played with fire and imperiled all parties concerned? The effect of his intrusion could spread disaster by physical contagion and lead to veritable havoc.

And from this very real, original fear evolved the idea of immorality. Adultery had to be shunned, in a Buddhist phrase, like "a pit of live coals." An adulterous wife did not just cheat her owner-husband, and her lover was not merely a thief, but both —by their sexual contact—unleashed the most frightening forces. Punishment, therefore, was not an act of vengeance on the part of a jealous husband but a desperate attempt at undoing, or at least confining, the harm done.

Early on, the consequences of adultery were taken to go far beyond the personal interest of the husband, for it could cause calamities of many kinds. It was thought that adultery in a very material sense could pollute the purity of the family's blood and thus offend the ancestors' spirits.

Magically it could effect the fertility of both man and nature. This is still reflected in the story told in Genesis (chapter 20)— and other of its versions—of the triangle between Sarah and her husband, Abraham, and Abimelech, the king of Gerar. Although no adultery is said to have taken place when the royal master took the patriarch's wife into his harem, the mere possibility had "fast closed up all the wombs." Parallel passages certainly suggest that the loss of sexual power was not due to any psychological, moral scruples but the conviction that adultery brought on barrenness.

There was equally a causal link between infidelity in the home and infertility in the field. Adultery could result, it was firmly believed, in the ground staying barren, the crops withering and the cattle becoming sterile. According to an Eskimo tradition, whales, musk-oxen and reindeer had abandoned a certain region because "men had too much to do with other men's wives."

Imagined repercussions of adultery thus extended far beyond the individual's home, which made its severe punishment all the more understandable. Its atonement (or prevention) concerned the entire clan. It is no wonder, therefore, that some societies punished a husband who refrained from punishing his wife. In China, for instance, a husband who did not divorce her was whipped.

* * *

Inevitably, early society feared that a husband's justified anger at the outrage committed might go too far. To avoid a miscarriage of justice and damage to the tribe, it began to control the punishment for adultery.

Thus, though the code of Hammurabi decreed the drowning of an adulteress and her lover, it demanded proof of her infidelity. No court would pass sentence on mere suspicion. The couple had to be caught in the act or make a written confession.

Soon further safeguards were added. When the punishment of the guilty parties was stoning, the witnesses of the adulterous act, on whose evidence alone sentence could be passed, had to throw the first stones and thereby become personally involved in the execution. This would make them think twice in giving their testimony.

The man who had led the wife astray could be castrated, his face permanently mutilated and his legs speared. His wife could be raped—a reprisal in like kind as it were.

There were many ways also in which the adulteress was punished once, because of its severity, the death penalty was abolished. She, too, could have her face permanently marked, so that she should never attract another lover. Other penalties introduced (for instance, in Roman days) were banishment, loss of property rights and corporal chastisement. Justinian decreed that an adulteress should spend the rest of her life in a convent!

Sometimes punishment was graded, according to the frequency of the offense or the standing of the cheated husband in the community. Thus, among South Australian aborigines, a first case of infidelity on the part of a wife was avenged by the branding of her face; a repetition of her misconduct, by the spearing of her legs; the third time, she was killed. The Incas of Peru commonly punished adultery by divorce, but if it concerned the wife of an Inca chief, the interloper was not only killed—by burning—but his parents as well, while his home was completely demolished.

The interpretation of adultery varied. At times, actual coitus between the adulteress and her lover was not even necessary. In New Caledonia, for instance, merely to have glanced at the wife of the chief was regarded as adultery and punished by execution. In its extreme, adultery itself was thus seen not only in having extra-marital relations but even in the mere lustful coveting of someone else: "that whoever looks on a woman to desire her has committed adultery with her already in his heart" (Matt. 5:28).

Lack of knowledge led to false accusations of infidelity. Some primitive men just could not understand that one father could beget twins. Their birth proved to them the wife's adultery. One of the two children simply had to be illegitimate. No protest on the mother's part could ever convince the father otherwise, and the poor woman had to pay for her jealous husband's (and early society's) ignorance . . .

The belief that a wife was married to her husband for all time continued to control her sexual life after she was widowed. Intercourse with another man then was still condemned as adultery. From beyond the grave, the husband (or his spirit) would exact due punishment for her unfaithfulness!

It took a long time to change the entire concept of infidelity and to remove its punishment from savagery. Many centuries had to pass before adultery finally became a moral offense, as contemptible in a husband as in a wife.

Adultery Tests

Earliest codes legislated for mere suspicion of adultery.

Thus Hammurabi of Babylon decreed that if a husband accused his wife of (unproven) infidelity—"she had not been discovered lying with another man"—he was not obliged to justify his charge. The burden of proof rested on the suspect, who was regarded as being guilty until she herself had provided proof that invalidated the accusation. In a solemn oath she had to affirm her innocence.

If, on the other hand, the suspicion had some justification, and was based not on her husband's jealous inclinations (or imagination) but on rumors spread abroad, linking her with another man—"if the finger had been pointed at the wife"—the oath was insufficient. Only a "trial" could now clear (or condemn) her. It consisted of the ancient water ordeal. To ensure the proper and irrevocable divine judgment, she had to throw herself into a sacred river. If she drowned, this was the unmistakable confirmation of her guilt and its simultaneous punishment. However, if she kept afloat, she had proved her innocence and at the same time saved both her life and her good name.

Purity and water were thus linked in early times in a most specific way and, to the cynical mind, could have fostered in very primitive days the practice of swimming as a lifesaver.

No doubt the Bible adopted and adapted the Babylonian trial by water—only changing it in several features.

The husband, having lost faith and trust in his wife, even without the slightest grounds and solely on the basis of his jealousy, had to take her to a priest at the Temple. And then a lengthy and trying ordeal commenced.

The priest on her behalf and for her alleged sin prepared a sacrifice consisting of coarse meal. He then led the woman toward the altar of burnt offering—"before the Lord"—and loosened her hair, an action which has been interpreted as symbolic of her (unproven) shame and expressive of mourning and regret.

The suspect was now asked to hold the vessel with the offering, while the servant of God kept in his hand a bowl of holy water, taken from the brass laver, into which he had previously mixed dust from the floor of the sanctuary. Confronting her, the priest pronounced an oath. Had she been faithful, nothing would happen to her and these "waters of bitterness" would have no effect. If, however, she had been guilty and had slept with another man, the concoction would cause her belly to swell and her thigh to rot.

Once the oath was uttered, the priest would call on the wife to affirm it twice with the word *amen*. (And this, in fact, is the very first time that the Bible mentions this word which was to become so prominent in the worship of three world religions, and whose faithful followers certainly do not always realize its original link with infidelity.)

Having pronounced the oath, the priest would write its words on a parchment, immediately thereafter to dissolve them in the dust-water. The ordeal would now conclude by the woman drinking this potion, the priest meanwhile burning the meal offering on the altar.

No factual reports exist as to the application of this extraordinary trial. However, we know that a royal convert to Judaism in Roman times, Queen Helena, presented to the Temple a golden tablet inscribed with the words of the biblical chapter on the ordeal of jealousy. From it the priest was to copy the text whenever the occasion arose. Perhaps this was one of the strangest royal gifts ever made.

The Talmud regarded the entire subject as being important enough to reserve for it a complete treatise.

It is interesting to speculate as to whether the treatment (if ever applied) had the desired effect. Did its very threat guard the sanctity of the home and frighten wives so much that they refrained from adultery? Did the trial's actual performance—if no ill effects ensued later on, apart from vindicating the humiliated wife—pacify the distraught mind of a suspicious husband without afterward damaging marital harmony? Or did its very severe, solemn and impressive ritual psychologically bring about the predicted result?

Rather regretfully, surely, nothing is recorded about any punishment of or even a reprimand to a husband who thus had falsely accused and calumniated his wife. He indeed was not even expected to, as it were, pay "court costs," by bringing a sin offering.

The Adulterous Birth of the Lapdog

Fads and fashions may be designed ingeniously for economic interests or by extrovert dandies. Sometimes they just "happen" or are the unexpected result of factors that aimed at a totally different object.

Lapdogs, some authorities have claimed, were first conceived by irate husbands as a queer sort of punishment for their adulterous spouses.

It all began, so the story goes, during the Russian campaign of King Boleslaw II, the Bold, of Poland. When the royal head and his noble supporters had been away too long, their wives got lonely and felt sexually frustrated.

As their complaints went unheeded, they proceeded from vociferous protest to the next "best" thing they could think of and —do. If their husbands were unable or unwilling to return forthwith to carry out their marital duties, they could quench their thirst at a source near at hand and most willing to oblige: the male staff who, after all, had been left with them to be "at their service."

News travels fast and when the absent soldier-husbands heard of their wives' infidelity, many of them deserted the army to save their marriage.

The king well realized that unless he stopped the rot at once, he was bound to lose two wars: against the Russians as much as on the home front. He hastened back and, to his disgust, discovered that meanwhile many of the lonely warriors' wives had become pregnant or given birth to illegitimate children.

With great cruelty he had all the "bastards" collected and taken to a wood to be abandoned to their fate. But he also decreed that as punishment the women who had committed adultery had to nurse—puppies. To display their shame publicly as well (and as a warning to potential offenders), they had to carry the dogs about wherever they went.

Designs, however, often misfire, and the punishment turned into a pleasure. To carry a lapdog in one's arms became so much the fashion that, conceived in shame, it gave birth to joy. Soon other women adopted the custom (maybe they did so to protect their own sex) and lapdogs became the vogue and no one could ever guess what type of mistress owned them.

Sexual Hospitality and Wife-Swapping

Hospitality to complete strangers used to play a significant role in social life. To show them respect and friendship was good manners. It is more than just a beautiful legend that tells how Abraham's home had doors facing in every direction. A passing wanderer should not have to search for the entrance but know that, no matter who he was, he was welcome. Arab hospitality went further. It demanded the protection of the life of even an enemy, once he had passed one's threshold.

Such eagerness in opening up one's home, however, was not quite unselfish. Obviously it established new bonds in a lonely and hostile world. In addition, in ancient days people often wondered whether the passing stranger was not in reality a superhuman being, perhaps an angel, or a god in disguise. Entertaining him "unawares" would bring blessings manifold (or a son to a barren wife, as in the case of Abraham).

At times, in some regions of the world, such hospitality did not include only board and lodgings. It went "all the way" and even invited the visitor to sleep with the female members of the household. In the case of a god as guest, this might (and in ancient tradition actually did) result in the birth of an extraordinary being. Thus sexual hospitality was not then the symptom of a permissive society but of a god-fearing age!

At that early stage, too, one variation of hospitality extended to the exchange of wives, or, in its modern slang, "wife-swapping." This, however, was not done haphazardly, clandestinely or out of sexual lust, in the modern sense of free and easy entertainment. A man expressed genuine friendship by making available his wife to a kinsman who (for one reason or another) was in (sexual) need. Once again, this strengthened the ties of a group and ensured its survival. (Of course, such arrangements were not possible in societies in which the attitude toward adultery excluded such "mores.")

Eventually the custom would grow into a reciprocal sort of agreement. When in need himself, he could expect his friend to pay back the debt in like coin and provide him with his wife. There was mutual profit in wife-swapping. It should be understood here that such cases arose only in special circumstances. For instance, it would apply when a man was far away from home.

Eskimos without horror or shame practiced this "exchange of wives." A child born of such union had a special name for its father. Without reproach but very factually it spoke of him as "the man who slept with my mother."

10.

The Male Organ

Phallic Worship

Conspicuous indeed is the erect male organ. Once its purpose was understood, it came to represent fertility, the eternal procreative force of nature—in man, beast and crop. On it depended man's very life. It ensured the growth of his fields and herds as much as the existence of future generations. And that was the reason why man began to worship the phallus.

He did so with even greater awe because of the mystery of its fecund power. To his mind it was a religious duty and nothing sinful. How could man ever be ashamed of what the gods had not been ashamed to give him.

Phallus worship was not only universal but took on the most diverse forms.

Its original practice was the veneration of a phallus still attached to a figure, of extraordinary, giant size however, and out of all proportion to the rest of the body. In many cases, the lingam was at least as large as the entire figure. Sometimes it could even be moved.

The next step soon followed. The penis, as it were, became independent and was now revered all on its own, as a huge pillar, a pole or a monolith. Yet the way these erect "monuments" were shaped could leave no doubt in the viewers' minds as to what they represented. They were put up at all kinds of sites: at the entrance of homes and shrines, under the foundations of buildings, in front of altars, at crossroads and in fields.

Then, as if further to emphasize the supreme importance of the generative power in man, the phallus image was provided with some human features, a face, hands and feet. The penis, once a mere adjunct of the body, had now become its very vehicle, so to speak!

Some authorities actually claim that the creation of the earliest statues of man was the result not of an artistic instinct but of the pursuit of this phallic worship. Its very idols were the first sculptures. When statuary apparently had become completely "secularized" and was no longer part of sacred sex promotion, for many centuries still and unknowingly its base, the plinth and column continued to represent the phallus on which were only superimposed the bust and head.

It is believed that even tree worship grew out of this type of fertility cult. The tree's very features were suggestive of the penis. Was not the tree like a living emblem of man's erect generative organ? It stood upright and firmly planted in the soil. It grew ever more. Its foliage and the fruit it bore, crowning its very top, were unmistakable manifestations of its fertility. A tree, deeply rooted, withstood tempests and blizzards. All the more so, it was a vivid image of the penis, the source of strength and virility.

That, in fact, is also the background of the biblical tree in Paradise (no matter whether it grew apples, apricots or figs, a question never settled). The eating of its fruit, meaning the phallus, symbolized sexual experience.

The cross, in its various shapes, has also been interpreted as an early fertility emblem. It was the stylized male member and, originally, venerated as such.

The serpent, so ubiquitous in sacred tradition, found its place there as well as a living figure of the phallus. Its ability of erection, most of all, contributed to its symbolic use and sexual deification.

Because of its phallic shape, even the mushroom became an early object of fertility worship. Its widened, bell-like crown, reminiscent of an enlarged glans, its sudden and fast growth after a downpour of rain, were some of the factors that led to the inclusion of this fungus into the rich pantheon of phalli.

Numerous phallic symbols—of wood, metal and stone—

were worshiped throughout ancient Egypt. A legend explains their introduction and deification. Osiris, brother and husband of Isis, was murdered by the treacherous and jealous Seth. With seventy-two accomplices and by a ruse, Seth slew the powerful god. But to make sure that his death was final, he dismembered the body into countless parts, scattering them all over the country.

Heartbroken, Isis went about in search of them. One version relates that she buried each piece wherever she found it. Another speaks of how she triumphed over death and achieved her husband-brother's resurrection. But, significantly, one tradition tells that she was able to reassemble Osiris' entire body with the exception of its most vital part—the penis.

When, after a renewed frantic quest she remained unsuccessful, she had a replica of his penis made out of wood, as a sacred object of veneration. And that is how, the legend suggests, Egypt took up phallus worship.

The Bible contains numerous traces of phallic worship as well. Certainly the prophets tried their very utmost to eradicate it. But in many cases they fought a losing battle. The *asherah* (literally a "pole") mentioned in Scripture was, to begin with, a branchless tree trunk, worshiped in such a vegetation cult. Against all opposition and in spite of all protest, the Israelites set these *asherot* up on hills—just as the Canaanites before them had done.

The dance around the golden calf was not mere animal worship. It was a sexual orgy in which men and women, stripped naked, ecstatically gyrated around the object of their veneration —the most powerful symbol of fertility. Most probably this was not the image of an entire bull but the representation of its phallus: a huge cone, shaped out of the gold donated by the women.

This would all the more explain Moses' wrath. He realized the overwhelming force of the ancient fertility rite that threatened the spiritual ideas he tried to teach his people. To idolize sex was still so much more natural to them than to serve an invisible God.

Even King Solomon's Temple—for those able to understand its biblical description—had its sexual symbolism: not hidden inside but conspicuously displayed at its very gate.

The large twin pillars that flanked the gate, and which have played so important a part in solemn rites (it has been claimed), were originally two giant-sized, stylized phalli. Their very names, though later interpreted ecclesiastically, were sexually suggestive. *Jachin* (the pillar on the left) stood for "he will erect," while *Boaz* (the pillar on the right) means "in him is strength."

Certainly the penis appears in the most unexpected places of the Bible. Sometimes it is so well camouflaged that its presence could hardly be expected. And this, of course, does not even take into consideration the symbolism discovered (or imagined) by psychologists and psychoanalysts in their interpretations of dreams and myths.

Who would ever guess the rhetorical use of the penis—and of all places—in biblical writings? Many readers might have been somewhat puzzled by a passage in the Books of Kings in connection with the fight between the north and the south after King Solomon's death.

It tells how Rehoboam, the late monarch's son and rightful pretender to the throne, discussed his course of action with his young friends, asking them how he should answer rebellious popular demands to ease burdens his father had imposed. They strongly advised him against the counsel for moderation given him by the elder statesmen (an early generation gap!) and encouraged him to show his strength.

Not tax deductions and less work but, on the contrary, his policy should be "the strong hand." Say to them, his impetuous young friends suggested: "My little finger is thicker than my father's loin." That, at least, is the traditional rendering of the text which sounds rather strange and certainly unimpressive, particularly so if used as a belligerent threat. But its original and true meaning was: "Tell them, my little finger is thicker than my father's [erect] penis." Such language will be all the more appreciated if it is remembered how renowned Solomon was for his sexual prowess.

No one could mistake the statue of Priapus, the Greek god promoting fertility in crops, cattle and women. His penis was always erect. Frequently it was of stupendous size. Or—a striking example of the independent phallus image—he was portrayed by a giant dummy lingam alone, in which human facial and bodily features were imprinted.

Typical also of the many other fertility gods in whose worship the phallus played a central role was Liber, ancient Italian deity, often identified with the Greek Dionysus. His festival, called after him, was the Liberalia, observed on March 17. A large wooden phallus, mounted on a wagon, was then carried across the country. The population followed wherever the phallus was taken. In exuberance they sang lewd songs and broke forth in passionate exclamations, all "appropriate" for the occasion. Finally it was deposited in a city, and there it was solemnly crowned with a wreath. This task was reserved as a privileged honor to one of the most respected matrons.

An account of one such phallic procession is preserved in Augustine's writings. Naturally this Christian leader and author denounced this worship of the male genital in honor of a god and vehemently decried the use of "this disgraceful effigy." With strongest words he castigated the practice as immodest, immoral, licentious and depraved.

But even the condemnation of so renowned an authority seemed powerless against man's vital urge and natural instinct and could not, as it were, remove the penis. Records testify that phallic worship continued to flourish—in one way or another.

Repeatedly Church authorities had to threaten and punish offenders who would not give up venerating this, to them, sacred "member." A typical penance was the eating of dry bread and drinking of only water for three consecutive Lents.

Worse still, phallic worship entered the Church. Statues of Christian saints were provided with large penises. In southern France, for instance, phallic worship took place within the very precincts of a shrine. Women, denied the joys of motherhood, invoked St. Foutin—an ithyphallic saint, reputedly the first bishop of Lyons. When Protestants captured the town of Embrun in 1585 and destroyed the local church, they found relics of the saint's phallus. Its tip was colored red, it was said, from the many libations of wine poured over it by childless women in their desperate quest for St. Foutin's help. (It is also claimed that afterward they drank the wine thus used. They believed that it would be an unfailing remedy for their sterility.)

When Jews, on the Feast of Tabernacles, ceremoniously shake palm fronds and then hold them tightly to the round fruit of a citron, this, too, might be a survival of primitive phallic worship, with its obvious implications. Of course, no one nowadays would suspect this background, as the practice has been completely reinterpreted and spiritualized. The same applies to the palms of the Christian Palm Sunday, equally a vestige of ancient sex adoration.

Even hot cross buns were originally pagan genital mascots. To conceal their erotic source, they were stamped with the sign of the cross.

There were traditions of airborne, flying phalli in ancient Mexican lore. The famous "feathered serpent" of Toltec and Aztec culture—Quetzalcoatl—has been seen as the plumed penis-lord of Mexico.

The pre-Inca Mochica race, likewise, in ancient Peru paid solemn homage to the male organ. Excavated Mochica pottery displays not only phalli of extraordinary size in the state of erection but shows women in apparently devout prayer invoking the penis.

Ubiquitous, indeed, was the phallus, in the sky, on earth and —in the water! All over the Pacific area was known the myth of an eel. And the eel, like the serpent, assumed phallic symbolism because its very shape was so suggestive of man's penis.

A frequent theme, recurring in many versions throughout the region (from Polynesia to New Zealand) tells how the eel was slain and his head implanted in the soil to grow into a mighty coconut palm. Its size was so enormous that it nourished and quenched the thirst of the whole world.

The phallus extends from "pillar" to "post." No aspect of life seemed too strange for its intrusion. The dance around the maypole, in its essence, too, was nothing else but phallus worship. It was so fitting on the day that celebrated the growth of crops, and it is not to be wondered at that the Puritans stopped the practice.

That the penis also found a place on graves, however morbid, can easily be understood. Those who believed in the life-giving force of the lingam and hoped for the survival of the dead could not but feel that the one needed the other!

Phallic worship was not restricted to its mere replicas, of whatever type. It included the veneration of the penis of living men. Pagan priests exposed it, so that the pious might pay due homage to it. In parts of India holy men walked about naked, announcing their approach by ringing a bell for the faithful to come out of their homes to worship the "living" phallus, often by devoutly caressing it!

The Magic Penis

The phallus, so omnipotent and universal, was not only worshiped but also came to serve as a potent agency against evil forces. Because of its life-giving properties it assumed, next to extraordinary sizes, magic dimensions as well.

The phallus became a most-sought-after amulet. It was made of every type of material: clay, wood, silver, gold and glass. Sometimes it was even baked of dough. No doubt those who ate the pastry-penis believed that it was not only food for sex but for strength altogether.

Greeks and Romans used to suspend the replica of a penis outside their shops. Women and children wore it as a necklace. They did so not for decorative reasons, as an ornament, but to ward off evil forces.

City gates were guarded by a giant phallus, positioned like a sentry. Inscriptions reminded those entering that—because of the phallus—"happiness dwells here" (*hic habitat felicitas*). And although this inscription is so ambiguous that it could easily be misinterpreted to indicate some orgiastic, licentious habitation, in reality it meant to say that by the magic power of the penis-mascot no misfortune would ever be able to pass this gate.

Not least because of its rigid strength while erect, the phallus became a token of courage and was regarded as its very producer. That is how Maoris saw in this "ancient one" (as they termed the male organ) the very emblem of virility and invincible power. If a war leader, for instance, woke up on the morning of a battle with his penis stiff, he welcomed its erection as an omen of victory.

The effects of witchcraft and the nefarious intentions of sorcerers, it was believed, could be annulled by the chant or recital of a magic verse, if simultaneously the threatened man tightly grasped his penis.

There is among Ulithian lore the story of "The Wooden Phallus of Ifaluk." It tells how the hero, after having been badly beaten up by some men, was cast by them into a refuse pit. A woman, by urinating on him, revived him. He asked his friends, who then joined him, to pursue his aggressors, magically indicating the direction in which they had gone by letting his penis slowly grow and point the way . . .

The extraordinary phenomenon of man's use of the penis as a magic wand has hardly an equal. It served him not only as a potent charm that protected him (or her) against threats of sterility and frigidity but entire communities against any sort of attack. The power of the penis thus went far beyond the realm of sex, embracing the whole of life.

Circumcision

It is generally assumed that only Jews are circumcised—for religious reasons—and that (some) other modern communities adopted the operation for hygiene alone. The fact, of course, is that circumcision is much more ancient and widespread.

Circumcision was practiced—independently—in many parts of the world from prehistoric times. It was known from Africa to the Philippines, among Australian aborigines and American Indians. An Egyptian inscription of c. 4000 B.C. refers to it and archaeologists unearthed the mummified body of a circumcised man from a tomb dated c. 1600 B.C. Significantly the hieroglyphic character for phallus shows the penis without its foreskin.

Frequently the uncircumcised was stigmatized and excluded from his group. He could not marry, take part in the deliberations of his tribe, bear arms or receive a legacy. The act of circumcision was deemed so important that sometimes only after it had been performed was a man given his permanent name and the years of his life were counted from that date.

Mostly every male of the group had to be circumcised. However, cases are equally known where circumcision was a privilege reserved for the ruling class and the rich, thereby expressing their state of superiority.

Certainly a custom so worldwide and regarded with such awe must have fulfilled a deeply rooted human need.

That circumcision concerns sex goes without saying. But there is still a diversity of opinion as to which primary function it served. The operation was originally practiced either to bestow positive benefits on the circumcised or to protect him against evil of many kinds. Whichever way, the importance of sex and the sexual act were realized.

Man treasured his sexual prowess. After all, without it he was not a man. But he also believed that it was a gift from the god of fertility on whose favor he depended.

Nothing in life is for nothing. To pay the price for his virility man gave part of the member that was the very instrument of propagation. The forces of fertility had to be bought and their good will ensured. Without their cooperation no copulation could take place or be successful. They were indeed entitled to (and demanded) the gift of man's entire generative organ.

But such offering would defeat the very purpose of the "transaction" by making any future intercourse impossible. Therefore merely a symbolic offering was made: part of the whole. Solemnly and ceremoniously the loose foreskin covering the glans was detached and dedicated to the deity. Thus coitus was not only still possible but (it was often believed) it became more effective and virile.

By circumcision, man's sexual organ, as it were, was sanctified and henceforth the joys and excitement (and reproduction) of sex would be his. That is why most of the tribes that practiced circumcision, circumcised boys at the time of puberty or young men prior to their first intercourse. The practice belonged to the sacred initiation rites when the youth was made a full member of his group, and the foreskin was presented as an offering. It was like a fee paid in advance for one's reproductive activities.

One theory goes far beyond the assertion that, originally, circumcision took the place of castration. In the beginning, it claims, the gods demanded the very life of the youth and he was sacrificed. But this would have meant the eventual extinction of the tribe and that is why circumcision was introduced as a (so much more acceptable) substitute.

Circumcision was an essential preparation for the sex life of man. To have his first intercourse without the penis being properly "ready" was thought unsafe and inviting disastrous effects.

Anything done for the first time exposed man to enormous risks. It activated malevolent forces who, jealous of the occasion, would do their utmost to spoil it. They therefore might inflict irreparable harm on man's procreative power. To propitiate or drive them away, man sacrificed part of his penis, as the most appropriate preparation for marital relations. The blood thus shed magically acted as a devil-repellent as well. Circumcision accordingly immunized male prowess against potential interference and —beyond it—any future children against demonic attack.

Once circumcised, man could carry out the sexual act without fear. This also explains why circumcision was frequently practiced at the time of a boy's sexual maturing or actually before his first coitus, or around the date of his marriage, always giving the wound time to heal. In Hebrew and Arabic, in fact, the very term for bridegroom stems from a root meaning circumcision. The modern Hebrew for bridegroom (*chatan*) literally signifies "one who is circumcised."

That many tribes circumcised a youth during his initiation, led authorities—erroneously—to assume that the rite was introduced as a test of bravery. In reality, in such cases it was merely part of it, being just another of the variety of mutilations and ordeals the young man had to suffer to prove himself worthy of becoming a member. Certainly the initiate had to show his courage. Any sign of cowardice, and the slightest indication of the discomfort and pain he suffered while being circumcised, would disqualify him. In some communities girls would refuse to marry a man of whom it was known that he had winced during the operation. However much circumcision was a means to establish a man's power of endurance, its real purpose went far beyond it.

* * *

Circumcision served as a tribal mark. Impossible to remove, it branded the loyalty of a man and identified him with his group. That is how, according to the Bible (Gen. 17:9–14), circumcision became a sacred obligation for Abraham and his descendants. It was to be "a sign of the Covenant between Me and you." In fact, to this day, Jews refer to the initiation of a young boy (on the eighth day after birth) into Judaism by the rite of circumcision briefly as "the *b'rith*"—"the pact." It was (meant to be) an indelible "signature" to a contract, imprinted into the genital of every male. At the same time, however, circumcision also became a sign of divine protection.

To begin with, among the Jews, it was not as permanent as suggested. When assimilated Hellenistic Jews shared the gymnasia with their Greek friends, exercising in the nude, they often became the butt of ridicule. Seeing the Jews' circumcised penis, the Greeks taunted them, calling them "demanned." Even worse, they derided them because their organ seemed in a state of constant erection. To avoid this unpleasant situation and experience, Jews underwent painful "plastic" surgery to restore an uncircumcised appearance of their genitals. This operation was known as "stretching," as by drawing forward the residue of the severed foreskin the crown of the penis (and thereby the "seal of Abraham") was covered up.

Rabbinical authorities, naturally, were greatly perturbed by such camouflage, which they condemned as a violation of divine law. They therefore extended the surgery on the penis in a manner that made any later "rectification" impossible.

As a common bond, circumcision was even thought to be a means to assure the survival of the people. The philosopher Baruch Spinoza (in his *Tractatus Theologico-Politicus*) thus stated that "the rite of circumcision, I fain persuade myself, is of such moment . . . that it alone, I think, is sufficient to preserve this people [the Jews] as distinct forever."

* * *

By a process of practical evolution, circumcision, too, at some time and in several parts of the world, became an emblem of subjugation! The virile member of man was his proud possession, and to have it visibly maimed was an indestructible sign of shame. At first, the victors of battles slew their enemies. But then they realized that a live, defeated foe could be of much greater value than a dead one, for he could be made to work and increase —without any extra cost—the country's labor force. To brand him perpetually as a prisoner of war destined to hard labor all his life, he was circumcised. In addition, such "mutilation," because of its similarity to castration, further humiliated him. Also, within the imagination of primitive man, it made him look a little more

like a woman, which stressed his being weak and effeminate.
Certainly the very act of amputating however small a part of his
penis must have been associated early on with the dreaded act of
castration.

* * *

Hedonistic reasons have been proffered as well for the introduction of circumcision. Some said that the removal of the prepuce increased man's pleasure of intercourse. It enhanced and
prolonged its enjoyment.

Others, equally strongly, voiced the opposite opinion. They
were convinced that circumcision reduced sexual pleasure by
blunting the sensitivity of the penis.

Philo Judaeus, in his allegorical interpretation of the Bible,
thus saw in circumcision "first of all . . . a symbol of the excision
of the pleasures that delude the mind" and "of all delights which
pleasure can afford, the association of man with woman" was the
most exquisite. Therefore, he reasoned, "law givers introduced
the mutilation of the very organ that ministered to such connection." This led man to cut down on all superfluous and excessive
pleasures.

Almost twenty centuries later, Moses Maimonides (who
apart from being the renowned philosopher was also a medical
authority in his time) reiterated and reemphasized this explanation of circumcision. One of its (main) objectives was "to limit
sexual intercourse and to weaken the organ of generation as far
as possible" and thereby cause man to be moderate.

Neither assumption is correct. However, it has been suggested that circumcision reduced enjoyment of quite a different
type: it made masturbation less exciting. But this, in effect, encouraged intercourse, with the resultant legacy of children.

A very popular and comparatively old theory traces the origin of circumcision to medical considerations. It was hygienic,
authorities claimed, disease-preventing and progeny-promoting.

Egyptians practiced circumcision, the Greek historian
Herodotus wrote, because it avoided unpleasant infections. Philo
Judaeus thought that the removal of the foreskin generally served
cleanliness, as germs could easily lodge under it.

Circumcision, it was believed, facilitated intercourse by making erection and ejaculation easier. It also removed possible

physiological obstructions. These could be caused by several factors. The foreskin might grow too long or too tight. In the specific case known as phimosis, the contraction of its orifice could make it impossible to retract the prepuce.

Philo added that circumcision made conception more certain. He believed that "by the penis being circumcised the seminal fluid proceeded in its path more easily," "neither being at all scattered, nor flowing on its passage into what may be called the bags of the prepuce." Therefore, he further asserted, nations which practiced circumcision were the most prolific and the most populous.

Such therapeutic and hygienic arguments, however, might easily attribute "modern" concepts to the primitive mind to whom this "reasoning" was completely foreign. (After all, even baths were something unknown to the medieval courts of Europe!) Nevertheless, it might be possible that a "healthy" instinct led primitive man—without actually knowing why—to introduce the operation with those very objectives which we now regard solely as rationalization.

In modern days, certainly, circumcision was adopted by the Gentile world because of its sanitary benefits. At one time it was suggested as a compulsory operation in the Prussian army. Prince Charles of Britain was circumcised by the official Jewish *Mohel*, the circumciser appointed by the orthodox Jewish religious authorities of England!

There is a medical opinion that circumcision might avoid uterine cancer, possibly contracted by intercourse with an uncircumcised man. A carcinogenous substance was contained in the smegma secreted in the coronary sulcus between the prepuce and the glans penis and then retained inside the foreskin. Circumcision removed this possible source of malignancy.

* * *

Psychoanalysts, ever since Freud, have given their own (and various) interpretations of circumcision, its origins and effects. They linked the operation with the Oedipus complex. To begin with, it was said, fathers, jealous and afraid of their sons' (sexual) rivalry, actually desexed them. Circumcision was merely the (harmless) remnant and substitute of this primal castration. Eventually, by undergoing this operation, sons symbolically expressed their submission to the father. "Whoever accepted this symbol,"

Freud wrote in his *Moses and Monotheism,* "showed by so doing that he was ready to submit to the father's will, although it was at the cost of a painful experience."

No doubt the mere act of "cutting around" (the Latin *circumcidere*) the penis must have reminded people—if only unconsciously—of the fearsome castration. This, too, had its deep and lasting effect on the psyche of man, who was always in fear of losing his manhood. Anti-Semitism was caused at least partially, psychoanalysts claimed, by circumcision. Because Jews were circumcised, they raised in the minds of the Gentiles thoughts of castration that filled them with loathing and horror. Hence they hated the Jew. But ignorant of this cause or unwilling to admit it, they rationalized their antipathy and invented new and unreal explanations.

The circumcised penis—by the absence of its prepuce—resembled the erect phallus with its retracted foreskin. To attain an apparently permanent state of erection by circumcision seemed to primitive man an assurance of constant "fertile sensuality and thence the continuity of the group." Therefore, one school of psychoanalysis claimed, he practiced the operation. The ever-erect appearance of the penis enhanced it and was the greatest bonus for the tribe and its procreative possibilities.

Psychoanalysts (quoting ancient myths) even blamed the woman for the institution of circumcision. She had envied man his penis and to take revenge for possessing this potent organ, she enforced on him the operation which, if not robbing him of the entire member, at least partially injured and shortened it. Women also wished to see man bleed (at least once) from his genitals, as they themselves had to do regularly from the moment they reached puberty.

In fact, man himself, it was suggested, had established circumcision at that period of his life to serve as an equivalent to the female's first menstruation. By the flow of his blood he was to demonstrate his attainment of sexual maturity. Circumcision thus, in the words of Bruno Bettelheim (which supplied the very title of his book on the rite), was a "symbolic wound." It publicly displayed that the boy had reached the most significant stage in life's cycle. After all, human fertility, and the procreation it assured, was one of the most prominent functions in the life of man.

* * *

Judaism made circumcision a religious act, adapting it to this purpose. To divorce it from any sexual context, it was ordained to take place on the eighth day after birth. Islam, its daughter religion, adopted the rite as well, although some think that it took it over not from the Jewish religion but from pre-Moslem Arabs. Actually, it is not mentioned in the Koran.

Jesus was born a Jew and (as recorded in Luke 2:21) his parents had him, like any other Jewish boy, circumcised on the eighth day after his birth. Subsequently the Church observed January 1—eight days after Christmas—as "the festival of the circumcision of Christ." His "holy prepuce" was venerated as a sacred relic in at least twelve different churches in Europe! It was believed to bestow fertility on the barren and to lessen pain at childbirth.

That Christianity eventually discarded circumcision had practical reasons. The new religion was anxious to convert the pagan world, a task already pursued by the Jews. It realized that to demand the painful surgical operation of an adult pagan proselyte, apart from reminding him of castration, would act as a powerful obstacle. St. Paul, in his Epistle to the Romans (2:28–29) thus pronounced that circumcision was "that of the heart, in the spirit, and not in the letter," not outward in the flesh but "inwardly." The Apostolic Council in Jerusalem (c. A.D. 50) ruled that Gentile proselytes need not be circumcised.

* * *

The diversity of reasons (and times) for circumcision is equaled by the variety of instruments used for the operation and the multiplicity of "circumcisers."

In the earliest days, the "surgery" was performed by means of a sharp flint, a stone knife or a bamboo splint.

The circumciser could be a priest, the future father-in-law, a prominent member of the family, a woman or a circumcision "specialist" (later on among the Jews the—Hebrew—*Mohel*).

Even the place where the circumcision had to take place varied. It included the "home" of the child, a secluded site away from the settlement, the sanctuary or a special circumcision hut. There were single and group circumcisions.

The Fate of the Foreskin

The disposal of the severed prepuce took many forms as well. In the case of the original fertility worship, of course, it was solemnly presented to the deity as a precious offering. Fears that nefarious powers may acquire this valuable part of man's source of virility and use it for magic purposes directed against the very person who had grown it caused others (like in the case of cut hair and nail parings) to hide, burn, bury or cast it into a river. The prepuce was also fed to cattle or the youth himself had to swallow it. And all this was to ensure that the potentially dangerous piece of skin was securely "put away"! Underlying this was the ancient superstition that if a vital part (filled with the very essence of the former owner) fell into the hands of the wrong person, it could be used to do him untold harm.

Some tribes, believing in reincarnation, even linked the future resurrection of the circumcised with the fate of the foreskin. Its preservation (often within a rock or a tree) was thought to facilitate his rebirth. After all, it was a very power-point of his being. It could be of paramount importance when, one day, his disembodied spirit, greatly weakened by having discarded its ephemeral shell, needed extra strength for its rebirth. Therefore the careful "keeping" of the foreskin was a significant insurance for the days to come.

The belief that the prepuce had absorbed a man's essential energy also made it a treasured trophy to victorious fighters. They thought that by obtaining the foreskins of their defeated foes, they added to themselves some of the enemies' strength.

But foreskins also served as dowry!

The original custom to purchase one's wife had led to the introduction of many types of dowry. Well known among native people was the (sometimes not insubstantial) number of cattle charged as the "common fee." Jacob—instead of paying in kind —gave so many working hours (the Bible says fourteen years) to acquire Leah and Rachel from their father Laban. But sex "in the raw" was the dowry demanded by King Saul from young, amorous David.

When the melancholy monarch realized that his younger daughter Michal was in love with David, he agreed to "sell" her.

The price he asked was the presentation of a hundred foreskins, slashed off Philistine warriors.

The Bible gives these data quite factually, without any comment or condemnation. It relates how the young man in love, aided by his friends, undertook this mission and, eminently successful, returned from battle with double the number of "trophies" (I Sam. 18). Saul, who had actually hoped that the suitor would be killed in carrying out this mission, honored the bargain, and on receipt of the dowry, handed over his daughter . . .

It is rather an idle and nauseating speculation to ask who checked up on the right amount of prepuces. Commentators have expressed doubt whether the demand was actually for the Philistines' foreskins alone. This would have required careful surgery on the part of David and his party. They suggested that Saul expected not just the prepuce but the complete (uncircumcised) genital of the foe.

Circumcision, concerning such a small piece of skin, is thus tied up with an enormous amount of human if not cosmic objectives, expectations and obligations.

Semen

Semen, the seed of the male, "sows" (from the Latin *serere*) the future generation. Magical power has been ascribed from earliest days to this thick milky fluid from man's procreative organ, containing the reproductive spermatozoa.

Primitive man did not realize that it issued from the testes. The scrotum, indeed, was regarded as merely a decorative bag, ornamental in purpose and nothing else.

Simultaneously sacred and taboo was the seminal discharge. Unless ejected in actual coitus, it rendered man "unclean" and contaminating. The Bible contains strict injunctions how he who has had an "emission of semen" (perhaps through an erotic dream) had to be isolated and purified.

Ancient rites demanded a daily offering of semen to the gods, and to provide the vital fluid, orgiastic frenzies took place. To meet the demand, men masturbated—often in rhythmic "chorus" with appropriate musical accompaniment.

Semen not only was the generating power in conception but a source of strength. Its retention invigorated man, adding to his physical, mental and, not least of all, his spiritual stamina. Hence, those dedicated to the gods (or God) observed strict abstinence.

Romans employed semen as an ingredient in their magic, aphrodisiac concoctions, reasoning that "seed" would beget "seed."

Swearing by the Genitals

Modern courts of law administer the oath by asking the witness to place his hand on the Bible. However, the solemn biblical method of swearing demanded the putting of one's hand on the penis of the person to whom the promise, statement or vow was made.

Later periods, regarding this system (or even its very recollection) offensive, changed the text, calling the penis—innocuously to our ears—the thigh or loins. Those familiar with biblical terminology know that these interchangeable words were generic terms for the organ of reproduction.

Thus, speaking of his descendants, the ancient Hebrew would refer to them as "those who come out of my thigh." That is how Abraham asked his servant to swear "by the Lord, the God of Heaven and the God of the earth" that he would choose for his son Isaac as wife not a Canaanite girl but one of "my kindred."

And again when, on the eve of his death, Jacob asked Joseph solemnly to promise him under oath that he would make sure that in the days to come his body would be interred not in Egyptian soil but among his ancestors' graves in the Holy Land, he, too, asked him to put his hand "under my thigh."

As the organ of reproduction a man's genitals were regarded as his most sacred possession. To expose them to view caused not shame but awe. Therefore swearing by (and literally on) the penis presupposed extra sanctity and inviolable obligation.

The obvious meaning of the procedure implied that should he who was taking the oath ever break it, his "issue"—the yet unborn generations—would punish such disloyalty and dishonoring of a pledge.

Great and mysterious power was thus associated—at the beginning—with man's putting his hand publicly and demonstratively on what was to become known as his "privates." But this very tradition survives—etymologically—in the "Testament" and "testimonial," in fact in anything that "testifies." All these words "bear witness" to the ancient method of taking an oath—on the testicles *(testes)*.

Castration

One of the earliest and crudest methods of depriving a male of his generative power gave castration its name. From the Sanskrit (via Latin) it speaks of the "cutting off" of man's scrotum or the "amputation" of his penis. This term, however, was also applied to other types of removal of man's virility. These included the crushing of the testicles with a stone or flint knife, searing them with a red-hot iron or carefully pulling them out by means of a sharp bamboo stick.

Castration was so ancient a practice that it even figures in the Egyptian *Book of the Dead* and in Greek mythology. Cronus is said to have used a sickle to sever the genitals of his father Uranus, and to have flung both the genitals and the sickle into the sea. Indeed, it was believed that the foam caused by the genitals hitting the water had given birth to Aphrodite, while the blood dropping onto the earth had created the nymphs and the furies.

That the origin of castration leads back thousands of years must have weighty reasons. These can be traced to early religion, dynastic concern, penal measures and the establishment of a corps of guards for women, themselves put beyond the bounds of temptation.

Without doubt early man first learned the facts of castration from his experience with animals. Gelding was practiced in far-off days in almost every ancient civilization. Once an animal had been castrated, it was so much more docile. Why not do likewise with men to render them more loyal slaves, rulers reasoned. And that is how, in remote times, man began to emasculate his own kind, hoping that he would gain slaves that were all the more servile.

War and conquest soon taught the victor the advantage of

removing the manhood of his beaten foes. A slain enemy was of little use, but a castrated one could serve as a slave laborer, while his being desexed ensured the eventual extermination of his tribe. Literally, his source of reproduction had been effectively and permanently cut off!

The earliest war trophies, therefore, were not scalps but severed penises. To return home with a bag filled with such spoil established a warrior as a hero. Herodotus related how, throughout the empires of the Middle East, Assyrians, Babylonians, Persians and Egyptians systematically deprived their prisoners of war of their manhood.

Is it any wonder that Oriental custom introduced a like kind of dowry? A suitor presented to his future wife (or her father) as his bride-price, not cattle or money but genitals he had slashed off the tribe's foes. Nothing could exceed their value and endear him more to his new family circle.

*   *   *

Castration played yet another significant part, almost from the start of civilization, in fertility rites. The sacrifice of the phallus, the organ of generation, was seen as the finest token that could be offered to the god or goddess of procreation. The belief that the gift of one's own fertility would ensure continuance of life belongs to the paradoxes that abound in the history of mankind.

In the cult of Astarte, the Semitic goddess of fertility, love and pleasure, the devotee demanned himself. Carrying in his hands the severed organ, he ran through the city. Eventually he threw the penis into one of the homes. Its owner, thereby greatly honored, had to pay for the privilege by presenting the new eunuch priest with a (female!) vestment.

Similar features distinguished the worship of the Greek Cybele, that "great mother of nature." In frenzied orgies and wild dances and to the accompaniment of raucous music, men slashed their bodies and cut off their penises, which they presented on the altar of the goddess. From then onward they served her as sacred eunuchs, also clad in female attire.

Apart from thus dedicating their manhood to the goddess (of whichever name), several reasons accounted for the self-mutilation. The deity jealously demanded the uninhibited, unrivaled and permanent attention of her servants. This could best be assured by removing any possibility of unfaithfulness.

The act of castration also mysteriously strengthened the godhead, it was believed. After all, it was a fertility rite, and thus the sacrifice of their manhood contributed to the fruitfulness of nature, assisted in (if not ensured) her resurrection and the bursting into bloom of all verdure.

Yet more so, it has been suggested, the castration was motivated by man's desire to be transformed into a being closest to the goddess and thereby most worthy to become a vehicle for her gift and power. Nothing could prove his genuine desire more than the very removal of his male genitals. The donning of female attire was merely another step in man's quest of impersonation. It is interesting to consider here how the frenzy itself must have acted like a strong anesthetic on the victim of the self-inflicted and most painful surgery.

Castration was practiced as well, later on, by fervently religious men who saw in sex only evil and who were afraid of becoming slaves of their passion. Not trusting themselves and never to fall into temptation, they underwent the operation.

St. Matthew's Gospel thus recorded (19:12) the existence of "eunuchs who have made themselves eunuchs for the sake of the kingdom of Heaven." Significantly, and obviously approving of it, the Gospel added that "he that is able to receive it, let him receive it." Although most later commentators explained this passage metaphorically, some members of the early Church were influenced by it to practice self-mutilation. In the words of St. Augustine, they thought "thereby to serve God." Deprived of sex, they were sure exclusively and absolutely to dedicate their lives to their faith.

However praiseworthy Christian authorities at first regarded the sacrifice of manhood, Judaism and Islam strongly condemned it at all times. In fact, the Jews' was the only culture in antiquity expressly to legislate against the emasculation of both man and animal, later to be extended even to fish. The Hebrew Bible excluded from "the assembly of the Lord" anyone that "is crushed or maimed in his privy parts" (Deut. 23:2).

Moslem tradition tells how Uthman, to escape temptation, had asked Mohammed's permission to castrate himself. But the prophet had severely reprimanded him, saying that "he who castrates himself or another does not belong to my followers." The only type of castration permissible in Islam was fasting.

* * *

Castration became, too, part of the penal code of many countries. Egyptian law thus punished adultery. Indians desexed those guilty of insulting men of high caste. Frisians enforced the operation on the rapist and temple robber. The Welsh made castration an alternative for a heavy fine: condemned criminals could pay either in cash or in manhood.

Dynastic considerations were also responsible for the carrying out of castration. Rulers, anxious to ensure their power and that of their progeny as rightful successors, enforced the emasculation of all possible sources of future trouble. Roman tradition asserts that the first act of castration ever was practiced for that reason by Semiramis, the legendary Assyrian queen and founder of Babylon. When assuming authority after the murder of her husband, she had all male infants of the royal household desexed. This, she reckoned, would put a stop to any rebellious claims to the throne.

* * *

Castration played an important role even in "social" life. Wealth was once expressed by the number of wives and concubines a man could afford. Their care and protection created its own problems, not least in the engagement of reliable guards. Who, after all, could be trusted to look after them without, unbeknown to the master, collecting an extra bonus—not in money but in kind? The temptation was too great.

The most obvious and safest means was to put in charge men who were no longer men. This need created the unenviable profession of the eunuch who sold his manhood (or was deprived of it under force) to fulfill this most trustworthy mission.

Accordingly the etymology of the eunuch's name has been explained—from the Greek—as meaning "bedchamber guard." This claim, however, has been refuted. "Eunuch," much more likely, stems from a Babylonian-Hebrew root, *chanuch,* describing someone who is "proficient" and "trained" and therefore utterly dependable. Experience certainly underscored such derivation.

Eunuchs proved themselves not only reliable guards in the "sleeping quarters," but became equally loyal and responsible in public service. Xenophon recorded how Cyrus, the great Persian emperor and conqueror of the Babylonian empire, felt that no one could excel the eunuch in loyalty. He had no family ties or affections, therefore he would appreciate all the more anyone who gave him a position of trust. "Besides, inasmuch as eunuchs are objects of contempt to the rest of mankind, for this reason, if for no other, they needed a master." Cyrus therefore "selected eunuchs for every post of personal service to him, from the door-keeper up." (And it must be remembered that, at the time, a doorkeeper was a most responsible official.)

Eunuchs were chosen for most important positions and executed their tasks with competence. They were employed all over the world: in Assyria, Persia, India, China, Greece and Rome. To produce eunuchs at times became almost an industry and special "operation centers" for their constant supply were established in the Greek islands of Delos and Chios.

Castration—at least partially—was inflicted on men for superstitious reasons as well. Some primitive tribes—such as the Hottentots—believed that the birth of twins brought bad luck. They also imagined that twins could be fathered only by a man who had two testicles. Therefore—according to their mind—the problem could easily be solved (though, in the father's case, not without pain) by the removal of one testicle. And thus, conscientiously, men offered themselves for the operation. After all, a temporary discomfort would avoid later misfortune. Above all, no woman of their tribe would otherwise marry them! This, of course, is a case of demi-castration.

*   *   *

Castration, once so widespread and practiced for so many and diverse reasons, eventually became generally decried as inhuman and against the law of God. Even the Church spoke up against it and in A.D. 325 the Council of Nicaea excluded voluntary castrates from the priesthood.

And yet it was in the Church that—in the sixteenth century —castration was revived and for the most peculiar purpose.

To serve God adequately only the best of song was good enough. But as at that period no women were permitted to join a church choir (or the stage), their pitch of voice had to be provided otherwise. Only young boys could do so or those of their sex who never grew up into manhood. Castration could attain the latter aim. It prevented the development of some of the characteristics of the male including, significantly in this case, the lengthening of the vocal cords. Thus the boy's "falsetto" voice was perpetuated.

Italian parents presented their sons for the operation to preserve their precious soprano voices for the glory of God, the stage and—a good income. France commercialized the supply of *castrati,* as these singers became known, and opened up (especially in Verdun) "eunuch factories," exporting the "deballed" singers to Italy and Spain.

As grown-up men—in stature but not in sex—they became renowned for their beautiful voices and were proudly advertised. Their gain of a melodious (adult male soprano) voice outweighed their loss by mutilation.

Castrati formed a significant part of eighteenth-century choirs and became the most vainglorious stars of the stage. Over two hundred castrati alone sang in Roman church choirs, including the Papal Sistine Chapel. Famous composers, such as Gluck and Mozart, wrote special roles for them. Only an edict of Pope Clement XIV in 1770 outlawed the then almost two-hundred-year-old practice and both on stage and in church women eventually took over the part of the castrati. As it were, the wheel had come full circle.

Forever now, it was hoped, castration was at an end. The very idea came to horrify man. His emotional reaction was deeply rooted and personally conditioned. Somehow he himself was afraid of losing his manhood which he treasured above all. This, according to Freud, even created a phobia—the castration complex. Once having been prepared to offer his virile power as a sacrifice to the gods, now man will go to no length to preserve —and even increase—it.

11.

Prostitution

Sacred Prostitution

The prostitute, for so many centuries ostracized by society as a despised woman of low and disreputable standing, who led a hole-and-corner existence and was considered beneath contempt by the self-righteous, was originally a person of high dignity, in fact, a priestess.

If prostitutes have been called members of the oldest profession, so were some of the earliest brothels part of temples. Just as the majority of man's arts, crafts and learning originated in the realm of religion, so, in no small measure, did sexual indulgence!

Not only women but men also served at shrines: not to burn incense, sacrifice animals or chant hymns, but to offer their bodies: man to woman, woman to man, but also without compunction or shame—man to man.

Sex was a sacrament and the experience of intercourse holy communion with the gods. The prostitutes considered themselves as married to the divinity, and all they performed (sexually) was in his—or her—name and honor. The coitus was a pious act and an integral part of the official religious cult.

Their services were available at the shrine at any time to all the worshipers, but particularly so to total strangers. Could not that visitor (it was believed here as well) be a disguised god, or at least his messenger? And to please him—sexually—would gain the officiating prostitute additional merit and favor.

They gave their bodies (whether openly or in the dark) not for monetary reward but in pious dedication. Likewise, those seeking them out cohabited with them not out of lust (so they claimed) but out of a yearning for the most intimate contact with the gods.

The majority of the harlots actually dwelt within the precincts of the temple, where they served their time and were fully provided for. Others were not attached to the shrine but, so to speak, practiced their profession independently, charging a fee for services rendered. However, they did not keep the money. They handed it on without deductions to the priests who thus— without blasphemous thought—could be regarded as the original pimps!

Sacred prostitution was widespread and obviously so, as, apart from its religious association, it served a common human need. It was known in Africa, India, Greece and all over the Middle East. Ishtar, the Babylonian goddess of love and war, was believed to have remarked that "a compassionate prostitute am I." She—like many other goddesses of similar kind—was the mother who succored and helped. And she gave her loving gift to any of her sons who felt the need of it.

The Bible records how the Canaanites and their neighboring tribes worshiped their idols in sacred prostitution. No wonder that their Israelite conquerors were strongly attracted by their type of religion and, against their own leaders' vehement opposition, were ready converts to the ancient "sex cult." It is significant to note here that the Bible's protest against prostitution proscribed its practice not so much for its immorality as for its idolatry.

A typical example of the continued observance of sacred prostitution in Hebrew times relates to the sons of Eli. They (ab)used their priestly office to sleep with women visiting their sanctuary.

Prostitution persisted (overtly or in secret) among the Hebrews for many generations and it was occasionally even pursued in the Temple itself and fostered by (what the Bible calls) "wicked" kings. Only the most stringent measures eventually abolished the cult.

It is therefore not surprising that one of the original terms by which the sacred harlots were known referred to their priestly status. The Hebrew biblical word for prostitute (derived from the Babylonian) has its root in "consecration" and "holiness": *kadesh* for the male and *k'deshah* for the female!

There were various reasons why a girl or a woman chose (or was enlisted) to enter the profession. At times her own parents dedicated her for this peculiar type of holy service. In other cases young women in a spirit of true awe and solemnity felt the urge to take up the vocation which, after all, in their own eyes and those of the public, was considered most worthy and pious.

Again, other girls gave their body only once. They did so prior to their marriage, to sacrifice their virginity to the god, represented by a priest, a pilgrim or a total stranger just then calling at the shrine. A girl's sacred prostitution was thereby a unique event in her life.

On the other hand, the Babylonian worship of Mylitta (identified with the Phoenician goddess Astarte), according to Herodotus, demanded of every woman to give herself sexually once in her life at the temple to the very first stranger approaching her. The recipient of her favors would start the "transaction" by throwing into her lap—as remuneration—a piece of gold, accompanying the action with the phrase that he claimed her "in the name of [the goddess] Mylitta." Some matrons of high standing and too proud to mix with the vulgar crowds proceeded to the sanctuary brothel in a closed carriage.

Married women as well, possibly because of dissatisfaction with their own home life, took up the sacred task.

Even mass-conscription of temple prostitutes has been known. The consecration of those women to the gods was, as it were, the offering of a multitude of sacrifices. Thus Xenophon relates how fifty courtesans were presented to the Corinthian Venus as the result of a vow made by a victor in the Olympic Games. Identical votive offerings were made to other temples as well, such as in Cyprus and Abydos.

Payment for services rendered naturally varied at the different centers—just as the takings on church plates nowadays. Some men merely threw a small coin to the woman of their choice (and, indeed, temple prostitutes often lined up for the men to take their pick, just as their profane successors continue to do in the red-

light districts). Other worshipers had to pay dearly for the privilege of a coitus with the divine delegate. In the temple of Aphrodite at Corinth, for instance, charges were enormously high. Nevertheless, or perhaps even because of it, the number of callers was
so vast that, as Strabo records, more than a thousand priestesses
were employed in sex worship. Their presence not only gained
the city a record tourist traffic but with it unequaled wealth.

The temple authorities themselves welcomed all candidates
for prostitution, and every possible provision was made for their
comfort. They were not only given excellent accommodation but
also received an intensive course of training, which taught them
every aspect of their profession.

Views differ about the origin of the holy practice. It is one
of the paradoxes of religion that while some faiths, from the
earliest days, demanded absolute chastity from their devotees,
others consisted almost completely of licentious cults.

One theory claims that the women and men indulging in
intercourse in the temple precincts as priest-prostitutes were convinced that by giving themselves voluptuously, they would increase the power of reproduction and the fruitfulness of all that
grew. It was a case of sympathetic magic. Their gift of excessive
sex bestowed a divine blessing on earth. (Cynics may see in such
a belief not only a superb example of rationalization, but also an
explanation of why early pagan worship never presented its
priesthood with the modern worry of empty "pews.")

Finnish anthropologist Edward Westermarck traced temple
prostitution to a common social phenomenon, now termed
"greatness by association." People's status grows by "name-drop-
ping" and their rubbing shoulders with the famous. Westermarck
claims that those seeking carnal knowledge with holy women (or
men) equally imagined that by their intimate contact—in cohabitation, and by their actual intercourse—some of the sanctity of the
holy prostitute would flow into their lives and enrich them supernaturally. After all, those consecrated priests and priestesses
represented the godhead and as her (or his) delegate transferred
divine power to the person with whom they slept.

To consort with a prostitute therefore, at the beginning, was
never a furtively undertaken sidestep but a sacred act. Most certainly, in this case, Lord Shawcross' condemnation of our "per-

missive society," that the "new morality" was merely the "old immorality," must be reversed.

Modern immorality here is ancient religiosity. People with a strong sense of sarcasm might claim that the change of the ancient sacred profession into a profane occupation presented the most stunning symptom of the modern secularization of life.

Finally, the fact that in spite of repeated efforts to stamp out prostitution it has never died out and the "sacred one" survived as the "woman of light virtue" shows that even in our technological age nature still has the upper hand.

Sex for Sale–How to Call a Prostitute

A wealth of names has been given to the woman who sells her body. The modern "call girl" is merely the latest adaptation of the courtesan of the Italian Renaissance (at first a very decent female member of the royal *court*) and of the *hetaira* of ancient Greece (a feminine form of "companion").

A prostitute is pure Latin (as a word, that is). Joining the *pro* to *statuere* (still found in any "statue"), she publicly announced herself as being "set up" or "exposed"—for sale.

And, no doubt, the hiring out of her sex and the economic exploitation of her womanhood gave her the professional status she desired. The word "prostitute" was a later euphemism, though it could not but help becoming equally tainted—by association—as were (the terms for) her sisters, the harlot and the whore.

The word "harlot" originally did not apply to females only but served both sexes. To start with, it simply referred to a vagabond, a rogue, a cheat, a base fellow. In fact, the earliest harlots, linguistically, presented a liaison between the old High German *hari*—"war"—and the Old English *loddere*—"beggar." These women followed the army in droves, constantly ready to oblige any soldier, so long as it was for some small consideration. They were the original "camp followers" of history.

A further, unfounded, but scurrilous folk etymology has suggested that a harlot was a slightly corrupted version of Arlotta, none else but the mother of William the Conqueror—for reasons that had better not be further explored. If true, it would be yet another example of the linguistic phenomenon to create words out of names.

Three different terms thus describe the identical person. However, they are used on a sliding scale of popular value. This leads from the most vulgar of them, the whore, via the still rather common harlot to the professional prostitute.

Trade Methods—Ancient and Modern

The prostitute's methods of approach, psychology and enticement have altered little since it all began. She did not just wait for men to feel hungry for her goods, but tried by every means to whet their appetite and understood everything about the modern concept of impulse buying. Surely no book better than the Bible itself could testify to this fact and it does so very realistically at various places.

It seems that this millennia-old profession has hardly changed in its conduct through the ages. We watch the prostitute sitting on the doorstep of her home, calling out to the passerby (Prov. 9:14–15). She is seen "lying in wait at every corner" (Prov. 7:12).

We witness her moving about the streets, standing in plazas and at busy intersections (Prov. 7:12; Ezekiel 16:24–25). She is never lost for words and speaks in most seductive detail of how her bed is ready for her guest, promising a good time, not for a rushed few minutes, but "until the morning" . . .

She does not passively wait till she is approached. With luring glances she solicits her client, "capturing him with her eyelids" (Prov. 6:25). She is adept at accommodating herself to every type of man: either brazenly displaying herself or addressing her potential visitor with smooth words (Prov. 2:16; 5:3).

Some of the Greek prostitutes certainly must have been most helpful and enterprising in "showing the way." Lest their clients might be "misled," they marked their path to wherever they were at the moment. They did so in the most simple, unmistakable and inviting manner. The soles of their shoes had embossed the Greek words for "follow me." These left their imprint in the sandy road.

The Red-Light District

As the prostitute's trade was regarded an essential part of social life, she had no need to advertise nor, on the other hand, to sell her wares in hidden corners. Frequently her abode was strategically positioned, at times in the very city wall, and easily to be found. Licensed brothels used to carry as their distinguishing sign the most obvious representation: a red penis.

Perhaps the Bible, responsible for so many of our ideas and customs, may be given the credit as well for having inaugurated the "red-light" district, that is, its striking color to attract the customer.

It may all go back to the famous Jericho woman of light virtue who had been contacted by Israelite spies prior to the invasion of the Promised Land. She had been most cooperative, even hiding these secret agents from the people of her city. The Bible honored her by recording her very name, Rahab, the easy-going, "broad"-minded permissive one.

In acknowledgment of her collaboration (so the Bible further tells), she was promised protection at invasion time. All she had to do—to avoid being overlooked—was to mark her "residence" with a scarlet thread! Then, indeed, none of the soldiers would miss it.

The Brothel

Sex has led to so much confusion—even in the designation of the brothel. This word is ill-chosen and has really no place at all in the nomenclature of love. Its presence there is merely the result of (yet another linguistic) corruption.

A brothel described not a place or building of any nature. It referred to a low type of person: a scoundrel, a wretch, a good-for-nothing.

Originally, the site of commercialized sex transactions was known as a bordel house. This term recalls that early houses (even those that were not a home) were made of timber, of boards. *Borda,* its root, is Old Saxon and the *bordel* (from the Old French *borde* and its diminutive *bordelet*) pointed to "a little abode."

But somehow the slurring of the name of the prostitutes' dwelling—the bordel house—caused men to change it into a brothel house. And by the frequency of its use, "house" was eventually dropped. All that remained was the shortened form "brothel," with the original personal meaning (of the word) having become obsolete.

What was to develop into a house of ill fame, to begin with, was sacred ground. As priests—both of the male and the female sex—served as the earliest prostitutes, they naturally pursued their (sacred) profession within the very precincts of their sanctuary. Thus the first brothels (whether most private and intimate, or exceedingly large and well organized) were part of shrines and temples.

Many of them were open-air affairs, often on top of a hill, around the conspicuous phallus erected in honor of the god. It is equally known that in ancient Babylonia in the temple of Marduk, a room high up in its monumental, towerlike structure was specifically reserved for "sex." It was furnished with a couch, and every night a priestess was in attendance for holy consummation.

Still many centuries later, Greek and Roman sanctuaries had their famous quarters for prostitutes. One of the best known and most extensive was the brothel at Corinth, in the temple dedicated to Aphrodite.

But temples did not keep the monopoly. Sacred shrines were soon joined by other institutions that catered to man's sexual appetites (and equally those of women), now completely divorced from religion. Wine shops, in ancient Babylonia, for example, did a voluminous trade in spirit and sex, offering both any quantity of wine and type of whore. In fact, possibly to eliminate difficulties of employer-employee relations, some women owned and ran the establishment, themselves quenching their customers' thirst of every kind.

Another favored and most suitable location of early brothels were the public baths. In Rome they became so much the prostitutes' haunt and the site of all sorts of licentious living that bath and brothel became almost synonymous. Mixed bathing, of course, in the nude was the fashion. Indeed, anyone merely coming to have a bath was looked on askance. He was regarded as queer or suspected of impotence!

However, brothels, completely independent and not as an adjunct to other organizations or institutions, also go back to very early days. Babylonia had some of them as well. They were privately run and staffed by female slaves. Often the original "madam" (a wealthy gentleman then) kept three quarters of the girls' takings.

But to Solon, seventh-century B.C. Athenian statesman, legislator and poet, goes the credit of having established the first public, state-licensed brothel (in Athens). He felt that though prostitution may be evil, it nevertheless fulfilled an essential service.

Every aspect of its functioning was well organized. Clients were given the choice of a wide range of girls, most of them slaves. These waited for their customers, either completely naked or clad in a see-through dress. They were fully maintained by the state. A special taxation was levied and met from the fee charged. This was fixed at a common, low level. Part of the moneys collected were duly used to build a temple to Aphrodite. (But it is also recorded that Solon himself did well from the business.)

Special, state-appointed brothel supervisors had many duties. They were responsible for the payment of taxes, looked after the public image of the establishment (which had to be "dignified") and, in cases of disagreement and quarrel, acted as arbitrators.

Solon's innovation was a success. Brothels (known as *dicteria*) spread all over Greece. At times their inmates became almost overanxious to ply their trade and procure customers. Scantily dressed, they stationed themselves at street corners, in gateways and at stalls, trying to attract their prey and entice it indoors by every possible means. Certainly there was no reason (or need) for customers to sneak into the brothels. On the contrary, as Athenaeus recorded, the girls might even "drag you, almost with violence, into the house."

Brothels came to play a significant part in Roman civilization. At first frowned upon, they became a much-sought-after institution which pandered to every type of erotic want. Services were provided as much for the homosexual as for the heterosexual. Every vice was catered to. Even young children were employed to satisfy perverted lusts.

Most of the prostitutes, whether male or female, were slaves.

The elder Seneca recalls a typical purchase of a kidnapped girl for brothel duties: "She stood naked on the shore to be criticized by her buyer; all the parts of her body were inspected and handled. Do you want to hear the end of the sale? The pirate sold, the pander bought."

However, some of the women offering themselves were free citizens, at times of the highest class. Among them was Messalina, Roman nymphomaniac empress, the third wife of Claudius and mother of Britannicus. Renowned for her debauchery, she is said to have frequented the brothels, to present her body to lusty men. In his *Satires* Juvenal has left a vivid description of her brothel expeditions:

Claudius had scarce begun his eyes to close,
Ere from his pillow Messalina rose;
(Accustomed long the bed of state to slight
For the coarse mattress, and the hood of night;)
And with one maid, and her dark hair concealed
Beneath a yellow tire, a strumpet veiled!
She slipped into the stews, unseen, unknown,
And hired a cell, yet reeking, for her own.
There, flinging off her dress, the imperial whore
Stood, with bare breast and gilded, at the door,
And showed, Britannicus, to all who came,
The womb that bore thee, in Lycisca's name!
Allured the passers by with many a wile,
And asked her price, and took it, with a smile.
And when the hour of business now was spent,
And all the trulls dismissed, repining went;
Yet what she could, she did, slowly she passed,
And saw her man, and shut her cell, the last,
Still raging with the fever of desire,
Her veins all turgid, and her blood all fire,
With joyless pace, the imperial couch she sought,
And to her happy spouse (yet slumbering) brought
Cheeks rank with sweat, limbs drenched with poisonous dews,
The steam of lamps, and odor of the stews.

In fact, people said that all brothels (whether primitive, grimy rooms or stately mansions) had the identical smell. This "brothel stench" was due not to lack of cleanliness but to the various odors associated with intercourse. Patrons could not rid themselves quickly of it, so that one could easily tell who had visited a brothel.

Nonetheless, even a Cato recognized the usefulness of the brothel in the maintenance of morality! He congratulated a nobleman who had just been to such a "house" for his virtue. After all, it was so much better for a youth whose veins swelled with gross lust to drop in there than to "grind some husband's private mill."

For many centuries and all over the world brothels, whether privately owned or run (and licensed) by ecclesiastical, municipal or state authorities proved a rich source of revenue. They were strictly controlled and heavily taxed. Numerous and intriguing records survive of their existence and prominence.

Once again, as in classical times, baths served as favorite venues. They offered "accommodation" for any number of clients. There were tubs that could take three, four or even seven people. On the other hand, those anxious to be on their own could choose a tub for a "twosome."

City authorities, as part of their hospitality, often invited renowned visitors to enjoy the brothels—free of charge. Not a few royal palaces in Europe had their own, private brothel.

The public bordel founded in Avignon by Queen Johanna of Naples in 1347 became well known. Its strict regulations looked after every aspect of the young prostitutes' lives and their clients' behavior. The girls received, apart from a fixed wage, free board, lodging and clothing. They were not permitted to walk the streets. Their mark of distinction—or professional badge—was a red knot they were compelled to wear on their shoulders.

Visitors, on being admitted, were warned to abstain from anything that might create a disturbance or give fright to the girls. In case of misdemeanor they would be duly arrested by the beadle and punished. No "business" was allowed on Friday and Saturday of holy week or on Easter. Girls ignoring the ban and, clandestinely, supplying sex on such days were to be flogged and dismissed.

A weekly medical examination of the charges assured their good health and isolated girls found to have contracted "any illness by their whoring." The prostitutes were admonished never to quarrel, engage in petty jealousies or loud brawls and reminded to "live lovingly like sisters."

For some period of time even England had its (controlled) brothels. Most of them were situated in the Borough of Southwark, within the jurisdiction of the bishop of Winchester who actually licensed them. Once again public baths, known as stews, became the homes of prostitution. (Originally the stew was a type of Turkish steam bath, brought to Europe by the returning Crusaders. But their frequent use for immoral purposes led to the plural of stew, "stews," to become in fact just another word for a brothel.)

Indeed brothels were sanctioned by Parliament in 1161 during the reign of King Henry II. A special Act regulated their "transactions." A prostitute had to spend the entire night with her client—"till the morrow." She was not permitted to solicit customers outside. Girls suffering from the "perilous infirmity of burning" were immediately to be suspended. No woman of religion or any man's wife was to be employed. A single girl could be kept only as long as she was willing to serve professionally. The moment she expressed the wish to change her—sinful—way of life, she had to be released. Brothels had to be kept closed on public holidays and an officer of the law had to inspect them weekly.

The influence of the Reformation made King Henry VIII— in 1545—shut down all English brothels. Officially they have never been reopened.

Thus brothels have been an institution throughout the world at least for some time everywhere. No matter what they were called—bordels, whore houses, wench houses, or, as in China occasionally, prostitute shops and blue chambers—they all tried to satiate sexual desires.

At times, however, their purpose went far beyond the mere supply of sex. Authorities also used brothels to stabilize man and social life. French kings, for instance, fostered bordelets to counteract sexual aberrations and fight conventicles practicing abnormalities and vice. When, in 1421, yet another "house" was established in Venice, the magistrate opening it expressly stated that it was meant to combat sexual perversion and marital infidelity. The new brothel, it was hoped, would diminish homosexuality among the young men and adultery among housewives.

VD

What caused man to appropriate a most beautiful name for a dreadful disease? Venus, the Roman goddess of love, was rightly exalted by bestowing her name on the morning star. To debase her and, as it were, cast her down from Olympic heights to venereal connotations, of course, suggests that even venereal disease was still the result of "loving." The name of Venus herself is derived from the Sanskrit *vanas*, the description of (physical) desire.

Promiscuity (of terms) certainly abounded in the early stages of the scourge. Gonorrhea and syphilis, its most frequent manifestations, suddenly appeared on earth. But no one knew which was which. For many centuries, in fact, both diseases were confused, if not regarded identical. And even when, as in the case of gonorrhea, its name can be found in early writings, we still are not sure whether it truly referred then to what we mean by it now.

That VD has afflicted man from earliest times is almost certain. However, no one can prove it. Numerous references and descriptions stemming from antiquity seem very much to point to gonorrhea or syphilis. Though, of course, they cannot be absolutely identified with either disease.

A sixteenth-century pre-Christian Egyptian papyrus thus speaks of a genital infection which it even named (*Uchedu*). The Babylonian mythical hero Gilgamesh and the Hindu deity Shiva are said to have suffered from similar trouble.

The Hebrew Bible very explicitly and on several occasions deals with venereal afflictions: either in historical tales or hygienic legislation. Pharaoh is said to have been plagued thus after he had cast "a lustful eye" on Sarah, Abraham's wife. Job's illness, it has been suggested, showed symptoms of VD. The Book of Ecclesiastes discusses not only the prostitute but also her diseases.

"Rotting genitals" are mentioned in the writings of Hippocrates. Under the Roman Emperor Tiberius "noble men" are reported to have suffered from venereal disease, caused by kissing. An inscription in Pompeii leaves little doubt in the readers' minds. Found in a ruined building adjacent to a former brothel, it speaks of a girl of ravishing beauty who, nevertheless, was discovered to be "a dunghill within."

Gonorrhea

Whether or not gonorrhea is actually mentioned in the Bible has been a topic of controversy. The passage in question (Lev. 15) speaks of an abnormal discharge from the male or female genitals. This was considered so contagious that every effort was made to isolate and thoroughly disinfect the afflicted. In fact, anything he (or she) had touched was declared contaminated. Wooden vessels had to be cleansed and earthenware ones destroyed. His bed, the seat he had used, anyone who had come into contact with him, his very saliva also, were thought to be infected.

The patient was quarantined for an entire week and had to wash his body and all his clothing in running water.

Confusion as to the real identity of the disease was made worse by the Greek rendering of the relevant Hebrew passage. The Septuagint translates the Hebrew for "discharge" (usually called in the Authorized Version "issue") with "gonorrhea." But this Greek word originally and literally solely meant to "run" or to "flow" (*rhein*) "semen" (*gonos*), a term which was equally ambiguous.

For a long time gonorrhea and syphilis were regarded as merely two different aspects of the same venereal disease. It was only in 1793 that (in a treatise on the very subject by Benjamin Bell) their complete separateness was shown. Still, for many years afterward, Bell's claim was ignored. It was Philippe Ricord, a Baltimore-born doctor in Paris, who finally (in the 1830s) proved gonorrhea to be a distinct disease. He demonstrated its existence by extensive experimentations, and his investigations involved twenty-five hundred inoculations.

Syphilis

Syphilis (as a name) was conceived in poetry. The very first time it appeared (in print) was in the title of a Latin poem. This was called *Syphilis sive Morbus Gallicus* ("Syphilis or the French Disease").

Published in 1530 in Verona, Italy, its author was Girolamo Fracastoro, a physician and astronomer who also wrote verse. He tells the story of Syphilis, a shepherd, who became the first victim of the disease which has been called after him.

Fracastoro was convinced that only a sickness clearly defined would become the subject of serious study. A wishy-washy description would only delay the final cure. His treatise in verse of thirty-six small quarto pages was thus much more than fiction. It not only explained the symptoms but explored the possible treatment to be adopted against so grave a pest.

In his introductory words to the poem he spoke of this "fierce and rare disease never before seen for centuries, which ravaged all of Europe and the flourishing cities of Asia and Libya, and invaded Italy in that unfortunate war whence from the Gauls it has its name." He promised to tell in a song "the new treatments . . . how human wisdom has proudly fought the grave calamity, and what was the divine aid and the reward." Indeed, he would "seek the secret cause in the profound mystery of the air and the stellar spaces . . ."

Fracastoro became so famous that he himself became the subject of legends, particularly linked with his birth and earliest childhood. Originally his mouth had been so small that it had to be widened surgically with a razor. His mother, while carrying him in her arms, had been struck by lightning. She was killed on the spot but the boy—miraculously—escaped unscathed.

Yet in spite of those tales and his many achievements, eventually all was forgotten about Fracastoro—all, that is, except his one claim to fame—that he created the word "syphilis"!

His poem recounts the adventures and terrible fate of the handsome young shepherd. Many of Syphilis' cattle had died of a severe drought. In anger he had blamed the sun god for his loss. But no one goes unpunished for insulting the gods. To chastise him, they sent down to earth a poison that infected him (and later even his royal master) with the terrible disease.

Limbs were stripped of their flesh, exposing the bare bones. The mouth lost its teeth, the breath became fetid, and the voice was reduced to a feeble whisper.

Well aware of the cause, the king decreed the culprit's death. But in divine mercy, at the very last moment, a goddess took pity on the shepherd and struck a bargain. If men would promise in payment for the sin to sacrifice an entire white heifer to her and a black one to Mother Earth, the gods' wrath would abate and they would be prepared not to go on wreaking vengeance.

The king was only too happy to agree and thus to avert a dreadful fate from his country. He not only immediately arranged the offerings but they became an annual institution.

The sin, however, had been too grievous for the gods to stay the disease altogether, and so it remained on earth. But to eliminate its worst features, the gods caused at that very time the guaiac tree to grow. Its bark—the "holy wood"—though not healing altogether, would at least render less virulent the effects of the scourge.

So much for the legend. Why Fracastoro chose the particular name of Syphilis for his shepherd (and hence for the sickness) has never been fully explained. Certainly it is neither a scientific nor a medical term.

Some authorities believe that he adopted it from Greek legend. According to Ovid, Sipylus was one of Niobe's fourteen children, all of whom were slain by Apollo whose anger she had provoked. Also, Mount Sipylus was the mountain to which Niobe, distraught by grief through the death of her children, had wandered. There Zeus had changed her into a marble statue, with her face constantly bathed in tears.

Whether called after the child or the mountain, "syphilis" would still obviously be a slight linguistic corruption of the original "Sipylus." However, some early manuscripts of the legend have been traced, possibly used by our author, where this is the word's (incorrect) spelling.

Other derivations of "syphilis" have been added. One links the name with a southern Italian township from which the shepherd might have come. Syphilis thus could mean "a native from Sypheum." His name may equally be a description of his occupation, it has been said. He was a "lover of pigs" (from the Greek *suphilos*), a swineherd. Finally, syphilis, also from the Greek (but *syn philos*), might merely be an appelation of "a companion in love."

Even more mysterious than the name is the origin of the disease itself. No one really knows how, where and when it first made its appearance.

Some thought that God had sent it to punish man for his sins, just as once before he had smitten the Egyptians. Pride of place, again, was given to the devil or some related malevolent force. They used the disease magically, it was claimed, to inflict man.

Man had caught it "out of the air," astrologers asserted. It was a case of planetary radiation. An unfortunate constellation of major planets (mostly said to be Saturn and Mars) had putrefied the earth's atmosphere which, inhaled by men, had infected them with the scourge. (It would have constituted the first type of air pollution.)

Likewise, it was seriously believed, and as renowned a scientist as Francis Bacon repeated the view, that cannibalism was responsible for the sickness. Soldiers participating in the siege of Naples had suffered from food shortage. To keep alive they had fed on human flesh and thereby contracted the malady.

That leprosy had been the cause of syphilis was yet another assertion made and given in various versions. One of them blames a single leper. He had slept with a prostitute who had herself at the time been afflicted by venereal buboes. By their intercourse she had developed the syphilitic germ which she then transferred to all her future clients.

Again, it was said, the disease had been created deliberately to poison men. When the French had invaded Italian territory, the population of one township before evacuating it had infected a store of wine by mixing it with the blood of lepers. And when thirsty French soldiers drank of it, they imbibed with it the fatal germs.

Authorities have voiced the opinion of its spontaneous creation. It arrived without any definite reason and certainly not as the result of any evil intent on the part of men, God or the devil. Syphilis had suddenly manifested itself, "ready-made" as Athena is said to have sprung out of Zeus's head.

Medical research considered the possibility that syphilis was the outcome of mere chance and may be as old as man himself. An accidental mutation in the human make-up had led to its appearance. One hypothesis—given by Alfred W. Crosby, Jr., of Washington State University—suggested that with man populating the world, treponematosis, originally a single disease, had developed into some related but distinct sicknesses, of which syphilis had been one strain.

Most farfetched is the recent suggestion that syphilis was possibly introduced to this world by visitors from another planet. Out of space they had brought man this most terrible gift . . .

* * *

It is not surprising that the many cures suggested for hundreds of years were equally fanciful, weird and, at times, outlandish. "Sweating," for example, was thought the most natural remedy. It was bound to chase away the devil. The patient was not just kept warm in bed but, to make it hotter for him, the entire family would lie on top of him! Going one better, he was shoved into a well-heated oven. Once again anticipating modern methods of isolation, sufferers from the disease were strictly segregated. And even if not they themselves, at least their genitals: by locking these up in the well-known chastity belt.

There are two views (and at times they have caused heated controversy) as to where syphilis really came from. One claimed that it had existed in Europe many years prior to Columbus' return from the New World. However, until then it had either been dormant or had afflicted people merely in a very mild form.

But as syphilis spread with such frightful rapidity after the discovery of America, many have blamed Columbus and his sailors. They had contracted the malady from the natives in the West Indies and brought it back to the Old World. It would have been a most costly price mankind had to pay for his discovery.

Crosby, in fact, was convinced that syphilis had evolved in America and that from there it had been brought to Europe by Columbus.

Indeed excavations of bones with syphilitic lesions have provided undeniable evidence of the existence of the disease in both South and North America in pre-Columbian days.

Furthermore, records exist of a report by a Barcelona doctor who claimed that in 1493, immediately on their return from Haiti, he had treated several of Columbus' men (including his pilot) suffering from the disease with "frightful and bizarre eruptions" covering the skin.

No one can deny either that, two years after Columbus' return to Europe, the scourge took on epidemic proportions. This certainly was not by accident but, as so many misfortunes, the result of warfare.

At the time Italy was not yet a united country, but a conglomeration of numerous city-states, republics, kingdoms and papal possessions. Each was the other's rival and tried jealously to keep its own independence. Even more so, some were threatened to become the victim of adventurous power politics.

Charles VIII of France then claimed that in reality Naples should be part of his realm. And when his demand to hand over the city fell on deaf ears, he gathered an army of fifty thousand men to take it by force. The soldiers were mostly Frenchmen, but there were also many mercenaries from all over Europe: Swiss, German, English and Italian.

Naples, on the other hand, because Alphonso II, its reigning prince, was a Spaniard, was backed by King Ferdinand and Queen Isabella of Spain. Duly they sent an expeditionary force from Barcelona. But these very troops carried with them not only their equipment but also the disease, so recently imported from the New World.

Meeting hardly any resistance, the French captured Naples on February 2, 1495. In no time the war was over. The soldiers returned to their various homes but, on their demobilization, took with them not only the booty they had captured but the germ they had caught.

Terrifying indeed is the record of how quickly the disease grew into a worldwide epidemic. In the very year of the victory, it took hold in France, Germany and Switzerland. Within twelve months it had arrived in Holland and England. With Vasco da Gama's sailors it rounded the Cape and had reached India by 1498. And in 1505 it had found its way to Canton, China.

National animosities made citizens of one country use the disease as a vehicle for their antagonism against neighbors. Thus Italians soon called it *morbus gallicus* (the alternate title of Fracastoro's poem)—the "French disease." The French, in turn, described it as Neapolitan. No wonder that the Turks referred to it as the "Christian disease." Each, of course, by the choice of the name, inferred that the scourge was caused by (or at least caught from) those wicked people.

However contagious the sickness, Fracastoro's name did not catch on for many years. "Syphilis" was generally adopted only at the end of the eighteenth century. The fact that it finally came to replace all the other descriptions was due in no small measure to its "neutrality." Syphilis disparaged no particular nation. It was at home everywhere.

12.

Talking Sex

S ex, being so all-important, has been most fertile in the
realm of language as well and has produced a wealth of
descriptive words. Its vocabulary covers every shade of
meaning, every situation and circumstance. Many of its
words are so direct and obvious that no one could mistake them.
Others sound very scientific and perhaps, to the uninstructed, also
equally nebulous. As it were, they have been created or invented
if not to neutralize sex, at least to take all emotion, joy and passion
out of it. Another category of terms is ambiguous, and whether
the word really belongs to sex or not depends on the individual
case of application and context.

All About Intercourse

Cohabitation may purely and simply refer to a mere "living together" of members of a clan or a family. On the other hand,
technically and legally, the "living" may connote "sleeping," in
which case, however, both parties are very much awake.

Likewise, the term "intercourse" can be interpreted in many
ways—socially, commercially and conversationally—so that its
sexual type needs specification. After all, linguistically the word
solely describes some sort of "mutual dealing," though, oddly
enough, originally it was not the "lying together" that the Latin
roots suggested but a "running" *(currere)* "between" *(inter)*!

The term "copulation" is much more correct and to the point. It speaks (still in the favorite Latin form) of the fastening of a link or tie *(co + apere)*. Realistically it describes the "joining together" of two beings into "one flesh."

"Coitus" is yet another—Latin—synonym for this "going together," this merging of the two sexes in the final act. "Consummation" merely emphasizes this "supreme" and "utmost" *(summa)* "joining" *(co)*.

Togetherness inevitably dominates all sexual contact, in the way of speaking and in its most intimate phase. That is why when we talk of conjugal rights, though literally this refers to being "yoked together" implying some type of slavery, the term was really introduced to establish perfect cooperation. Its being misunderstood can be compared to the fate of wedlock. The uninitiated imagined that this synonym of marriage speaks of people being "locked up" together, like prisoners. But in fact the original "lock" is no lock at all. Derived from the Anglo-Saxon, it means a present, just as the word "wed" refers to a pledge. Wedlock therefore is merely the "promise of a gift."

Though sex is as old as nature, "sexy" as a word has been traced back only to 1925, when it first appeared, quoted as an English expression, in a French magazine.

The Sex Organs

The vulva stems from the Latin for "covering" or "sheath." It describes all that is visible of the female external genitals when the lips of the cleft are parted. It is the outer part of the organ of generation—its opening.

The linguistic history of the phallus equals the antiquity and variety of its worship. The word's root is an Indo-European verb *(bhel)* that spoke of a "swelling." It is linked with the Greek for "whale" and a "pair of bellows," almost suggestive expressions of tumescence. Its Sanskrit ancestor *(phala)* expressed the very moment in which a fully ripened fruit was about to eject its seed. The Sumerian *bal*—meaning "borer"—has also been quoted as a possible source of "phallus." In that tongue the identical word was also used to depict the weaver's spindle. It was said to convey how the penis penetrated the vagina.

In its later evolution, "phallus" gave German its *Pfahl* and English its *pole*—words of identical meaning.

"Penis"—an alternate for "phallus"—is simply the Latin "tail." Its description as lingam goes back to the Hindus. It was the Indian name for a phallic emblem they worshiped, which was representative of their god Shiva. Also from the Sanskrit, it referred to a "token" and "mark."

Four-Letter Words—Sacred and Profane

Is it mere coincidence that "four-letter words"—so taboo, so unpronounceable and so carefully guarded—belong to both the world of faith and the realm of the obscene?

In Hebrew sacred lore God was known as *YHVH* (most likely pronounced as Yahveh, though so often mistakenly rendered Jehovah). For that very reason theologians have come to call the term the tetragrammaton, being Greek for "four-letter." It was so holy that only the High Priest was permitted to utter it. He did so once annually on the most sacred day of the year in the Holy of Holies of the Temple in Jerusalem. But Judaism and Hebrew are not the exception. In fact, in a great number of tongues the divine name is expressed by a four-letter word: the Greek *Zeus* and *Theos;* the Latin *deus;* the Spanish *Dios;* the Scandinavian *Odin;* the German *Gott,* and the English *Lord.*

Going from one extreme to the other, from the supremely sacred to the most profane, the greatest number of so-called obscene words are equally known as four-letter words. They describe urinating (piss), defecating (shit) and breaking wind (fart). They are used for the penis (cock) and the female pudenda (cunt). Thus the most vulgar reference to the organs of sex and of elimination (and their functions) share the four-letter linguistic oddity with the most reverent appeal to the deity.

Heading the list of tabooed sex terms, no doubt, is *the* four-letter word "fuck." Its modern obscenity is equaled by the obscurity of its origin. No one really knows its etymological source. Only suggested "ancestors" can be cited. These include the Latin *futuere*—to "copulate"; the German *ficken*—a verb describing a fast movement "to and fro" and to "push into the pocket," and in German vulgarly applied to intercourse; and the French *foutre* —"to spurt."

To add to the mysterious origin of this four-letter word is the circumstance of its first literary evidence. This goes back to a poem attributed to a former Franciscan friar, William Dunbar (1460–1525), who was also a court bard and famed as "the rhymer of Scotland." Entitled "Brash [bout] of Wowing [wooing]," it was published in Ramsay's *Ever Green* in 1724. It deals, as the title indicates, with the wooing of a maiden by her lover:

He clappit [fondles] fast, he kist and chukkit [bobbed under the chin]
Yit be his feirris [gestures, sexual desires] he wald [would] have *fukkit:*
"Ye brek my hart, my bony ane [pretty one]."

Following this first occurrence of the word in poetry, it reappeared in numerous Scottish folk songs and seemed to gain wide popularity. However, toward the end of the sixteenth century, its employment suddenly stopped and no respectable work dared use it. Thus, for reasons that can only be guessed, a word of common usage became befouled and disreputable. It is an early example of—linguistic—pollution. Hundreds of years later, attempts by James Joyce and D. H. Lawrence to resurrect it were unsuccessful. The four-letter word remained an obscenity symbol which many a government declared punishable to use in print. All writers could do was to suggest it by innocuous dots.

Only second in shame and offensive use is "cunt"—the four-letter vocal representation of the pudenda, though in Chaucer's writings it still appeared most expansively as *Queynte.* Of medieval vintage, it could have been fathered by the Latin *cunnus* (a "split" or "cut") and is related to *cuneus*—the (Roman) "wedge." Polite society shunned its use ever since the fifteenth century and by 1700 it was considered obscene. Only *Lady Chatterley's Lover* and the modern twentieth-century cult of vulgarity gave it a new lease on life.

The question arises: what causes a word to become profane? Several explanations offer themselves. For a long time it was thought that, just as still nowadays, newcomers in a strange country acquire their earliest knowledge of the new tongue by its worst slang, so archaic man learned his language by swearing. Frustrated in an ambition, injured painfully or terribly frightened, the (so far) dumb creature opened his mouth and out of his anguish or in protest formed his first words! And there is no doubt as to their implication. That is how authorities came to assume the birth of language in swearing. It was a healthy drainage channel, a vent and a safety valve. And out of those first words man learned to talk . . .

More acceptable (and certainly more respectable) is the view that man's swearing belongs to a later stage of his evolution. Man always fought. He did so to prove his superiority and supremacy, if not to ensure his very survival. But slowly man also learned somehow to sublimate (though still in primitive form) his initial acts of cruel vengeance or attempts at scaring off adversaries by means of attack. Thus, it is claimed, he took up swearing as a most potent substitute, a form of bloodless combat. Unable actually to attack his opponent, he wished to frighten him off by what would shock him most.

Now, at a time when religion was a predominant force, its representatives, laws and vocabulary occupied a prominent place in the life of man. No one would dare to question their authority or lightly (if at all) appropriate to himself any of their rights or privileges. To employ a word loaded with sanctity (or blasphemy) would be sacrilegious and its effect shattering. And that is how in a religion-orientated and saturated era the most revered terms of the religious vocabulary became swearwords!

By hearing them, people were so awed that all their opposition crumbled and they were confounded as in a mighty battle. That is how "by Jove," "Christ" and "Holy Mary" became swearwords. And, if people, too scared to use the actual words in their fullness, still felt their need in the battle of life, they slightly varied their pronunciation and employed approximations which sometimes were so well camouflaged that the real name was no longer apparent. An example at hand is "Holy Mackerel"—a cleverly disguised substitute for "Holy Mary." "Crikey," of course, stands for "Christ."

But times changed again and when sex, once considered a

natural function of which man had no reason to be ashamed, became something regarded as unclean, unworthy and unmentionable, its terms or their circumlocution took the place of the erstwhile swearing vocabulary of religion. But fundamentally there is no difference between the (ab)use of the four-letter words of either sphere.

The Uterus in Hysteria

Much food for thought is the variety of interpretations given to the identical sexual organ by different cultures. This found expression even in the coining of words. Though based on the same "root," their meaning may be worlds apart.

To the Hebrew mind the womb *(rechem)* suggested motherhood and its affectionate warmth. The term portrayed in its association love of the highest type—unconditional and not expecting anything in return. Hence the Hebrew word for womb gave birth to the word describing the qualities of "compassion" and "pity" —*rachamim*—which, in its literal form is the plural of "wombhood."

To the Greeks, on the other hand, the womb conveyed an entirely different concept. Instead of being the seat of loving emotion, they saw in it the cause of nervous tension. (Perhaps they had observed premenstrual irritability and linked this "naturally" with the womb.)

The Greek word for uterus was *hystera*. That is why we still call the operation performed for the excision of this organ a hysterectomy: a "cutting out" of the "womb."

In ancient Greek psychology and medicine specific states of mind were traced to definite organs. As women were taken to be usually more excitable than men, it was reasoned that this must be on account of a purely female part of the anatomy. The choice fell on the uterus. That is how hysteria came into existence and why we (so wrongly) continue to call a psychoneurotic condition hysterical.

The Testicles in the Orchid

Sex is ubiquitous. No wonder it has penetrated into almost every aspect of life, and duly camouflaged by usage or by the ignorance of the user, has passed even the most fastidious of censors.

Who would ever suspect the presence of testicles also in the beautiful orchid? But that is exactly the meaning of its name, formed from the Greek *orchis*.

Pliny the Elder, Latin author of thirty-seven books on science, art and natural history, recalled how the plant with its double roots was distinguished by its striking resemblance to the testicles. Hence its name.

Full of Beans

Nothing could suppress the progress of sex which has found its way into the most unlikely places. It has dwelt there so long that it has lost all its original erotic implications and is as innocent as a newly born babe.

Even as impeccable-sounding a phrase as the exhilarating "full of beans" may have a sex basis.

Nowadays people speak of being "full of beans" to depict the vital and vigorously active. The expression is used in a horsy sense and, in fact, has been interpreted to stem from the sight of spirited equine creatures that have had their fill of oats (or beans). But dig deep enough and you will reach the erotic zone!

Pythagoras exhorted his disciples to abstain from eating beans. Many have wondered why. Early commentators explained it oddly enough as a warning, to keep away from politics. Election techniques for public office at the time used for the casting of votes the throwing of beans into a helmet. If it was "full of beans," this augured well for the candidate, who had every reason to be pleasantly excited.

Aristotle, however, claimed, in an almost Freud-anticipating vein, that beans stood for sexual indulgence. No wonder, therefore, that as pious and studious a man as St. Jerome (c. 342), centuries later, very much concerned with nuns' chastity, also forbade them to partake of beans.

The question why, of all things, beans were regarded as it were as an aphrodisiac has led to several theories. Beans, it was asserted, produced (apart from wind) amorous feelings because they secreted a body fluid that roused erotic passion.

A psychological interpretation traced the sex basis to the very shape of the bean. This reminded men and women (by a likeness) of testicles and thereby excited them sexually.

Even our so sex-conscious age with all its titillations, and with the most vivid imagination would not recognize testicles in the bean. Yet like a monument of the distant past it survives semantically.

A Sexual Perversion of Architecture

"Fornication," an obsolete word now, forcefully once condemned sexual intercourse between two unmarried people or with anyone else than one's lawful spouse as a grave sin. A sexual term, it owes its existence to architecture, yet not without reason.

"Fornication" pointed not to a lusty couple of lovers—but from the Latin *fornix*—to the "arch" of the vaulted chamber of Roman brothels or the arch of an aqueduct under which prostitutes and their clients "fornicated."

The Compleat Bugger

Many a term of abuse was born out of national prejudice. The loom of language helped here—rather unkindly—to perpetuate regrettable dislikes and antagonisms. Frequently the original intention and circumstances are obvious, or at least easily ascertainable as, for instance, when we speak of Dutch courage or French leave. In other cases, however, words have become so "disfigured" and thereby disguised that they no longer calumniate those they were meant to defame and accuse.

The most striking example is "buggery." Who would suspect that this strong pejorative disparages, of all people, Bulgarians. But that is the correct meaning of the original bugger. From the

Old French *bougre,* all he described, unrecognized now, was a Bulgarian!

Buggery as a term of abuse can be traced to religion and its fanatics. Eleventh-century Bulgarian Christians had been converted to the Albigensian "heresy," which itself showed an implacable hatred of the traditional Church.

The Albigenses taught that all matter was bad. They did not believe in procreation, as children would increase the realm of Satan. Hence they condemned marriage as evil. But as most men could not completely suppress the weakness of their flesh, the heretical leaders turned a blind eye on those members of the "ordinary" class of believers who relieved their strong sexual urge in promiscuous and homosexual ways.

No wonder that their doctrine and way of life was regarded a terrible menace by the rest of the Christian faith. Soon it identified all Bulgarians (and the very name of their country) with wickedness and vice.

And that is how the Bulgarian (in its pronunciation of "bugger") assumed its new, disparaging connotation. It thus became a linguistic curse and has remained such ever since. (Oddly enough, on American tongues, it has gone to the other extreme, and to be called a bugger expresses amiable friendship.)

In the technical modern meaning a Bulgarian—the "bugger"—has come to mean a variety of erotic techniques, particularly penis-anal sexual intercourse.

The Bastard

The bastard's illegitimacy is apparent from the etymology of his name. The word points to his out-of-the-ordinary sort of cradle, though where the "bastard" actually was conceived is still doubtful.

Authorities agree that it was not in the usual kind of bedroom. Some look as it were for a German father and see in the bastard a corrupted form of the German *Banklink*—a child begotten on a "bench" *(Bank)* and not in a marriage bed.

Others derive the word from the Old French for a "son of a packsaddle" *(fils de bast).* It was the custom of mule drivers to bed down on their saddle. And, obviously, they did not do so always on their own . . .

A third suggestion goes even further in the calumniation of the bastard. True, it says, the word stems from the French for packsaddle. However, it has nothing to do with any improvised bed. It associates the illegitimate child with the mule that carried the saddle. The animal was the result of the crossing of a horse and a donkey and he of a similar improper alliance.

The Genesis of Gender

How sex began to divide even the world of vocabularies into male, female and even neuter nouns is a question that has puzzled the expert. It goes back to the history of linguistics thousands of years before any literary tradition existed. Was the power of sex so strong that it extended to the realm of mere words as well and exerted its influence in "sexing" them? No final answer has so far been given and only possible reasons have been suggested for this mysterious intrusion of sex among words.

At the beginning, it was said, man's fantasy not only personalized but personified everything and hence bestowed on every object, even the most inanimate one, qualities of a man or a woman. The great and powerful was seen as possessed by male attributes, while, accordingly, the female attached herself to the smaller and weaker. Eventually, in dry grammar, the results of man's early vivid imagination (and his regrettable discrimination against women) survived in the (grammatical) gender.

Another theory asserts that, in fact, the objects themselves were sexless at first. It was the pronoun that accompanied them which was responsible for the introduction of the grammatical gender. The sex of "his" or "her" by its close proximity was transferred to the noun it preceded.

However, a much more intriguing solution has been advanced. It is based on the recorded fact that among some primitive people (for instance, Latin American tribes) two languages existed side by side: a male and a female one. Men used a totally different vocabulary from that known to the women. An identical object would thus be described by different words, dependent on whether a man or a woman spoke of it. In less drastic cases, though the actual words were identically written, women pronounced them differently or gave them a distinctive ending.

With the passing of time the two vocabularies or dialects became intermingled. Even language abhors wastage, and as duplicating a vocabulary was uneconomical, only one of the two possible nouns for the identical object eventually survived. This was not the result of logical, deliberate choice but merely of chance. But the recollection that the word once belonged either to the realm of women or the conversation of men for all time determined its sex. That is why up to this day and without any obvious reason, words were either feminine or masculine.

A further question arose among those who adopted this explanation: to start with, what made women have their separate speech? It certainly was not for any secretive purpose. Also, and most unsatisfactory, is the hypothesis sometimes advanced that women, usually more conservative than men, had preserved an archaic form of speaking.

Much more likely is the suggestion linked with the circumstance that a tribe's females originally came from some other part of the country or even from some other (hostile) tribe. Their presence might first of all be the result of (human) plunder. In warfare their menfolk were not only vanquished but killed. But they, the surviving women and girls, were taken back to the victorious country as a most welcome booty. In their new and enforced habitat they continued to use their former tongue and that is the origin of the double language. (A historical parallel showing the tenacity with which people hold to their original tongue is the creation of Yiddish: German Jews driven out from their country continued to speak their language wherever they made their new home.)

The language the (captive) women spoke was therefore merely "foreign" and not indigenously female. But the fact that only the women spoke it impregnated the words with their sex!

Talking to the men, of course, they knew how to make themselves understood. But among themselves they went on to cherish their native tongue.

Exogamy, the practice of marrying women of other tribes, no matter whether obtained by capture or purchase, is the other possible explanation. Coming from another region, they talked a language alien to their husbands' people.

Examples have been cited from many parts of the world: Latin American Indians, African Zulus and Australian aborigines. In Greenland women pronounced common words differently. Whether by mere inflection, the addition of a suffix or the actual use of a different vocabulary, men and women thus varied in the way they spoke.

It was the transference of the sex of the speaker to the words he (or she) used (from the subject to the object, as it were) that "fathered" the grammatical gender.

Another interesting topic of speculation concerns specifically English and the fact that it eventually (again) discarded most of the gender of nouns. For instance, the original masculine "foot" and "day" and feminine "hand" and "night" became sexless—neuter.

The cause might have been a combination of circumstances. Most of the English words never themselves indicated their sex, as it happens in Latin, Greek and French. This was done by the accompanying adjective and personal pronoun. But throughout the years, usage made those distinctions disappear and, with no noticeable differences in spelling or inflection left, the nouns themselves lost their gender, and became "desexed."

13.

The Obscene

The Writing on the Wall

Obscenities scrawled on walls are referred to as graffiti. This Italian word, the plural form of *graffito,* solely points to the fact that the writing or drawing is "scratched" on a surface. Originally this was literally true. The graffitist used a sharp instrument—a stylus, knife or nail —to scratch his "message" into the stucco of a wall or a pillar.

The term then came widely to be applied to any type of casual writing or drawing, no matter whether actually scratched, daubed or painted with chalk, charcoal, ink or paint. And the graffitist came to utilize almost every opportunity that availed itself.

Graffiti included political slogans, the names of candidates in an election, scurrilous remarks, messages, short lines of poetry, shopping lists and memoranda of every type and nature.

A large amount of deeply religious graffiti have survived. Short prayers were scratched on the walls of pagan temples. During their persecution by the Romans, the early Christians scratched the fish, the original symbol of their faith (preceding that of the cross), on the walls of the Roman catacombs.

Graffiti have indeed been of tremendous importance to the archaeologist, the historian, the sociologist and the linguist. They have helped to date excavated artifacts and buildings, to recapture the way of life of lost generations, to confirm events until then only hinted at by legends and to study the vernacular of ancient races. For instance, runic graffiti discovered on the Orkneys testified to the presence of Norwegian crusaders on the islands which until their discovery had only been a legendary tradition.

It is revealing of the working of man's mind and the attraction of sex that, in spite of the multifarious use of graffiti, the very term is often specifically reserved for the erotic type. And this goes back to earliest times as well.

When primitive man covered cave walls with his first scrapings, scratchings and drawings, these undoubtedly included the sexual element, scenes of love play both among men and animals. Their aim was not that of crude pornography in the modern sense but a solemn concern to perpetuate life and to ensure offspring.

These original erotic drawings, some well over thirty thousand years old, are the ancestors of modern graffiti, now clandestinely and furtively penned and drawn on lavatory walls and doors. To begin with they served worshipful, sympathetic magic.

Geoffrey Grigson in his *Painted Caves* speaks of those earliest "emotions about impregnation, pregnancy and increased abundance, and so about life and death" which "determined most of the Upper Palaeolithic art, from the renowned 'Mother Goddesses' which the Gravettians carved in three dimensions, to the bulls of Lascaux and the bisons of Altamira."

Primitive man was convinced that by depicting the male and female genitals, separately or jointly in the sexual act, he would magically ensure fertility in man and nature.

Fertility cults were superseded by a more "enlightened" faith. The original motive thus became redundant and was forgotten. But, largely as a vestige of the former magic, people continued to draw graffiti of that type. These accompanied man throughout the ages. No doubt in some people they came to satisfy an inner craving and expressed an almost magical obsession on the part of the graffitist. Their evocative sexual power is evident.

The presence of graffiti in the brothels of excavated Pompeii certainly requires no explanation. Obviously the obscene portrayals and erotic remarks were good advertising and sales promotion. Sex was a natural instinct and those unknown authors of

Roman and Pompeian graffiti merely recorded unashamedly what they had seen, experienced or hoped for.

Typical examples, for instance, record how "Colepius kisses the ladies where he should not" and expressed the hope of another graffitist to be "always and everywhere . . . as potent in dealing with women as I was here." A satisfied visitor to a brothel recalls that "here I enjoyed the favor of many girls." On the other hand an unfortunate victim of venereal disease factually states that he suffers from "a sort of rheum."

Yet another "author" addresses a certain Fortunatus as "you sweet little darling, you great fornicator" and attests the veracity of his claim by adding that "someone who knows you writes this."

The fact that in later centuries such drawings and inscriptions were regarded as offensive only added—psychologically—to their attraction and gave both the graffitist and the viewer of his "art" extra pleasure and sexual arousal. Obscene sketches particularly became favorites. After all, as the Chinese say, a picture is worth a thousand words.

Even modern primitive tribes know graffiti. Robert Suggs in his anthropological study of Polynesian practices, recorded the popularity of "obscene" graffiti among the Marquesans which gave their young men a physical pleasure. In his *Marquesan Sexual Behaviour* he described how the sight of the written word for the vulva, for instance, provoked gales of laughter among young males. Sexual terms (especially the vulgar vernacular for copulation) were scrawled on almost every available empty space.

Often the words were accompanied by the stylized representation of the sexual organs. It was not a hidden "art" but openly displayed and caused apart from amusement a sexual physical response. Any type of elongated object was used to carve phalli on it. In most cases these were shown in the state of erection, with the foreskin drawn back. But this, too, caused neither blushes nor whispered exchanges of obscenities but only loud hilarity.

The Italian term *graffito* linguistically stems from the Greek *graphein*—"to draw" or "to write" (hence graphology). Indeed those scrawlings—whether of stone-age man, twentieth-century savages or the modern "educated" graffitist, in hidden cave, on tree trunk and rock or in public lavatories—can all be traced back to the earliest aim to release and relieve sex. At its basis is the worship of sex: whether in its original magical form or its later vulgarized profanation.

Certainly the original motive is now forgotten. But as a vestige of the primitive fertility cult, graffiti for some people still express and satisfy almost magically an innate urge and rather innocuously but graphically assert their aggressiveness.

Graffiti thus act as a substitute for real sex. Man might use it to get sex off his mind and out of his system. Its very compulsiveness is truly reflected by words scribbled two thousand years ago near the entrance to a Pompeian shop. The graffitist confessed that "the man who wrote this did it because he wanted to."

Somehow graffiti liberated man of sexual tension. Vernon Scannel in *Walking Wounded* versified on this happy release of sexual refuse:

> The cell is small and mainly functional,
> Yet something more: this privacy is rare . . .
> This, and of course the business why we're here,
> May be the reason why the mental bowels
> Move to expel dark cargo of their own.

Pornography and the Obscene

If the Bible contains countless sexual symbols, references and intimations, its Song of Songs is the most outspoken of erotic love poems. Had it not become part of Holy Scripture, many a censor would have banned it. Almost nothing is left to the imagination, and hardly any part of man's anatomy is ignored. Down-to-earth language befitting those closely associated with the soil and the beasts of the field, is used—realistically and not merely metaphorically.

The very beginning of the poem reveals its theme: an invitation to making love. The girl calls on the young man to kiss her "with the kisses of his mouth," which taste sweeter than any wine. Her longing for union makes her feel almost faint so that she is in desperate need of some stimulant.

In an overabundance of sensuous description, both man and woman praise each other's voluptuous body. The girl's lips are compared to a thread of scarlet, the whiteness of her teeth to newly washed wool and pure snow, her rosy cheeks to a freshly opened pomegranate.

The young man eulogizes her beautiful figure, the shape of her neck and the suppleness of her limbs. He relishes the firm roundness of her breasts, which he likens to a cluster of sweet grapes, and is dazzled by the ivory hue of her bared belly which to him seems like freshly thrashed wheat. He praises the smoothness of her round full thighs and even her navel, which is like a well-rounded goblet . . . And so as not to leave any doubt as to the final aim, the Song tells of the readily stored aphrodisiac—a mandrake!

To the young man's regret, no doubt, we also hear that though the girl's lips drop honey and her scent is bewitching, so far she has remained like a "shut-up garden," "a sealed fountain." (Interpreters have explained this passage as proof of her virginity on the wedding night.)

Nevertheless, to rouse the youth's sexual desire even further and make herself irresistible for the beloved to come into his "garden," to quench his sexual thirst in her "fountain," she applies every available cosmetic aid and perfume.

She herself is not reticent either in depicting vividly and without shame her lover's body: his ruddy complexion, wavy black hair, his lips distilling liquid myrrh and his legs strong like alabaster columns.

In spite of all efforts at rationalization, the "green bed" of which the Song of Songs speaks refers to their making love in the open on the grass. Modern dream interpretation finds good material in the girl's nightly recurring search for her lover . . .

No wonder that the ecclesiastical authorities had great hesitation in including such an outspoken, erotic tract in the canon of Holy Scripture. Heated controversies raged for a long time.

Only a subterfuge of a double fiction and casuistic interpretation saved the book for posterity.

First of all, King Solomon was claimed as its author. And no one would dare to exclude any of his works. Then, in veritable mental acrobatics, it was explained that everything written in this Song, even the most realistic and erotic, was mere metaphor and each verse—truly overflowing with sensuality—had to be allegorized. In reality, therefore, the Song of Songs was not an ex-

change between two lovers but a dialogue between God and man
—God and Israel, so Judaism said; the Church and Christ, Christianity taught.

At times the theologians' efforts to prove their point overreached limits of propriety. When, for instance, the Song unashamedly describes the girl's attractive breasts, ecclesiastics seriously asserted that these were purely symbolical for Moses and Aaron!

Just as through the breast a baby partook of all its mother had fed on, so all that those two spiritual giants had learned they imparted to their people. As a mother's breasts were filled with milk, so Moses and Aaron were saturated with the knowledge of God. As the breasts ensured life and growth to the suckling child, so the two brothers caused Israel to live and to prosper. As the two breasts of a woman were of identical size, there was no difference in the stature of Moses and Aaron, neither excelled the other.

The "kissing" too surely did not point to the passionate caress of the lips but to a historical incident at Mount Sinai. There every word spoken by God had been miraculously transferred to the lips of every Israelite standing at the foot of the mountain.

Such manipulative and forced interpretation, however, could not convince even all theologians. Sebastianus Castellio, sixteenth-century translator of the Bible into Latin and French, though still believing in the traditional fiction of King Solomon's authorship, nevertheless decried the book as a lascivious and obscene account of the king's shameless and lecherous love affairs.

Yet it was perhaps in acknowledgment of the all-importance of sex and the sanctity of love that, two thousand years ago, a religious leader could remark that "if all Scripture is holy, the Song of Songs is the Holy of Holies."

*   *   *

In its most literal sense, pornography concerns only the prostitute. *Porne* is the Greek for "whore" and *graphos* (so ubiquitous in our tongue, from the graffiti to the autograph) for "written." Pornography therefore, etymologically, refers to writing about whores, and their customers. In fact, to start with, the term applied to "literature" specifically disseminated by brothels for business reasons, to rouse men's sexual appetite and make them seek its satisfaction in the arms of a whore.

That, no doubt, is how the word began. But its meaning eventually broadened and came to embrace many types of eroticism—written, portrayed, danced, uttered or sung—all of which caused sexual titillation and arousal. Pornography is part of the obscene, a phenomenon in existence much earlier than the word.

In the beginning, pornography was enjoyed uninhibitedly and without shame. Nothing bad was seen in it. On the contrary, it was welcomed as an aid to make man face an arduous existence. It helped him in finding pleasure and belonged to his natural way of life, but even more so, to his religion. Did not the phallus, indeed, play such an important part in primitive worship with its fertility cult? Early Indian writings are saturated with the erotic. Certainly in numerous cases it served the promotion of sex. Typical was the employment of pornographic art by a former Chinese emperor of the (fifth-century) Nan Ch'i dynasty. To keep himself and his many women in a "permanent state of arousal and further increase their sex drive," he had the walls of his palace adorned with huge obscene murals.

But when sex and all pleasure came to be identified with sin, pornography inevitably was condemned as pernicious and evil. This in itself however had its reaction and, as it were, backlash. The forbidden fruit is all the more tempting and "under-the-counter" pornography came to be sold at a premium.

The question, still not settled and which goes beyond the scope of this book, is, how much good or bad pornography does. Whether it can serve as an innocuous outlet, to ease people's sexual tensions, or incites sex crimes. Whether it is a harmless source of sexual pleasure (at worst, making men masturbate) or depraves or corrupts the mind and warps a person's view on sex and love. No matter what the present attitude and final solution may be, pornography and the obscene played a vital role in ages long past. They had a significant place in some primitive cultures, at times almost ensuring their survival.

* * *

It is wrong to assume that, initially, the obscene offered lewd men "dirt for dirt's sake." Modern governments in some parts of the world still ban pornography as inimical to morals, claiming that it destroyed the moral fiber of a nation. In primitive groups, however, the obscene at certain periods was not only permitted but fostered and even prescribed with weighty reasons.

Studies have been made, for instance, of African native groups, among whom obscenity was prominent in song, gestures and general conversation. No expression was barred, and the most lascivious thoughts were voiced, often accompanied by telling actions. Enormous wooden phalli were carried around and suggestively manipulated. Coitus was dramatically reenacted in public.

All this happened on special occasions alone, which were of the most varied kind and yet seemed to share a common factor. They included rites of circumcision, the initiation of girls, rain ceremonies, funeral feasts, the completion of heavy building operations (such as the carrying of a roof to a hut or the making of a canoe) and every stage in agricultural work from the preparing of the ground for sowing to the final making of flour.

Henri A. Junod in *The Life of a South African Tribe* (second edition, 1927) deals with a typical funeral feast among the Ba-Thonga of the Transvaal. He tells how a couple of months after death, all the family of the deceased gathered. The mortuary hut was destroyed, and after a goat and some hens had been sacrificed, the party broke forth into lewd songs. A woman performed an erotic dance which she accompanied with a no less salacious song. She displayed "a strange mimicry with her thighs" which "took on a more and more lascivious character." Her song "described an adulterous woman going during the night from one hut to another, seeking for lovers . . ."

An important point to remember is that at other times those very words, actions and displays would have horrified the members of the group. What then was the purpose of such obscenities?

Several reasons have been advanced. It has been suggested that all these obscenities occurred on occasions that were out of the ordinary. Therefore, it was said, that by going to the other extreme, the natives tried to normalize the situation, striking the happy medium.

Professor E. E. Evans-Pritchard in "Some Collective Expressions of Obscenity in Africa" (included in *The Position of Women in Primitive Societies,* Faber & Faber, 1965) comes to the conclusion that the obscenities were caused by three factors, each essential for the well-being, if not very survival, of the group. They were meant to ease tensions; to highlight special occasions; and to lighten grueling tasks.

Certain events in tribal life were so supercharged with emotion that they could easily wreak havoc. Some lightning conductor was needed, as it were, to take the electricity out of the air. But this had to be something available in the majority of people and easily used. Sex was the most obvious choice. Therefore, at times of crisis, such as during the "passing rites," tribes prescribed obscenities. No doubt these fulfilled the desired purpose and directed otherwise highly dangerous passion into controlled channels.

Modern society still celebrates events of great national importance, when rules are relaxed and restrictions canceled. The very liberties then permitted underscore the significance of the occasion. But primitive people already employed this technique. To mark the "red-letter days" of their life, they removed potent taboos and thereby made the event all the more memorable for the people. And which taboo was stronger than that which concerned sex! Actually the very withdrawal by society of its normal prohibitions, in the words of Evans-Pritchard, "gave special emphasis to the social value of the activity."

The sugaring of the pill has always been a clever method to render palatable the unsavory. People are bound to forget or ignore the ardor of a task and the harshness of labor, if these are accompanied by pleasant sensations and experiences. These divert their attention all the more if they rouse and excite strongest instincts. Hence tribes invited their men and women, especially during hard labor, to join in lascivious songs. These made them not only forget all the extra effort needed and the exhaustion it brought, but the very rhythm eased their toil. The suddenly permitted lasciviousness gave "both stimulus and reward to the workers during [their] periods of joint and difficult labour . . ."

Obscenity thus—at the very beginning—fulfilled a positive mission. And, it is well to remember, that once the occasion had passed and the work was completed, the "feast" was over. Sex was then relegated to its previous limitations, and the taboos of yesterday were reintroduced.

*   *   *

People were greatly puzzled by yet another revelation of the obscene in most unexpected circumstances in a different part of the world. At excavations in Peru many hundreds of stirrup vessels were unearthed. They dated from ancient pre-Inca days and, in sculpture, vividly portrayed every possible situation in sexual activity and almost every type of sexual deviation. The objects certainly belonged to the category of the obscene.

The stirrup which gave the vessel its name had a multiple practical purpose. It served as a handle and, simultaneously, its spout provided an inlet for air and an outlet for the liquid. It was a clever construction to let the water or native beer (known as *chicha*) flow freely. In many cases the jars featured an erect penis (or vulva) as the spout through which the liquid was meant to be drunk.

The anonymous potters, indeed, used their art to model very realistically every aspect of sex and its aberrations. Situations of anal coitus predominate. Men proudly display their supersized penis, holding it with their hands. There are groups of two men with one woman, and of two women with one man, having intercourse.

The pottery equally graphically shows the practice of fellatio, the application of the mouth to the penis. There are scenes of masturbation, of animals' love-play and mating and of bestiality, men having coitus with the beast. One vessel presents the crouching figure of a man in the shape of the male sexual organ. His penis forms the head and the body, while his testes make up his rounded knees.

All this obscene pottery, produced by the Mochica and Chimu civilizations (and now exhibited in the Herrera Museum and National Museum of Anthropology and Archaeology in Lima), were discovered in—graves!

The first explanation of the weird phenomenon coming to mind is that those early races must have been obsessed by sex and all its manifestations. It certainly proves the ancient history of deviation. But to use drinking vessels, like Toby jugs, for the portrayal, it was said, might show that such sex practices were common among those people.

Another suggestion was that the vessels were originally meant to stimulate sex at orgies. But then it was found that, actually, the Mochica and Chimu races were what we would consider most moral and not perverts. In fact, they decried sexual excess and severely punished—with mutilations and death—lasciviousness. Thus the mystery of pornography in their midst (or rather, their graves) only deepens. What then made them produce their obscene pottery and, of all places, bury it with their dead? To increase the enigma even further, those "lewd" vessels were discovered even in children's tombs.

No one knows the explanation. Several possible answers have been given, however. It may be that what the Mochicas were prevented from practicing during their lifetime, they hoped to relish after death. Very much aware of the suppression and frustration of the erotic "on earth," the family and friends presented their dearly departed with those funeral gifts "with a difference," all the more to enjoy sex to the fullest in the world to come.

Sex was the potent symbol and source of life's perpetuation. Could not its dramatic presentation in its rich variety magically ensure survival for the departed? Therefore their entombment with the stirrup vessels could have also been meant as a religious act, aimed at the continuation of their life.

Finally, art in many of its expressions has been seen as a sublimation of sex. All the more so if it concerned the erotic. Renoir supposedly said that he had painted his warm-blooded nudes with his penis! Barred from all excess of love and the practice of aberrations, did those unknown artists of the Mochica and Chimu cultures perhaps try to sublimate their strong sexual drives by creating their type of erotic pottery? But unable to keep and display it on earth, they did the next best thing and hid it under the ground.

Whatever the reason, those hundreds of stirrup vessels of pre-Inca days are yet another phenomenon of pornography.

In one isolated case, indeed, pornography was assumed even to serve the annihilation of potential rebels. In the Honan province of China, archaeologists dug up earthenware vessels, dating back to the first century, which were decorated with unmistakable obscene drawings. Superstitious belief then had it that such portrayal would cause misfortune! Experts suggested that monarchs at the time were advised by their astrologer-counselors to employ the pornographic magic to forestall future revolutions. They had the jars and plates buried at the very sites which, according to those seers, would one day be the birthplace of men who might try to overthrow their dynasty.

*   *   *

The obscene thus, in earliest times, has had its prominent place in life. Originally and in various cultures almost at opposite ends of the world, it fulfilled a significant role and a supreme purpose. It was then far removed from the modern "sexploitation" of man with its commercialized, calculated obscenities which, nonetheless, do justice to the primary meaning of (the word) pornography.

14.

Out of the Ordinary

From Sodomy to Homosexuality

omosexuality—its very term and its condemnation as a perversion—has been based on and caused much confusion.

The word itself is not derived, as sometimes assumed, from the Latin *homo* for "human being" or "man." Its root is the Greek *homo,* meaning "identical." The name was coined to differentiate the desire for, and arousal by, a member of the *same* sex from "normal" *hetero*sexuality, aimed at the "opposite" and "different" sex. It just so happened that a word of identical spelling and pronunciation belonged to the two tongues —in a completely different meaning. This, of course, is a well-known occurrence in the story of language. A typical example is the word *gift* which in German (though spelled with a capital *G*) describes "poison" and in English a "present."

Even more intriguing is the fact that the condemnation of homosexuality by Judeo-Christian tradition as the most degenerate vice is based on a possibly wrong interpretation of the biblical passage which relates the story of the destruction of Sodom (Gen. 19).

Two strangers visited Sodom. By chance, Lot—himself an alien resident of the town—met them at the city gate. He urged them to spend the night in his home. After some hesitation, the two men accepted his invitation and hospitality. But the moment citizens of Sodom heard that Lot was sheltering the visitors, they became suspicious and objected to his action.

They surrounded his house, demanding not only an explanation but the handing over of the strangers: "Who are the men who came to you this night? Bring them out to us that we may *know* them!"

Lot refused to comply with their request. But to pacify the agitated crowd, he offered his virgin daughters instead, for purposes he did not leave to their imagination. In punishment of the wickedness of the Sodomites, the Bible tells, the city, with all its inhabitants (excepting Lot and his family) was annihilated.

It is a sad tale altogether. That Lot preferred the defilement of his own daughters to breaking the laws of hospitality makes odd reading. Sure, we know of the "sexual hospitality" offered among primitive races, when the host might give his own wife to his guests. But equally well known is the high regard paid to virginity in the Bible. No father, especially as righteous a man as Lot, would present his daughters to be raped.

There were other difficulties. To "know" in biblical Hebrew is often (though not always) used as the technical term for "having sexual relations." Students of the Bible thus took the passage to mean that Sodom's citizens were homosexuals. Their demand that Lot should deliver his two guests into their hands was taken to have only one purpose: to have homosexual intercourse with them. That is, in fact, why sodomy (after the city of Sodom) became an alternate description of the very deviation, heavily loaded with emotion and loathing.

A common feature in early biblical writings is their etiological motif: geological formations, etymologies and events are related to and explained by certain causes. Thus it was said that the name of Adam was chosen for the first man because he had been formed out of the "earth"—in Hebrew *adamah*. Isaac, meaning "laughter," was so called, it was claimed, because Sarah had laughed (either incredulously or, as later commentators believed, rejoicingly) when God's messenger had foretold his birth. After all, she was a woman well advanced in age whose periods had ceased, as she herself stressed. Even the narrative telling of woman's creation out of one of Adam's ribs was etiological in intention. It wanted to show how both man and woman originally had been "one flesh," which was why by destiny they belonged to (and therefore yearned for) one another.

It was a well-known tradition that the Dead Sea covered an area once populated by mighty townships of which Sodom was one. Seeking for a "religious" reason for the terrifying disaster that had overtaken the city, the biblical sources found it in the wickedness of its inhabitants. What then had been their vice, readers wondered, and imagined that it had been the people's homosexuality, so vividly displayed on the occasion of the visit of the two strangers.

All this was deducted by reading into the possibly innocuous word "to know," its sexual connotation. It was only a further link in this chain of argument to suppose that if God had destroyed an entire city in punishment for the homosexuality of its people, this must be a vile and most wicked sin.

Approaching the biblical text with an independent mind, without preconceived notions and uninfluenced by later exegesis, a totally different picture might present itself.

Lot, after all, was a comparative newcomer to the city of Sodom and xenophobia has been an age-old, unfortunate phenomenon. Foreigners were always suspect and perhaps Lot's own demeanor did not contribute toward allaying any latent distrust. But when, on top of it all, two total strangers arrived and, in no time, were claimed and sheltered by Lot, the fears were multiplied.

Who were those men and what did they want? Why, of all homes, did they visit the house of a relatively recent arrival? Therefore, quite naturally, they insisted on meeting the men, to "know" what they wanted. To "know" in such context obviously would point not to (homo)sexual intercourse but—merely—to making their acquaintance.

It is so simple an explanation and, according to some authorities, the correct one. But the vivid account explaining a catastrophic annihilation of an entire city as the result of sin (possibly erroneously taken to be homosexual aberrations) left its indelible impact and influenced the attitude and legislation of countless generations.

In other parts of the Bible, homosexuality certainly was described as an "abomination" (Lev. 18:22) and seen as a crime so grievous that both parties had to forfeit their lives: "They shall surely be put to death; their blood shall be upon them" (Lev. 20:13).

Yet another and most likely mistaken assumption of homosexuality is linked with the Bible. It concerns the relationship between David and Jonathan of which it was said (I Sam. 18:1) that "the soul of Jonathan was knit with the soul of David, and Jonathan loved him as his own soul." And, undoubtedly, because David had been so closely attached—in a genuine friendship—to Jonathan, he deeply lamented his death. Possibly in the exaggeration of the hour of grief, he gave voice to his feelings of loss by saying poetically, "Your love to me was wonderful, [sur]passing the love of a woman" (II Sam. 1:26). Readers were only too apt to see in the phrase an admission of a homosexual bond between the shepherd boy and the prince. In reality, such claim might merely read into the text something which is not there.

To decry the phenomenon of sexual inversion as "unnatural" is also incorrect. There are many examples of homosexuality in nature. As is well known, it is not uncommon among dogs, cattle and cocks. Young primates are notorious for it. Yet their (mis)demeanor differs in one important aspect. Homosexuality on their part is never exclusive. Even if practicing it frequently, the animal will still be attracted by, and respond to, the opposite sex. The inexorable and ultimate law of nature is sexual union with a mate of the other sex, as only this guarantees the preservation of the species.

Homosexuality of animals has not been completely explained. Several possibilities have been suggested, either as a single or a joint cause. In most cases, homosexuality may simply act as a substitute sort of sex, practiced out of desperation on the part of an animal which is bereft of, or temporarily misses, the company of the opposite sex. It might be a phase in the early life of the animal, preceding its attainment of sexual maturity.

Homosexual behavior has also been seen as a phenomenon of animal class-consciousness and self-abasement, or as a clever ruse to achieve an aim. The weaker and inferior animal offered itself—sexually—to the stronger and leading one (of its own sex) to show servility, to express respect, to get protection or some other award. Thus homosexual "service" even bought a meal!

Instances are known of how a weaker animal about to be deprived of its food by a superior "mate" (of identical sex) swiftly presented itself as a homosexual partner and as a reward could keep its "snack."

*   *   *

Homosexuality has been found among many primitive tribes, though there were others who decried it. Some of the groups not only permitted but expected its practice among their (young) men. They imagined that it strengthened their manhood. The Zuñis greatly honored such men-women and in some regions of the world (in Babylonia, Mexico and Peru, for instance) it was their class that often supplied a tribe's magicians, medicine men and priests.

Conscious of the need of "sex," in cases where the company of a woman was missing, some groups supplied, at least temporarily, a substitute female. This type of homosexual marriage was an institution among the Australian Aranda aborigines. It terminated the moment the elder partner acquired a wife of the "right" sex.

Homosexuals imitated the functions and features of the opposite sex. Men shammed pregnancies (by stuffing rags or dried grass under their skirts) and even simulated menstruation (by inflicting wounds on themselves to let blood flow). Herodotus records how men wore jewelry and rouged their faces and bodies in the manner of women.

Men copied feminine behavior and women masculine traits, especially so in the way they walked, stood and acted. They often donned the garb of the other sex (as transvestites) and preferred to engage in its activities and occupations. Marquesans called such men "homosexuals of the ridge pole," reflecting on their staying at home—like a woman—and doing her work.

This phenomenon led Edward Carpenter (in his *Intermediate Types Among Primitive Folk*) to raise a fantastic claim. The earliest notable advance in civilization, he asserted, was due to those homosexuals.

From the very beginning, he wrote, there was a division of labor between men and women. Tasks were specifically reserved for either sex, and this really never changed.

In the case of the homosexuals, however, they did not relish the traditional occupations of their own sex. The (deviate) man

loathed warfare and hunting. The (homosexual) woman abhorred housework and childbearing and all this implied.

But a vacuum cannot exist. Both sexes therefore searched for
some other enterprise that could fill their time, occupy their
minds and serve them as "new outlets for their energies." And
thus they began to scan the skies and study the stars, to compose
songs and to collect herbs. "They became students of life and
nature, inventors and teachers of arts and crafts, they became
diviners and seers . . . and so ultimately laid the foundation of the
priesthood, and of science, literature and art," Carpenter declared.

However farfetched and strange his theory may sound in
giving homosexuals the credit for the invention of astronomy,
religion, medicine and art, it caused no less sensation than yet
another speculation. This was put forward by the Reverend Hugh
Montefiore who was to become the bishop of Kingston, Jamaica.
In many ways a radical in the Church, he expressed the view that
possibly the love of Jesus toward his fellow men may have had
homosexual roots.

* * *

Primitive religion certainly featured homosexuality. It was
part of early heathen devotion. Male sacred prostitutes ministered
sexually to the worshipers at pagan temples. The castrated devotees of Cybele (specially dressed in female attire) offered their
bodies—like priestesses—to the male "congregants."

Greek mythology attributes homosexual acts to some of its
gods. Zeus himself is thus pictured. He descended, one tradition
says, in the guise of an eagle, from Mount Olympus to seize (and
make love to) Ganymedes, whose ravishing beauty had roused his
passion. He carried him back to his divine abode to serve not only
as a cup bearer but as a focus of amorous attention on the part of
the other gods. (In Latin, Ganymedes' name was—corrupted into
—Catamitus, which created the English term "catamite" for a boy
"kept for unnatural purposes.")

Apollo, the son of Zeus, is said to have had twenty male
favorites.

One hypothesis (given by B. Z. Goldberg in his *Sex in Religion*) even alleges that homosexuality might have been the effect
of an early stage of worship. The first gods were hermaphrodites

and men and women venerated them together, often doing so by "normal" sexual union. But when, eventually, the original bisexual deity was separated into idols of the opposite sex, men came to worship the gods and women the goddesses. That is how, finally, homosexual "service" at the various sanctuaries became a ritual, with, in either case, the priest or priestess representing the godhead.

Perhaps more likely (and certainly simpler) is the suggestion that homosexual practice at the pagan temples arose out of man's dedication of his highly prized generative power to his god and, once again, offering it to the priest, the god's delegate.

The severe condemnation and extreme punishment of homosexual deviation in the Judeo-Christian tradition, apart from resulting from the impact of the story of Sodom, was based on several factors.

Homosexuality, which belonged so much to the pagan world and worship, was rampant in biblical times. It was not just immoral but idolatrous. It contradicted the pure monotheistic faith and (by the very lewdness it encouraged) threatened its very existence.

More so, as the Bible saw the only justification for (the practice of) sex in the begetting of children, any other use of it was its abuse—a sin and a vice. As the later secular law was based on the conceptions of the ecclesiastical courts which, of course, had adopted the biblical view, it perpetuated and confirmed the condemnation of homosexuality.

There was yet another psychological element. Deviates—as the very term indicates—are always in the minority, exactly because they diverge from the (majority) standard. But in the nature of man (and even the animal) is the dislike of the like for the unlike. Therefore the traditional antagonism toward the homosexual was further strengthened by the suspicions and antipathy of the majority group.

*   *   *

Among the Greeks, so uninhibited in their sex life, homosexuality was not only allowed but highly respected. It went with their adoration of the boyish slim figure, which they made their ideal of beauty. It was part of their culture.

For their prominent and eminent "older men" to have their

cherished youths belonged to the accepted (and expected) way of life. In the view of Greek society, homosexuality could serve the noblest ideal. It inspired young men with a pattern of behavior that would make them worthy members of the community. Of such lovers Plato wrote in his *Symposium* that "they would be the very best governors of their own city, abstaining from all dishonor, and emulating one another in honor." When fighting beside each other, though smallest in number, they would "overcome the world." Their affection would turn even a coward into an inspired hero, equal to the bravest: "love would inspire him."

Horace confessed his passion for Lyciscus, a young man for whom he was "stricken with the heavy dart of love" and who claimed "in tenderness to outdo any woman."

The Romans adopted homosexuality. However, they came to degrade it by making it part of their orgies and debaucheries. The older Curio, a Roman senator, taunted Julius Caesar as "every woman's man and every man's woman." Examples of this type abound. Pleasure mattered to those Romans so much more than procreation. No wonder that a Roman writer attributed hemorrhoids to the excessive practice of (anal) homosexual intercourse.

Not surprisingly, therefore, Christianity again condemned the deviation most harshly, recalling the divine vengeance (allegedly) brought upon the city of Sodom. Homosexuality was against nature and the law of God. It was the result of decadence. In his Epistle to the Romans (1:27), Paul scathingly spoke of those men who "leaving the natural use of the woman, burnt in their lust one toward another, committing shameless acts with men."

However, all opposition did not succeed in eliminating the practice. Even Shakespeare addressed some of his sonnets to a male youth.

*   *   *

A diversity of views still prevails as to what is the origin of homosexuality.

Plato already searched for an explanation and found it in an ancient myth. This he relates (through the mouth of Aristophanes) in the *Symposium.*

It tells how, originally, humans were created in three sets: men, women and hermaphrodites (the two sexes joined in one body). Greatly roused in anger by the early creatures' attempt to ascend into heaven, Zeus punished them by splitting asunder each individual. Ever since, each half continues to search for his (or her) original counterpart. This accounted not only for the love of a man for a woman but explains as well why some men search for other men. Their yearning is therefore not an aberration or vice but a natural wish for reunion of those who belonged to one another from the very beginning.

Since Plato's days ever more opinions have been expressed, particularly so in modern times since the advent of psychoanalysis. Homosexuality may be congenital. It might be caused by the mere lack of opportunity to meet a woman and, starved for sex, man turned to man. Was there, in fact, not the tribal custom among some Australian aborigines to provide young (bachelor) natives who, through circumstances were deprived of getting married, with a boy-wife? Thus they too could gratify their sexual desires.

As in the case of animals, homosexuality could present a stage in the maturing of man which he healthily outgrows. But unfortunate experiences could retard or arrest the sex impulse and keep it permanently fixed at the level of emotional immaturity.

Accidental contacts and environmental conditioning have equally been held responsible for the deviation. Again, it is thought that homosexuality could result out of the malfunction of endocrine glands during the embryonic stage.

Homosexuals are thus either born or made. They might be the product of a combination of psychological and physiological factors. There just is not one simple and definite answer nor a sole cause.

The Legacy of an Island—Lesbianism

"Lesbianism," the most frequent description of female homosexuality, and today used with very little contempt, was first coined as a scurrilous term. It defamed an entire island—Lesbos, situated in the Aegean Sea, in the eastern Mediterranean, ten miles from the coast of Asia Minor. This all came about because of one

woman, Sappho, who lived on the isle of Lesbos in the latter half
of the seventh century B.C. (c. 612 B.C.) and who is reputed to
have loved other females and to have recorded and extolled her
"unnatural" passionate affections in some of the most glorious
poetry, of which only fragments survive.

Not only did (part of) Sappho's literary creations celebrate
this type of love but, at the time, no one was shocked or took
exception to her life and love affairs. On the contrary, she was
renowned and feted as the greatest lyric writer of the ancient
world and was named "the tenth muse." If Homer was "the
poet," she was called "the poetess."

But the outlook of later generations came to taint her memory, to decry her way of life and burn her works as a menace to
morality, so that not much more than a twentieth part of her nine
books of collected poetry remain. In 1900 some additional lines
were discovered on papyri in Egypt.

Sappho was an enlightened woman of great culture. She
attracted to her home females of like kind, mainly her juniors.
They worshiped her and tried to show their affection in many
ways. They gathered in what Sappho called her "house of poets."
There they practiced the arts: the writing of verse, the making of
music and dancing, as well as every type of intellectual pursuit
that enriched the mind.

Oddly enough, she called her young lady friends her *hetaerae*. This term in later years was specifically applied to the educated concubines of upper-class Greek men. In her case, however,
it referred to a mate, an intimate companion. But, no doubt, the
use of this very word was a contributory factor in her later condemnation.

Certainly a bond of fond affection and intimacy soon
grew between her and the female admirers who joined her in
the literary coteries. It remained no secret to the outside
world.

The range of Sappho's poetry was wide. It included hymns
to Aphrodite and the muses, wedding songs and a farewell to her
brother when embarking on a voyage. But interspersed were also
creations of a different kind. They were addressed to or dealt with
youths of her own sex.

One such poem she dedicated to an unnamed girl, another

to a young lady of great beauty who had migrated to Lydia and whom she likened to the moon outshining the stars.

Yet in a third one she speaks of the supreme happiness she had shared with one of her girl friends. Additional passages and contemporary records help to make certain conjectures regarding the close bond of affection that joined them. It is the story of a passionate romance between two women, condemned by later writers as shameful. Sappho's biographers had no difficulty in reconstructing the love affair.

Atthis was one of Sappho's hetaerae. They first met when Atthis was still a schoolgirl, while Sappho was in her late twenties. Later on, looking back on the very beginning of their relationship, she recollected how "I loved you, Atthis, long ago, when . . . you seemed to me an awkward little child."

With the passing of time, their bond grew even stronger and more passionate. Atthis, now a fully grown and mature woman of outstanding beauty, enthralled her "teacher" who did not let her go. They shared a voluptuous time in rustic seclusion away from the big city: "sweet with the beauty with which you made me mad." Eventually, however, Atthis was determined to leave her lover: "Sappho, I swear I will not love you any more."

Back in the city others (and this time men) attracted her. Sappho was beside herself with jealousy. It has been suggested that this was the immediate cause of one of her finest odes. In it she confessed that "if I but see you a little moment, my voice fails me, my tongue is broken, and straightway beneath the flesh impalpable fire runs . . . a tremor seizes me altogether, I am paler than grass, and death itself seems not far off. . . ."

When all her pleading had no effect and she could not move her (former) lover to change her mind, Sappho renewed her entreaties: "Go the way of your own happiness," she wrote, "but remember me, for you know how I loved you, or if you do not remember, let me remind you of what you have forgotten—how fond and beautiful was the life we had together."

And then she recalled how Atthis' perfumed young body used to rest on her bosom, "lying upon a luxurious bed," and how there was no hill, no grove and no stream which they had not visited together.

Her words went unheeded. Another's love had taken Sappho's place and she tragically admitted defeat. Despairingly she wrote: "Darling Atthis, can you then forget all this that happened in the old days?"

The sequence of events may have been different but the actual words survive beyond misunderstanding. They lend themselves to such reconstruction as attempted by Arthur Weigall in his *Sappho of Lesbos—Her Life and Times.*

Actually, few facts are known of Sappho's life and loves. But the very surmises based on those fragments of her work were widely publicized. No wonder that Sapphism became an alternate (and much more appropriate) term for lesbianism, though it has never been known or used extensively.

The Greeks themselves called women who engaged in lesbian practice tribades, literally from *tribein,* reflecting on the "rubbing" together of their bodies and particularly their genitals. It was a form of masturbation, most common in lesbianism. Other less frequent sexual relations include the insertion of an artificial penis or a finger in the vagina, or cunnilingus.

The Hebrew Bible does not mention love between females although, no doubt, it must have existed. However, the rabbis later on denounced it as a pagan practice, and saw it implied in the warning in Leviticus (18:3) against following "the doings of the land of Egypt . . . and the land of Canaan." Moses Maimonides recommended flagellation as a disciplinary punishment for such immoral behavior.

The New Testament specifically refers to lesbianism. When, in his Espistle to the Romans, St. Paul condemned male homosexuality, he also wrote against those women who exchanged natural relations for those that were "against nature" (1:26). They corrupted God's world and engaged in an act of idolatry in which they served "the creature rather than the Creator." It was thus almost inevitable that in the ensuing centuries the Church decried Sappho's writings as heretical and subsequently burned them.

The origins of lesbianism have been as much subject to controversy as those of male homosexuality. As is only to be expected, many of the explanations are identical. Plato's *Symposium* has been quoted with its myth of man's creation in three sets. In lesbianism a woman was searching for her lost half which, in her case, was another woman. To the Greeks, female homosexuality also was a natural and understandable phenomenon. The ancient pagan world certainly did not frown on it.

The Greek philosopher Parmenides (c. 450 B.C.) was the first to suggest a scientific reason. Like its male version, female homosexuality, he said, was something natural and inherent.

Congenital, hereditary and circumstantial conditions as well as glandular imbalance have been cited as the possible causes of the deviation. Lack of opportunity to meet members of the opposite sex, undoubtedly, has also led women to the practice. After all, such relationship was preferable to the frustrations of solitude.

Some women became lesbians, psychoanalysts claimed, because they were possessed by a fear of the penis. This made them shun the male and seek out female (sexual) relations. Freud pointed to the initial bisexuality of the foetus and the fact that rudiments of the opposite sex remain in the adult person. Was not the clitoris a miniature penis?

It is no wonder that Charlotte Wolff in her *Love Between Women* stated that in her research of the phenomenon she had arrived at a "mosaic theory of Lesbianism." There just is not one definite answer. Its origins belong to the spheres of psychiatry, gynecology, endocrinology and embryology . . .

While still in modern times male homosexuality has been the cause of much abhorrence, public outcry and numerous prosecutions, lesbianism, through the ages, has been tolerated and very rarely proscribed by law. Indeed, its very omission in British legislation, it has been claimed, was due to a queen's whim (or ignorance). When an Act of Parliament was about to be passed and duly presented for signature to Queen Victoria, she had been greatly upset that her own sex was suspected of practicing the abominable vice of homosexuality. In protest, she had struck out the passage concerning women. It has never been restored.

Sadism—the Pleasure of Cruelty

Sadism is a comparatively recent term. Yet as a phenomenon it is an age-old aberration: obtaining a perverse sexual delight from the infliction of pain on another person. This may result in a mere penis erection or an actual orgasm.

The modern description of sadism immortalized the "Marquis" de Sade, and provides another example of a name growing into a word. However, the Count was not the first to enjoy the sickness nor did he discover or identify it. He himself became (in)famous because of his indulgence in the abnormality and his vivid portrayal of it in his writings. And that is why a so far unnamed vice was called after him.

The Marquis of Sade, as he is usually referred to, was not his correct title. It was only the way he wished to be known. His full and real name was Count Donatien Alphonse François de Sade.

No doubt, and in no small measure, de Sade was the victim of circumstances. Born in Paris in 1740, he was brought up by an uncle who enrolled him as a boy of fourteen in the French army. He served in it for twelve years, participating in the Seven Years War. Numerous experiences there must have left their indelible mark on the impressionable youth. Early on, he and his peasant valet (older than he) indulged in mutual whippings. In the army itself he was a frequent witness of cruel beatings, soldiers (in punishment for small disciplinary offenses) being forced to run the gauntlet, and rapings and tortures, committed during conquests and occupations.

Before long he himself came to enjoy the most bizarre experiences. But while other men, doing likewise, kept quiet, the Marquis blatantly spoke of his adventures. Stories of his gross misconduct circulated everywhere, and he was accused of heinous crimes and obnoxious behavior.

Among the many allegations made was the notorious case of a prostitute. She claimed that, after making the Marquis' acquaintance, they had retired to his garden pavilion. After undressing, de Sade had cruelly beaten her up and then inflicted on her flesh wounds with a knife. Other prostitutes in turn accused him of having tried to poison them.

De Sade was arrested numerous times, sentenced to long periods of imprisonment and even, once, to death. Able to escape abroad, he eventually returned, to be incarcerated again. Altogether he spent twenty-seven years of his life in jail, for some time even in the Bastille. Finally he was committed to a mental asylum, where he died—seventy-four years old—in 1814.

It was while in prison, to pass away the time, that he embarked on his literary career and there most of his books and plays were written. Among the best-known titles were *Justine, Juliette* (a copy of which he sent to Napoleon!) and, perhaps the most notorious, *Les 120 Journées de Sodome*. Though the latter was written—in the Bastille—as early as 1785, it was published only (from a manuscript discovered in Germany) in 1904.

The chief characters of the book are four prominent persons in public life. They are a count, a bishop (who is his brother), a judge and a tax agent (who, for a fee, has acquired the right to collect all taxes due to the government). There is no doubt that de Sade, by selecting these people, intended to vent his spleen on some personal enemies.

The plot is very simple. This quartet of men joined forces with one aim. Within a period of one hundred and twenty days they want to find out all about every type of sexual deviation. To do so they meet in a remote castle where they are keeping as their "prisoners of pleasure" their wives, mistresses, daughters and maids but also specially chosen attractive boys and girls . . .

Though originally de Sade had planned to give in the book a vivid description of six hundred different perversions, he completed only one-twentieth part of the "investigation." But these thirty "case histories" resulted in a work that, without fear of contradiction, was claimed to be "the most lascivious story invented since the world exists." It was no wonder that this book (like all his works), abounding with abnormal sexual scenes, was banned in many countries.

Prominent among the vices explained and experimented with, were "sadistic" practices. The Marquis, however, merely brought to light and underscored the love of cruelty and of the infliction of pain that has existed in man from ancient days. In fact, in its earliest form it was part of religious ceremonial, the highly erotic cults of fertility in honor of Priapus and Bacchus and orgies of similar nature. They all contained sadistic features, indulged in with hysterical abandon.

Such mystery cults included sacred floggings which resulted in the wildest frenzies of "religious" excitement. Initiates to Bacchus, for instance, were handed over to the priests "like a beast for the slaughter." A cacophony of shrieks, hymns, beating of cymbals and drums was meant not least to drown the victims' cries for help.

Infliction of pain was also a feature in rites of atonement for sin. Those guilty of incest, for example, believed that their crime would be forgiven only if they were duly punished by whippings. Not only incestuous acts but even thoughts were thus expiated and if the offenders could not be apprehended, others had to suffer for them vicariously.

It was the (perverted) pleasure experienced during such rites or punishments—either as victim, executor or spectator—that finally made people seek erotic arousal by sadistic behavior for its own sake, completely divorced from the original reason.

Romans particularly came to delight in spectacles of human agony, and they made no secret of it. They gained immense pleasure from watching others suffer and dying the most grue-some deaths (arranged with every possible "refinement"), as ex-emplified by the gladiatorial "shows." The mob attending them went mad with excitement when they saw men thrown to, and torn up by, wild beasts or forced to fight each other to the death.

Significantly it is also known that this very experience aroused them sexually. Roman prostitutes were well aware of that fact and took due advantage of it. They made it their business to intercept those returning from the gladiatorial fights as their easy prey, ready for their type of entertainment. Brothels were spe-cially opened up in close proximity to the arena, lest time and distance cool down the ardor of the spectators.

A prisoner was sold to a gladiatorial school for the most trivial offense, with his final fate in the arena. Man's lust for cruelty made him devise brutal and horrible tortures. It was no wonder that from those communal feasts (both religious and secular) the hallowed sadistic delight found its way into the lives and bedchambers of the "great."

Caligula punished minor crimes with whippings to death. Whenever he kissed his wife (or a mistress) he is said to have accompanied his caress with the remark that a single word from him would cause her head to roll in the sand. No one excelled Domitian in the enjoyment of cruelty. Early during his reign, he spent one hour daily in catching flies and taking joy in piercing them with pins. Not without personal reason or merely figura-tively, he referred to intercourse as "bed-wrestling." One of his later preoccupations was to lie with his lovers in bed and one by one tear out their pubic hair.

That is how eventually sadism, originally a mere by-product, became an independent source of pleasure, pursued for its own sake and then linked with sex, that most powerful instinct of man.

In his writings Augustine gives a telling example of how a young Christian living in Rome, far removed from any desire to enjoy cruelty, in spite of himself was caught by the fever. For a long time he had avoided the amphitheater with its brutal and murderous displays till one day his friends insisted on his company.

He went but told them that though they may drag his body there, they could not do so with his soul. He was determined to see nothing, to keep both his eyes and mind closed. However, against his will, a fierce scream made him look and "with the sight of the blood he absorbed a lust for cruelty; he could not turn away; his gaze was fixed; he was drunk with the lust for blood."

Through the millennia sadism has never died out. It appeared either blatantly open or in ever-new disguises, justifications and rationalizations. Its path leads from antiquity through the Middle Ages to twentieth-century "civilization."

Legal tortures, witch hunts, the Holy Inquisition, religious flagellations, corporal punishment and Nazi atrocities are just some of its most typical manifestations. There is even a noticeable sadistic strain in modern comic strips and cartoons, including the so revealingly named "horror comics."

* * *

Sadism most probably started as an incidental pastime. Watching a fight, man suddenly discovered that he relished it, not merely for the sake of the combat but for the suffering that went with it. The added element of danger no doubt heightened his pleasure. And then sadism, as shown previously, divorced from its initial sources, grew into an independent phenomenon.

Psychologists have suggested that at its base was man's inborn desire to feel master and to dominate, which extended even to those in love. His instinct of aggression thus entered its field. Love and hatred as human passions are closely linked: "there is a kind of pleasure that is akin to pain."

A case quoted by Freud to support this claim tells of a child who, witnessing sexual intercourse between adults, imagined that they were having a terrible fight, an assault of the man on the woman. Sadism, according to this school of thought, was of a twofold nature. It was an attempt of those living without affection to compensate for their lack of love. It could also be an arrested early stage in the sexual maturing of a person who has never grown up.

At times, indeed, it may seem as if the enjoyment of brutality was innate in man. Sadism has been explained as well as an "atavistic throw-back to primitive savagery." After all, were not man's ancestors omnivorous predatory beasts?

The Lust for Pain—Masochism

Masochism and sadism have often been contrasted and compared. They share several features. An essential element in both is the erotic pleasure derived from the suffering of (physical or mental) pain which might lead to sexual arousal. The sadist relishes watching, or making, others suffer. The masochist delights in himself experiencing torture or cruelty, which may be self-inflicted, caused by others or the effect of impersonal forces and circumstances. Both masochism and sadism, also, though existing for thousands of years, have only been identified comparatively recently with their names. Finally, both are called after men who prominently presented in their writings, and conspicuously practiced in their lives, those very abnormalities.

Leopold von Sacher-Masoch was an Austrian novelist, who was born in 1836 at Lemberg in Galicia where, at the time, his father was chief of police. Masoch, the second part of his (hyphenated) name, was originally his mother's maiden name. He not only adopted but perpetuated it.

With his family, Leopold moved to Prague, where he matriculated at the age of sixteen, two years ahead of the average student. He graduated as a doctor of law and then obtained a position at the Vienna state archives. During the French-Austrian war he (is said to have) served as a cavalry officer, being decorated at the battle of Solferino.

By the age of thirty he was well embarked on his literary career. He possessed a facile pen and wrote many books, plays and tales. The best known among them (and the most notorious) were *The Legacy of Cain* and *Venus in Furs*. However, his sole claim to fame is his vivid portrayal of the excessive enjoyment of suffering pain (being "the anvil") and of the various means by which this perverted gratification could be attained.

"To suffer, to endure cruel torments," he wrote, "seems pleasurable to me, above all if such pain were inflicted by a beautiful woman . . ."

Von Sacher-Masoch left nothing to the imagination. Telling indeed is his description (in *Venus in Furs*) of the perverted yearning of Severin, the male character. When, soon after first meeting Wanda, she asked whether he would like to be her slave, he, the willing victim, agreed. In a serious tone of voice he explained that "love permits no equality between partners. But if I had to choose between dominating or being dominated, I should find it by far the most delightful choice to be the slave of a beautiful woman. . . ." She had to exercise control with the most deliberate tranquility yet implacability.

No doubt, in his books, Leopold echoed the experiences of his own life. No more typical example could be quoted than the odd "draft treaty" he offered to sign for "Wanda," his real lover and which he himself had composed. (Wanda was not her true name. She had specially chosen it, calling herself after the novel's heroine.)

He expected her to accept and tolerate him as her slave on the following conditions: he was to renounce his whole personality unreservedly; he was to have no individuality apart from hers; he was to remain in her hands as a blind instrument to execute all her orders without argument. If ever he forgot that he was her slave and did not obey her in everything without exception, she would have the right to punish and chastise him in any way she liked without his having the right to complain. She was to be allowed to inflict any torture upon him and even if she mutilated him, he had still to endure it without any complaint. "Your honor, your blood, your mind and your energy belong to me and I am mistress of your life and your death . . ."

*　*　*

Much speculation has been given to the question as to what induced Leopold to become the great masochist and how soon this peculiar bent of mind manifested itself in his life. Three different circumstances in his early youth have been cited as significant stepping stones in this evolution: the effect of early reading matter, of a dream and of an incident.

It is said that, as a young child, Leopold was fascinated by the stories of the ancient martyrs and their suffering.

A dream he had during puberty continued to haunt him, and he was convinced that it left its mark on his entire life. In the dream, he was the victim of a cruel woman. Tied up, he knelt in front of her as her slave.

The third factor was an actual experience he had, also as a boy, at the home of his favorite aunt. Visiting her, Leopold became the unsuspected witness of her marital infidelity—and its discovery. While hiding in a closet in his aunt's bedroom, he watched her making love with a strange man and then being caught in the act by her husband who, in his fury, beat her up. This was too much for young Leopold who, in his excitement, gave himself away.

His irate aunt, now wrapped in a fur-lined dressing gown (and probably nothing else), most likely was happy to have found a target on whom to vent her feelings. In turn she gave the little peeping Tom a good hiding. This produced in him a feeling of ecstasy. In fact, it might have been the final impetus for the deviations in his later life and writings.

Sacher-Masoch not only went on seeking such experiences— to be degraded, dominated and humiliated both mentally and physically—but for the rest of his life had a sexual obsession with fur. Frequently, to be especially aroused, he asked his lady loves to wear something with fur.

His first wife must have wondered what kind of husband she had married when, soon after the wedding, he insisted not only that she was to put on a fur-lined dressing gown but to maltreat him dreadfully. Such tortures became a common feature of his life. Equally, he welcomed mental agonies, including those of jealousy.

It is no wonder that Leopold's marriage did not last. He married for the second time and, with his new wife, acquired a large estate. On this he died, of heart failure, in 1895. Eight years previously, France (where twenty-four of his novels had been published) recognized his literary "achievements" and elected him a member of the Legion of Honor. After his death, not just one country but the entire world "immortalized" him by making his name part of the vocabulary of every language. That in English the term "masochism" first appeared (as early as 1893) in a medical work was most fitting.

*   *   *

Self-torture and the enjoyment of suffering have had their significant place in the history of man and, not least, of religion. The self-castration of the priests in the cult of Cybele is perhaps one of the most extreme examples.

Paul wrote in his Epistle to the Romans (5:3–4): ". . . let us also rejoice in our tribulations: knowing that tribulation worketh patience, and patience, probation; and probation, hope." Tertullian, that great African Church Father, challenged Christianity's enemies by telling them that "condemnation gives us more pleasure than acquittal."

Ingeniously, men and women sought out every type of pain which they "suffered" joyously for the glory of God. They inflicted on themselves wounds which they did not allow to heal but aggravated by rubbing salt into them. They donned hair shirts, slept on beds of thorns or did not sleep at all. They enjoyed long "bouts" of thirst, terminated by drinking contaminated water.

Monks withdrew into the burning desert, to mortify their flesh. Individuals tried to outdo one another in their search for ever more harassing methods of self-torture. Christine of St. Troud, for instance, "fastened herself upon a wheel, had herself wracked, and hung on a gallows beside a corpse. Not content with this, she even had herself partly buried in a grave." And in many a case, those men and women were praised for their saintliness and some were canonized.

But most typical was the phenomenon of flagellation. To chastise oneself or to be beaten up by others gave a feeling of bliss. It was already practiced among the Greeks and Romans. However, it reached its climax in medieval times, with veritable orgies of self-flagellations. In the thirteenth century particularly, bands of men scourged themselves in public processions for the sin of the world and did so often to the accompaniment of hymns and psalms. Their example spread like a wildfire all over Europe.

With the secularization of life, masochism did not die out.

New rationalizations took the place of the earlier pious ones. People's "lust for pain" made them welcome hurts. These gave them a feeling of superiority and of being right. They imagined that by their suffering they would gain love.

Even fairy tales include the motif of masochism. Their prototype is the story of Cinderella. Aware of her own goodness, she willingly and patiently suffered humiliations, convinced in her heart that one day she would be recompensed.

Minor degrees of masochism can be found in ordinary sexual relationships. Typical is the "love-bite." The sexual life of natives includes similar erotic elements, particularly the thrill of scratching and biting.

* * *

There are many points of view as to what makes a person become a masochist, always "ready to hold out his cheek when there is a chance of receiving a blow."

Generally it is thought that some early, unfortunate condition is responsible: "A Child Is Being Beaten"—in the words of the very title of one of Freud's papers. An experience of that type created in the young child a feeling of guilt and a sense of inferiority of which the (masochist) adult could never rid himself. In seeking relief he turned masochist, believing that by his suffering and humiliation, he expiated for his sin and restored his self-confidence.

But there is still much uncertainty. Even Freud changed his ideas. At one time he saw in masochism the sadism of the individual turned back on himself. Later on, he abandoned this theory and explained the diversion as a manifestation of a death instinct.

Other hypotheses have proliferated ever since, contradicting and superseding each other in their search for an answer. Among many other things, masochism has thus been seen as a character neurosis, a defect in the sufferer's ego and a specific manner in which a person tried to resolve guilt feelings about his own sadistic tendencies . . .

Psychoanalysts have also claimed that in some women masochism may be the effect of the severe shock they received from realizing that they lacked a penis.

No matter what causes masochism, the end result is the

strange phenomenon and paradox of people enjoying their misery.

Voyeurism—a Spectator Sport

The French term "voyeurism" refers to the enjoyment of "looking on" while others undress or copulate. It is a "delight" that may extend from a mere feeling of excitement to the experience of an actual orgasm attained through masturbation. Its Greek equivalent (but rarely used) description is *scopophilia* (or *scopophilia*), meaning the "love of observation." The voyeur is thus the person who—erotically—enjoys the visual stimuli.

The popular expression of "peeping Tom" goes back to the famous legend of Lady Godiva and (according to an ancient chronicle) the year 1057.

Her husband Leofric, Earl of Mercia and Lord of Coventry, had imposed heavy taxation on his subjects. They could hardly meet the demands of their lordly master and penury threatened them. However, Lady Godiva, a pious woman, sympathized with the impoverished people and repeatedly implored her spouse to ease their burdens.

Possibly merely to stop her nagging and certainly not really meaning it, he promised "tax deductions." However, he stipulated that his wife had to "meet the costs" in an unusual way. She had to ride through the city on a white horse—stark naked!

Unexpectedly she took him by his word and agreed to do so. Leofric had no choice but to stick to the bargain. Not to lose face by becoming the laughingstock of the city by his wife's public display of her naked body, he decreed that, while she was being taken for a ride, all citizens had to stay indoors and to keep the shutters of their windows firmly closed.

All did so except Tom, the city tailor. Unwilling to miss the sight, he "peeped" through a window. Another version blames not Tom but the lady's horse. While passing the tailor's home, it suddenly neighed and caused him, acting on impulse, to "peep" through the window—more to look at the horse than the woman . . . In punishment, he was struck blind (or, as another tradition has it, struck dead).

With some wise modifications, Lady Godiva's ride has been reenacted at intervals of seven or eight years ever since 1678. The "peeping Tom" himself has become a telling description for all those who know how it all began.

Modern voyeurism and present-day peeping Toms are the updated version of ancient fertility cults. To view nudity, sexual organs or actual intercourse was a sacred pursuit in the veneration and (imagined) promotion of nature's vital power. (In fact, even the legend of Coventry is said to be based on a fertility rite once practiced in that city.)

Early Canaanite worship, for instance, had as its significant feature the display of the sexual organs and the naked body. No wonder, therefore, that the Hebrew Bible was deeply concerned lest the Israelites adopt this practice. It vehemently decried it and did its very utmost to eradicate any trace of the pagan tradition.

That is why the Bible specifically demanded that no steps should ever lead up to the altar. Priests at the time wore short skirts and, while ascending a staircase, might easily expose their genitals. To witness such "revelation," however, in the circumstances was regarded not—as we would—as immoral but as idolatrous.

To avoid any possibility of "voyeurism" connected with priests, detailed instructions were given even to those sewing their sacred vestments as to the exact extent of the priestly breeches. These had to cover the naked flesh from the loins to the thighs.

The Bible contains a report on how the sight of a naked body influenced early man. Commentators rightly suspect that, going far beyond mere "observation," an actual sexual attack was implied which only later authorities "covered up" by bowdlerizing the original text.

When Noah, after having for the first time enjoyed the fruit of his vineyard, lay in his tent dead drunk, Ham, one of his three sons, found him "uncovered." The biblical tale suggests that the sight must have aroused him in an odd way.

To share the experience with his two brothers, he rushed out to tell them about it. They, however, refused to see their father in this state. They took a garment and laid it upon both their shoulders and, walking "backward," covered him. How strongly the Bible felt about the entire incident is shown by its repeated statement that "their faces were *backward* and they saw not their father's nakedness" (Gen. 9:23).

This very account has been used by fanatics of modern Apartheid policy as a scriptural basis and justification. When, eventually, Noah sobered up and heard what happened—no doubt through his self-righteous sons—he cursed Ham for his behavior. Forever his descendants should be punished for his lewd deed by being slaves to their brothers! (Gen. 9:25)

And as Ham was regarded as the ancestor of the black race, this chapter and verse has been quoted by Dutch Reformed Church theologians in South Africa as divine authority for and sanction of the supremacy of the white race. That is how even racial discrimination and segregation have their (scriptural) root in sex!

Once again, evolution led from the sacred to the profane, from religious ecstasy to sexual arousal. To view the genital or the naked body ceased to be part of a solemn worship ensuring the fertility of nature and all creatures. Secularized, it became voyeurism.

Apart from this ancient fertility ceremonial there were other sources as well that led to the peculiar phenomenon so innocuously called by the French term which, never translated, just pointed to "looking on" without need of further specification of the particular spectacle observed.

Curiosity is a strong instinct in every normal creature. Not least so is inquisitiveness about the sexual "parts" of the body. Even monkeys are known to be fascinated by the sight of their mother's genitals. Young children like to explore their own body, trying to find out all about it and showing a pride of possession in the "objects" discovered.

Thus voyeurism, too, is the arrested stage of early primitive desire (in both beast and man) to "know," which the adult voyeur has been unable to outgrow.

Psychoanalysts have seen in voyeurism a symptom of emotional immaturity resulting from an early experience in the subject's life. As an infant, the voyeur had witnessed his parents "making love." As it were, watching others "in the act" recalls that first but consciously long-forgotten sight. It is an aftereffect which has become an obsession. Feelings of genital inadequacy as well have been cited as a cause of scoptophilia.

Peeping Toms have been severely strictured throughout the ages, and in many countries voyeurism has become an indictable offense. Nevertheless, variety shows, the cinema and the stage in many of its manifestations (most conspicuous in the striptease) have pandered to those buried but always latent desires of a man to see and watch the naked flesh and its copulation—an heirloom from primitive times and infantile years. After all, such spectator sports are just modern adaptations of age-old ceremonies, provided for the peeping Tom hidden in many a man in need of some extra excitement and stimulus.

A harmless type of voyeurism, indeed, is part of early natural sex play. No doubt, it remains latent in every man. Only if it becomes an obsession which engages the entire erotic interest of a person at the expense of all other sex does a normal curiosity deteriorate into a deviation.

Incest

The very concept of incest is emotionally loaded. It carries a feeling of disgust and loathing. The word itself—from the Latin *incestus*—conveyed the meaning of being "unchaste" and "impure." It reflected the strong barriers man has raised against "inbreeding"—something that was obnoxious and abominable to his mind.

Incest was regarded a serious crime. It caused all types of harm not just to the partners and their offspring but to the entire tribe or country. No wonder that even a mere dream of incestuous intercourse (with a sister) haunted the savage's mind, leaving "a deep and painful memory."

The degrees of relationship that constituted consanguinity varied in different cultures and epochs. Some groups prohibited intercourse solely between mother and son, father and daughter, and brother and sister. Others extended the ban to the union between any member of the rank, caste or group.

The breaking of the taboo was severely punished, often by exile or death. Methods of execution also varied among the different tribes and areas. They included drowning (among the Dyaks), burning (in the laws of Hammurabi) and forcing the guilty parties to take their own lives (in Melanesia).

However strong an aversion against incest exists nowadays and in spite of the facts quoted, it was not an original instinct. To begin with, the very notion of incest was unknown.

No wonder that ancient myths of many cultures tell of incestuous unions among the gods. They can be found in Egyptian lore, the writings of Homer, the Scandinavian Edda and the Vedas. Isis and Osiris thus were not only husband and wife but also brother and sister, just as Yama, according to Hindu tradition the first man, married Yami, his sister. Even Zeus is said to have been Hera's brother.

For brother and sister to marry, particularly among the high and mighty, was in some civilizations not only a custom but a command. Such incest occurred among the Hittites, the Egyptian Pharaohs and Ptolemies, the Peruvian Incas and the followers of Zoroaster.

Mostly it was a matter of expediency and dynastic interests —to maintain the monopoly of the ruling caste. To ensure the retention of the country's rule within their own family it was essential to exclude "outsiders." The Pharaohs were not only permitted to marry their sister (or half-sister) but obliged to do so. (Cleopatra was the direct descendant of six generations of brother-sister marriages.)

At times, however, even genetic considerations—as this concept was understood then—played their part. Rulers imagined that only they possessed the most precious "soul power." This had to be retained at all costs and any admixture with lower and therefore inferior classes would spoil their noble qualities. Consequently they married their own sisters.

Even the Bible, in its early parts, tells without qualms of incestuous unions. After all, the very first men had to marry their sisters. Sarah, Abraham's wife, was also his half-sister, sharing one father.

What then was it that rendered incest so repugnant and caused it to be regarded as an unnatural vice and an abomination?

As in other aspects of life, not one single clear-cut reason but a complex of causes may account for the development of the taboo with its accompanying horror, so astounding in its intensity. Many, and at times contradictory, explanations have been given.

Often twentieth-century concepts have been applied to ancient prejudice. Psychological factors have thus been quoted. Closeness of living, it was said, created within the family circle sexual aversion. The primitive mind, unable to account for it rationally, had sought for a supernatural sanction and arrived at the taboo.

The prohibition of incest has also been explained as a healthy instinct, a dread unconsciously based on genetic forethought. Intuitively primitive man feared that the children of such union might perpetuate or multiply inferior traits or inherited diseases. Inbreeding, it was thought (or merely felt), would lessen the vigor of the tribe.

Though Westermarck rightly doubted that savage people could have had a knowledge of the physiology of reproduction, nevertheless an inbuilt sense could have led them that way. Savages have excellent powers of observation and they might also have witnessed the degeneration of a tribe that practiced inbreeding and, for the sake of their own survival, introduced the taboo. Once husbandry had become part of the community's life, men no doubt noted the deleterious effect of inbreeding among cattle. Soon they must have applied the lesson learned to their own home.

Diametrically opposed to the idea that familiarity bred contempt was the hypothesis that male and female living closely together in "family units," exerted a strong sexual attraction on one another. And if no law (or taboo) existed, why should a man have any compunction to have intercourse with his mother or sister, for instance?

Such incestuous union, however, threatened the very fabric of homelife. It undermined its very foundation, as it caused rivalries (particularly among the women and specifically so between mother and daughter) with their suspicions, jealousies and hostilities. The entire home would break up.

But this was not the end of the matter. Society itself was endangered. Its various stages—the clan, the tribe or the nation —were based on the stability and unity of family life. With its very foundation gone, it would be destroyed as well.

To avoid this, society learned to build up most highly charged psychological barriers: not just a law against incest but a taboo with all its phobias and resultant aversions. And that is how fear of incest became an almost instinctive part of life as well.

Primitive people, like "civilized" nations, saw strength in numbers. The more there were of them, the better it was. Marriage therefore increased the family: not only later on by the addition of offspring but by making "strangers" part of their inner circle. Thus it was only natural and wise to marry "outsiders." This certainly was one of the reasons for the system of exogamy and why incest was frowned upon.

Margaret Mead met this very attitude in her interviews with Arapesh people. They regarded incest not with horror or as a frightful sin but merely as utter stupidity. Those who married close relatives missed an opportunity of increasing "the number of people whom one can love and trust." She relates in her *Sex and Temperament in Three Primitive Societies* how the "old men" of the tribe explained to her that something had to be wrong with a man who married his sister. Did he not want a brother-in-law? By marrying another man's sister and another man marrying his sister, he would acquire two brothers-in-law! However, by marrying his own sister he would have none and "with whom will you hunt, with whom will you garden, whom will you go to visit?"

Marrying "in" created no new bonds. On the contrary, slowly but inevitably it might lead to the dying out of the clan. But marrying "out" forged new links, secured new alliances and —not least—added property. Considerations of "power politics" at that early stage thus also motivated—at least partially—the prejudice against incest.

The horror of incest is therefore not an original instinct. By merging in several themes, factors and attitudes, of genetic, psychological and power motives, it grew with man for millennia. And out of the complex of primitive attitudes evolved twentieth-century marriage regulations with their detailed tabulations of prohibited degrees of consanguinity.

Indecent Exposure

If language has been abused to conceal thought, it can be equally stated that clothes have been (and still are being) designed to rouse passion.

Early man had nothing to hide. He owned no "private parts." To him nudity was no cause for shame. Sex was a natural function like eating and sleeping and therefore to cover its organ would be as absurd as screening one's mouth.

Nudity certainly, among the most primitive tribes, did not foster immorality. Only when misguided missionaries, appalled to see "savages" entirely naked, had forced them to cover their bodies, did they open up their minds to thoughts of "indecency."

Greek athletes practiced in the nude. It was the natural thing to do, as any sort of garment would impede movement. That is why they called their exercise hall a gymnasium (from the Greek *gymnos*—"naked"), a term we still, though now inappropriately, use. Aristophanes relates how a boy getting ready for gymnastics did not oil himself below the navel so that "the first tender down bloomed on his privates like on fresh apples."

There was nothing implicitly indecent in people's nakedness. On the contrary, to the Greeks it conveyed divine beauty and with fully "exposed" statues they adorned their temples, public squares and buildings.

"Proper" indecent exposure for Greeks was not nudity but the display of the erected male organ, as this could leave no doubt as to its owner's state of mind.

The same offense, of course, was committed by anyone who intentionally displayed his glans. Such "stripping of the head" or "peeling one's penis" was decried as lewd, vulgar and immoral. Eventually anything even suggesting an erection was classified as indecent.

Yet it did happen that in some men, with advancing years and merely resulting from physiological causes, the prepuce receded and the glans was denuded. It was not up to the beholder to investigate its cause who quite inevitably, seeing the naked tip of the penis, was either morally shocked or sexually aroused.

Some regarded a bared corona (it is surprising by how many different terms this part of man's anatomy can be described) as an indication of a man's excessive practice of masturbation, sodomy or other decried vices. No wonder that men afflicted by such foreskin retraction—with its "sinister" implications—tried their utmost to remedy their defect. They did so by applying mechanical gadgets, a clasp or a "tie."

This Greek idea that the display of the tip of the penis was obscene also explains why Hellenized Jews practicing in the nude in Greek gymnasia were greatly embarrassed. Having undergone the rite of circumcision, the actual surgical removal of the foreskin, they appeared to the Greek pagan athletes like lewd men. Even if they realized the true (and religious) cause of the Jews' "exposure," their Greek fellow gymnasts used it to ridicule and humiliate them.

No wonder, therefore, that Jewish youths, anxious to continue mixing and exercising with their Greek friends without becoming the butt of their jibes, went back to the surgeon, this time to suffer yet another—remedial—operation that by due stretching of the foreskin re-covered the glans.

*   *   *

That is how "indecent" exposure began—either in the real fact of male erection, or in the imagination of the beholder's eyes. And that is how it ought to have ended. But man's mind never rests, particularly so if it is concerned with sex and the female at that.

What constituted the offense came to differ from age to age. Apart from the display of the actual genitals, it extended from the top (a woman's hair) to the legs. It all depended on where and when it happened.

Man's mind, once so directed, could thus link any and every part of a woman's anatomy with eroticism. Therefore these erogenous zones were never permanent. They have wandered all over the female body, at times suppressing or eliminating some of its features, and at others exaggerating or even artificially extending them whether by the "falsie" in front or the bustle at the back.

However, a woman's body, in spite of all its dimensions and curves, has its limitations. And that is why the taboos on nudity and erogenous zones eventually were forced to return to abandoned places—and fashions repeat themselves.

A woman's nipples, once inspiring thoughts of the beauty of

motherhood, were changed into sexual stimulants. They were not only to be touched and fondled but adorned with fitting jewelry and, like the cheeks, colored with rouge.

The leg so sexually obsessed Victorian society that Victorians felt obliged to cover up even the legs of a table in case seeing them a man's thoughts might go astray. On the other hand, and at the same time, it was regarded respectable and refined by that period to display the bust. It was just a matter of raising or lowering one's sights and sites.

Several reasons have been suggested for this continuous change. First and foremost, the economic law of diminishing returns applies. Constant exposure becomes a commonplace and loses its "shock" value.

But then, and still within the realm of economics, fashion designers became anxious for new trade, and felt the need to change the ideas of what was arousing to man. And the female, only too ready to keep her alluring power, quickly followed suit.

Only last in line comes the opinion that women are fickle and love change and, to serve their wishes, hemlines have to be raised and lowered like a stage curtain. And the more unstable the age, the more frequently this happens.

Thus indecent exposure has traveled a long way: in terms of historical time as much as mere bodily dimensions.

15.

The End of
Sex

Celibacy

C elibacy, by its very nature, would fit in at the end of a book on how sex began. Inevitably it would spell *finis* to sex and this world. And not without reason, therefore, its advocacy was most feasible, at least in the Christian realm, at an era which was believed to be the end of time and the beginning of the world to come. Nevertheless, it is neither indigenously nor typically Christian.

As a word, celibacy is derived from the Latin *caelebs* for "unmarried." However, it goes back to an even earlier, pre-Latin root, describing a state of "living alone." Originally, the term did not imply permanent chastity or virginity but was applied to anyone who, at the time, lived without a spouse. Voluntary and permanent renunciation of marriage was only its later and final connotation.

Celibacy was observed in many parts of the world from earliest days. It was known among primitive tribes and their wizards, shamans, priests and medicine men. Ancient Babylonians, Persians and pre-Columbian American Indians practiced it. It existed among the worshipers of the goddess Isis and of the Mithra cult and, of course, among Indian Buddhists whose monks and nuns became the prototype of Catholic monasticism.

The reasons for celibacy were several.

Savage and primitive tribes exercised it in their battle for survival as a school for self-denial and self-discipline. For them, not least, it was a preparation for warfare. Men who could be trained to resist and subdue their craving for sex, the strongest of human passions, surely would make the best fighters. For the sake of martial prowess thus, first of all, sex was suppressed—at least temporarily.

Its mystic and magic qualities rendered sexual contact perilous, particularly so for those set apart to commune with the spirits. It weakened their powers of receptivity for divine revelation and vision. Therefore abstention from sexual intercourse also became essential in the sphere of worship. It obtained sacral value. All the energy had to be focused on the spiritual task. Sexual relations not only incapacitated but defiled the "holy men."

The initial rule of a Buddhist order of monks decreed that "whoever shall have carnal knowledge of any living thing, down even to an animal, he has fallen into defeat, he is no longer in communion."

The duration of celibacy varied according to circumstances. Some had to stay "alone" permanently. Others were required to practice temporary continence, for instance prior to battle or worship. Southern India's holy milkmen who served as priests at the sacred dairy had to be celibate during the entire term of office.

Even the concept of celibacy differed. Occasionally it was extended to include any kind of contact with a woman. Algonquin Indian medicine men would impair their professional efficacy if their food was cooked by a married woman. St. Basil would abstain from speaking to a female unless compelled to do so. Buddhist monks were not permitted to travel any distance with a woman, stay with her at a secluded site or sleep in her vicinity.

The place of celibacy in the Christian (Western) Church has been a topic of heated controversy. Its advocates claimed that celibacy was divinely ordained, an assertion now held untenable. Nowhere does the Bible contain a law to this effect. Others regarded celibacy an apostolic institution. But here, too, historical evidence points to the contrary. Some of the Apostles themselves (Peter, for instance) are known to have been married. Indeed, many early synods and authorities not only approved of marriage but, if used properly, saw in it a way to salvation for all. Still, according to the Apostolic Constitutions (c. A.D. 400) a priest or bishop who deserted his wife "under pretense of piety" was to be excommunicated. Yet it is also true that from early times many Christian priests stayed celibate or, on the occasion of their ordination, left their wives.

In fact, celibacy in Christianity was one of its spiritual "takeovers."

No doubt one of the principal sources was the Jewish sect of the Essenes (now extinct for almost two thousand years). It exerted a deep influence on the very creation of Christian teaching, as has been confirmed by the finds of the Dead Sea Scrolls. This sect, according to Philo and Josephus, taught abstention from sexual intercourse. Possibly adopting the custom from the Persian magi, their immediate reasons have been variously explained.

The Essenes were not women haters, it was said, but they viewed any contact with them polluting. A woman's menstruation particularly, through the magic of the blood, made her potentially dangerous. As the period of her "uncleanness" was not known, it was best to shun her at all times. Additionally, there was again the ancient belief that sexual intercourse weakened spiritual power.

Next to the influence of the Essenes (merely presumed) was the effect of Manicheism, a combination of Greek Gnosticism and Persian dualism. Its philosophy taught a strict division between body and soul, the flesh and the spirit. All flesh was evil and the realm of the devil. Anyone giving way to it killed the soul. Therefore sex had to be extirpated altogether. Marriage was an inferior state and celibacy offered the only road to salvation.

Another contributing cause for the practice of celibacy among the early Christians was undoubtedly their missionary zeal. They were well aware of the abstinence maintained by pagan priests and the standing it gave them in the community. For the sake of the success of their faith, they had to prove that what heathens could do, they could also do—only better. That is how celibacy, in no small measure, was adopted as well as part of the psychological phenomenon of "imitation by opposition."

A last factor, however, played the most significant role. In the ordinary course of events sex and marriage were necessary for the survival of man. But Jesus' contemporaries believed in the imminence of the kingdom of God and with it in the end of the world. If earthly life was about to cease, the conception of a new generation was futile. Marriage assumed as an institution merely for the sake of procreation had lost its meaning. So, standing on the threshold of eternity, man's only practical attitude was—celibacy.

When eventually the expectation of the coming of the kingdom of God was proved wrong and with it the principal reason for celibacy invalid, this was forgotten and, instead of taking note of the reality of the (changed) situation, an "ad hoc" policy was retained permanently.

Celibacy was now praised as a gift of God. Jesus himself is quoted to have spoken of the men who "made themselves eunuchs for the sake of the Kingdom" (Mat. 19:12). Since the Church prohibits castration, the phrase has been interpreted to refer to the acceptance of the symbolic knife of voluntary chastity. Nevertheless, centuries later, Origen is said to have applied this passage literally by castrating himself!

Paul became the great protagonist for celibacy. He expressed the wish that all Christians would emulate him by staying single. Only "man"—the male—was created in the image of God. Woman was of an inferior nature. That, in fact, was why Eve and not Adam had brought sin into the world. After all, it was she who had asked Adam to eat of the forbidden fruit. But even Paul knew that he could not do away with marriage altogether. It was a concession for those weak in flesh—it was "better to marry than to burn"!

Celibacy became a superior state. Woman, as defined by Tertullian, was "a temple built over a sewer." "Woman! You are the devil's doorway!" he admonished her. "You led astray one whom the devil would not dare attack directly."

A Synod Council at Elvira, Spain (c. A.D. 300), demanded absolute continence from all the clergy under penalty of deposition. "We decree," read its resolution, "that all bishops, priests, deacons, and all clerics engaged in the ministry are forbidden entirely to live with their wives and to beget children." St. Jerome called on all priests "to cut down with the ax of virginity the wood of marriage."

In spite of these edicts and condemnations, it took almost a thousand years for celibacy to become finally adopted in the West. A solemn declaration by the First Lateran Council of 1123 pronounced marriage of the (higher) clergy unlawful and invalid.

Consequently married priests had to discard their wives. Marriage and priesthood were proclaimed incompatible. You could not serve a wife and God at the same time.

The Eastern Orthodox Church never introduced celibacy generally. A married man could be ordained to the priesthood. However, he could not remarry should his wife pass away. Once a bachelor had become a priest, he had to stay celibate. Bishops had to be single or widowed.

*   *   *

Sex is as old as the world and man is the product of sex in more ways than one.

Exploited by many and explored by not a few, it is a basic phenomenon that will never end—unless sex itself dies out. And that, of course, would mean the end of the world.

Index

Aaron, and Song of Songs, 195
Abdul Hamed II, Sultan, his harem, 108
Abimelech, king of Gerar, and Sarah, 127
Abortion, 87–92; social sanction, 87; motives, 88–89; and age of parents, 89; in Bible, 89; of first child, 89; methods in primitive society, 90–91; subconscious reason, 91; condemnation of, 91–92
Abraham: and circumcision, 58, 143, 144; and Hagar, 106; and king of Gerar, 127; his hospitality, 132; and oath, 151; and incest, 228
Abydos, temple, and prostitution, 160
Adam: his rib, 1–2, 64; and immaculate conception, 26–27; misled by Eve, 61; and inferiority of woman, 64; his navel, 85; no mother-in-law, 113; etymology of, 203
Adam and Eve, their nakedness, 37, 38–39
Ade, George, 114
Adultery, 125–32; and betrothal, 70; and Mormon polygyny, 110; etymology, 125; different application for either sex, 125–26; consequences of, 126–27; punishment of, 127, 131–32; interpretation of, 128; extending beyond death, 128; tests, 129–31; and lapdog, 131–32
Aeneid (Virgil), and soul of dying, 10

African natives: and birth control, 93; and polyandry, 111; and divorce, 117, 118; and adultery, 126; and circumcision, 141; and pornography, 197–98
Agger, and vestal virgin, 19–20
Alaska, and polyandry, 111
Albertus Magnus, on mandrake, 75
Albigensian heresy, and buggery, 186
Algonquin Indians, 235
Alphonso II, King, of Naples, and the French, 176
Altamira, 191
Amazons, 64
Ambrose, St., on chastity, 22
Amen, and adultery test, 130
America: and right of first night, 72; and syphilis, 175
American Indians: and bundling, 13; and puberty rites, 55; and female circumcision, 58; and mother-in-law aversion, 114; and circumcision, 141; and separate language of women, 189; and celibacy, 234
Amulets, phallic, 140
Anal coitus: and chastity belt, 24; and pre-Inca pottery, 199; and hemorrhoids, 209
Anatomy: rib, 2; philtrum, 79; navel, 84–87
Anglo-Saxon, and wedlock, 179
Animals: and sniffing, 8; and necking, 13; and hymen, 16; kangaroo and

subincision, 56; their ritual slaughtering, 60; monkey and first midwife, 80; and cesarean birth, 84; and umbilical cord, 87; and invention of condom, 97; tortoise and woman, 107; lapdogs, 131–32; gelding, 152; and the bastard, 186–87; homosexuality among, 205–8; and voyeurism, 226–27

Antagonism, national: and naming of male sheath, 98; and naming of VD, 176; and buggery, 185–86; and Sodom, 204

Anti-Semitism, and circumcision, 147

Antoninus Liberalis, and condom, 96

Apache Indians, and love potion, 79

Apartheid policy, and biblical justification, 226

Aphrodisiacs, 79; and the mandrake, 74–76; bracelet as, 78; jealousy as, 113; semen in, 151; beans as, 184–85

Aphrodite: and Hymen, 15; and Hermaphroditus, 48; her birth, 152; her temple at Corinth, and prostitution, 161; and brothel, 166; hymns to, 211

Apollo: and Hymen, 15; as divine father, 25; and Niobe, 173; and homosexuality, 207

Apostles, and celibacy, 235

Apostolic Constitutions (c. A.D. 400), and priestly marriage, 236

Apostolic Council in Jerusalem (c. A.D. 50), and circumcision of converts, 148

Aquinas, Thomas, on masturbation, 67

Arabs: on queen of Sheba, 51; their circumcision, 58, 143, 148, and aphrodisiacs, 77; and harem, 106–7; and divorce formula, 120; their hospitality, 132

Aramaic, for mandrake, 75

Arapesh, the, and incest, 230

Archaeology: and circumcised body, 141; and syphilitic bones, 175; and graffiti, 190–91; and obscene pottery, 200

Architecture, and fornication, 185

Aristophanes, 209, 231

Aristotle: on shame, 41; on woman's defect, 64; on beans, 184

Arlotta, Queen, and harlot, 162–63

Armor, and genitals, 45

Art: and first man's navel, 85; and castrati, 156–57; and graffiti, 191; pornographic, 191, 196; obscene, in Peru, 199; and voyeurism, 227

Asceticism: and castration, 154; and masochism, 222; and celibacy, 234–38

Asclepius, and Cesarean, 83

Asherah, and phallic worship, 136

Asmodeus, demon, 73

Assyrian code of law: and covering woman's head, 50; on abortion, 91–92; on rape, 124

Assyrians: and penis trophy, 153; and eunuchs, 156

Astarte (goddess): and castration, 153; and Mylitta, 160

Astrology: and syphilis, 174; and pornographic magic, 200

Atatürk, Kemal, bans polygyny, 108

Athens, brothel at, 166

Athletics, and nudity, 231

Atonement, Jewish Day of, high priest on, 70

Aton-Re (god), and masturbation, 67

Atthis, 212–13

Augustine, St.: on pudenda, 41; denouncing phallic worship, 138; on eunuchs, 154; on sadism, 218

Australian aborigines: on conception, 5; and subincision, 55–56; and birth control, 95; and mother-in-law, 114; and adultery, 128; and circumcision, 141; and homosexuality, 206, 210

Austria, and chastity belt, 25

Autobiography (Sanger), 101

Avignon, public brothel at, 168

Auxiliary wives, 105–106

Aztec Indians: code on abortion, 92; and divorce, 118; and phallic worship, 139

Babylonians: and "first night," 33; and concubines, 106; and adultery test, 129; and penis trophy, 153; and eunuch, 155; and brothels, 165; and VD, 170; and homosexuality, 206; and celibacy, 234; see also Hammurabi

Bacchus, and sadism, 216

Bachelors, taxed, 70
Bacon, Francis, on syphilis, 174
Baldur (god), and mistletoe, 11
Bantus, and polyandry, 111
Bar Mitzvah, and puberty rites, 57
Barrenness: and polygyny, 103; and concubines, 106; and divorce, 118; and adultery, 127; and phallic worship, 138
Basil, St., and women, 235
Bastard, etymology of, 186
Baths, public, and brothels, 165, 169
Bavairi, the, and eating, 41
Beans, 184–86
Bed: and bundling, 13; blessing of nuptial, 36; and clothes, 46–47
Bedouins, 30
Bees, and virginity, 30
Bell, Benjamin, 171
Bellifortis, and chastity belt, 24
Bells: church, 34; ship, 34
Benediction, at wedding night, 36
Benjamin, tribe, and rape, 123–24
Berg, Charles, on hair, 51
Betrothal, 21–22, 70
Bettelheim, Bruno, on circumcision, 147
Bible: on creation of woman, 1–2; and duties of sex, 4; and kiss, 8; and rejuvenation by virgin, 18; and virginity proof, 21; and chastity belt, 23; and first sin, 26; "Breeches," 37; on transvestism, 48; and hair, 51; and pubic hair, 51; on blood, 60, 63; and status of woman, 64; on masturbation, 67; and mandrake, 75; and birth stool, 82; on abortion, 89; and birth control, 95; and polygyny, 102; and concubines, 106; on jealousy, 112; on divorce, 119, 120; on rape, 123–24, 124–25; on adultery, 127; adultery test, 129–30; and phallic worship, 135, 136–37; on circumcision, 143, 145; and foreskins as dowry, 149–50; and foreskins as trophy, 149–50; on emission of semen, 150; on swearing by genitals, 151; condemns castration, 154; on prostitution, 159–60; 163; and red-light district, 164; on VD, 170; on gonorrhea, 171; love poem in, 193–95; and homosexuality, 202–205, 208;

and lesbianism, 213; and voyeurism, 225–26; and Apartheid policy, 225–26; and incestuous union, 228; *see also* New Testament
Birth: virgin, 25–26; and midwife, 80–83
Birth control: and virginity, 21; and abortion, 88; reasons for, 93–94; earliest prescription for, 93–94; and superstition, 94; earliest rhythm method, 95; and subincision, 95; and condom, 96–98; modern battle for, 98–101; the term, 101; and polyandry, 111; *see also* Contraception
Birth stool, 82
Bisexuality, 47
Blood: hymeneal, 16; as token of virginity, 21; drinking of, at initiation, 55; menstrual, 59–63; its magic power, 60; and "right of first night," 71; and Tobias nights, 73–74; of circumcision, 147
Boaz (pillar), 137
Boleslaw II, the Bold, king of Poland, and adultery, 131–32
Book of the Dead, Egyptian, 152
Borneo, and myth on midwife, 80
Bracelet, as aphrodisiac, 78
"Brash of Wowing" (Dunbar), 181
Brassiere, 41–45; its French name, 42; its forerunners, 42–43; invention of, 43–44; and the Chinese, 44–45
Brayette. *See* Sex glove
Brazil, and symbol of fig, 38
Breasts: display of, 42, 43, 44; of mother-in-law, 114; and nipples, 232–33
"Breeches Bible," 37
Bridal chamber; blessing of, 35–36
Bride: and devil, 18; separation from groom (on wedding day), 30–31; kissing, 33–34; carrying across threshold, 35, 122; purchase of, 69; price, 69–70
Bridegroom: and "right of first night," 71; his Hebrew name, 143
Bridesmaid, 18
Britain: and circumcision, 146; and licensed brothels, 169
British Columbian Indians, and menstruation, 62
Britons (ancient): and mistletoe, 11; and bees, 30

Brothel, 164–69; and temple, 158; name of, 164–65; in Babylonia, 165; in Roman Empire, 165–68; and public baths, 169; sanctioned by British Parliament, 169; and VD, 170; and "fornication," 185; graffiti in, 191, 192; and sadism, 217
Browne, Sir Thomas, and navel, 85
"Buckeye's Lamentation for Want of more Wives," 109
Buddha, his conception, 25
Buddhism: and hair, 51; and navel, 85; and adultery, 126; and celibacy, 234, 235; and women, 235
Bugger, etymology of, 185–86
Bulgaria, and buggery, 185–86
Bundling, 13–14
Burnaby, Reverend Andrew, on bundling, 14
Buttonhole, origin of, 32

Caesar, Julius: and Cesarean, 83; as homosexual, 209
Calf, golden, and phallic worship, 136
Caligula, Emperor, his sadism, 217
Call girls, 162
Canaanites: and phallic worship, 136; and intermarriage, 151; and prostitution, 159; and voyeurism, 225
Cancer, uterine, and circumcision, 146
Cannibalism: and foetus, 88; and origin of syphilis, 174
Capital punishment, and shedding of blood, 60
Capote, 98
Caribbean area, and midwifery, 82
Carpenter, Edward, his claims on homosexuality, 206–207
Cartoons, and sadism, 218
Casanova, Giovanni Jacopo, and sucking, 9
Castellio, Sebastianus, 195
Castrati, 156–57
Castration, 152–57; and adultery, 128; and circumcision, 142; etymology of, 152; in Greek mythology, 152; and gelding, 152; origins and reasons, 153–54; and warfare, 152–53; and fertility rites, 153–55; and asceticism, 154; and penal code, 155; and eunuch, 155–56; and Church,

156–57; and falsetto voice, 157; of Origen, 237
Castration complex, 157
Catamite, etymology of, 207
Cato: on adultery, 126; on brothel, 168
Celibacy, 234–38; in Christianity, 71, 235–38; the term, 234; practice of, 234; reason for, 235; Jesus on, 237
Cemetery: and find of chastity belt, 25; shells in, 40; love fixation from, 77; and phallic symbol, 139; at Cologne and 11,000 virgins, 27
Cesarean operation, 83–84
Ceylon, and divorce, 118
Chaldea, and divorce, 118
Charles, Prince of Wales, and circumcision, 146
Charles II, King, and condom, 97
Charles VIII, King, of France, and war against Naples, 176
Charm[s]: fig as, 38; love, 76–79; and phallus, 140
Chastity: cult of, 15; ideal of, 18–22; and white bride, 22; and female circumcision, 58; and beans, 184
Chastity belt, 22–25
Chaucer, Geoffrey, 181
Cherokee Indians, and contraception, 94
Chichen Itza, Mexico, and Well of Sacrifice, 18
Child: as purpose of marriage, 71; and oath by genitals, 151
Childbirth: and status of woman, 65; and midwife, 80–83
Chimu civilization, and obscenity, 199, 200
Chinese: and divine fatherhood, 25; and bra, 44–45; and birth control, 94; and umbilical cord, 86; and condom, 96; and divorce, 117; and adultery, 127; and eunuch, 156; and pornographic art, 196; and obscene pottery, 200
Chios, island of, and eunuchs, 156
Chiriguano tribe, and menstruation, 61
Christianity: and kissing under mistletoe, 11; on virginity, 22; on virgin birth, 25–26; and immaculate conception, 26; and unlucky Friday, 30; condemnation of the "flesh," 41; and hair, 50, 51; confirmation in, 57;

on masturbation, 67; and celibacy, 71; and Tobias nights, 74; on abortion, 89; and birth control, 95; and divorce, 120; on phallic worship, 138, 139; and circumcision, 148; and castration, 154, 156; and buggery, 185–86; on homosexuality, 209; and masochism, 222; and celibacy, 235–38

Christine of St. Troud, 222

Christmas, and kissing, 11

Church: calendar and St. Ursula, 27; bells, 34; and castrati, 156–57; Western, and celibacy, 235, 237–38; Eastern Orthodox, and celibacy, 238

Church of Jesus Christ of Latter-day Saints, and polygyny, 108–10

Cigarette smoking, 9

Cinderella, story of, 223

Cinema, and voyeurism, 227

Circe, and mandrake, 74

Circumcision, 141–48; at puberty rites, 54; female, 58–59; practice of, 141; reasons for, 141–48; and castration, 142; and devil, 143; and initiation, 143; as covenant between God and man, 143–44; and Judaism, 143–44; as emblem of subjugation, 144; and sexual enjoyment, 145; and continence, 145; and hygiene, 145; and psychoanalytic interpretations, 146–47; and anti-Semitism, 147; as religious act, 148; and Jesus, 148; and Christianity, 148; its performance, 148–49; and the foreskin, 149–50; and obscenity rites, 197; and indecent exposure, 232

Civilization, and homosexuality, 206–207

Claudius, Emperor, 167

Clement XIV, Pope, outlaws castrati singers, 157

Cleopatra, her descent, 228

Climate, and clothing, 38–39

Clitoris: and sexual excitability, 58; and female circumcision, 58

Clothing, 37–52; the "buttonhole," 32; invention of, 38–39; and shame, 40–41; nightshirt, 46–47; "sexed," 46–48; transvestism, 47–50; and hair, 50–52; and voyeurism, 225; and indecent exposure, 231–33

Cod-piece, 45–46

Coitus: and pregnancy, 5–6; anal, 24, 199, 209; and circumcision, 58; with a menstruating woman, 63; dangers of, 73; and sacred prostitution, 158–62; terms for, 178–79

Coitus interruptus, 67, 95

Coitus obstructus, 94

Cologne, and the 11,000 virgins, 27

Color, as chastity protection, 22

Columbus, Christopher, and 11,000 virgins legend, 27; and spread of syphilis, 175

Conception: through sun, 5; through food, 5; by spirit, 5; and coitus, 5–6; immaculate, 26; and circumcision, 146; *see also* Pregnancy

Concubine: and invention of bra, 44; and marriage, 105–106; and mass rape, 123–24

Condom, 96–98

Confirmation ceremony, and puberty rites, 57

Congress, U.S., and polygamy, 110

Constantinople, harem at, 107

Consummation: its dangers, 35–36; of marriage, time of, 72

Continence: and stored energy, 21; at start of marriage, 74; and circumcision, 145; of clergy, 237–38

Contraception, 92–101; reasons for, 92–93; methods of, 93–95; attitude toward, 95; and condom, 96–98; battle for, 98–101

Copulation: fertilization without, 26; terms for, 178–79; and voyeurism, 224, 226, 227

Corinth, brothel at, 165

Corona, its exposure, 231–32

Coronis, myth, 83

Cos, island of, and exchange of clothes, 48

Council of Nicaea, and castrates in priesthood, 156

Courtesy: pagan salutation, 12; and yawning, 10, 40–41

Courtship, 7–14; kissing, 7–10; necking, 13; bundling, 13–14

Couvade, 81–82

Coventry, England, and voyeurism, 224–25

Cowrie shells, and pudenda, 39–40

Crete (ancient), and fertility goddess, 42

Crikey, etymology of, 182

Cronus myth, 152

Crosby, Alfred W., Jr., and syphilis, 174, 175

Cross, as fertility symbol, 135

Crusaders, and chastity belt, 24

Cunt, etymology of, 181

Curio (Roman senator), 209

Customs: of penis ornament, 5; covering mouth and yawning, 10, 41; kissing under mistletoe, 11; kissing Pope's toe, 12; bundling, 13–14; of flower girl, 18; of bridesmaids, 18; of "white bride," 22; of separation of bridal couple prior to wedding, 30–31; of buttonhole, 32; red carpet, 32–33; kissing the bride, 33–34; tin can tied to wedding car, 34; carrying bride across threshold, 35, 122; of honeymoon, 77; of *couvade*, 81–82; circumcision, 141

Cuzco, Peru, and "Virgins of the Sun," 19

Cybele (goddess): her worship, and castration, 153; and homosexuality, 207; and masochism, 222

Cyprus, temple at, and prostitution, 160

Cyrus, Emperor, and eunuchs, 156

David, King: his rejuvenation, 18; and polygyny, 103; and concubines, 106; and foreskins, 149–50; and Jonathan, 205

De morbo gallico (Fallopio), and condom, 96

Dead Sea Scrolls, and Essenes, 236

Death, and soul, 10

DeBevoise, Charles R., and bra, 43

Defloration: and hymen, 15–16; its perils, 16–17; witnessing, 21; and female circumcision, 58

Delhi, India, and navel of the world, 86

Delos, island of, and eunuchs, 156

Delphi, and navel of the world, 86

Demons: and defloration, 17; on wedding day, 33

Deseret News, on plural marriage, 110

Devil: and virgin, 18; and wedding eve, 34; and wedding night, 35–36;

and fig charm, 38; and creation of navel, 85; and circumcision, 143; and the realm of the "flesh," 236

Dialogues of Courtesans (Lucian), 113

Dinah (daughter of Jacob), her rape, 123

Dionysus: and Hymen, 15; and fertility feasts, 38; and phallus worship, 38, 138

Divorce, 116–21; and priest, 70; and betrothal, 70; and non-virgin, 21; grounds for, 116–18; procedures of, 118–20; Bible on, 119; religion on, 119; and adultery, 125, 128

Doctrine, of immaculate conception, 26–27

Domitian, Emperor, his sadism, 217

Dowry: and bride price, 69–70; of foreskins, 150–51; of genitals, 153

Droit du seigneur, 17, 71–72

Druids: and mistletoe, 11; and virgin, 19

Dunbar, William, 181

Dutch Reformed Church, and Apartheid, 226

Dyak tribe, and incest, 228

Eastern Orthodox Church, and celibacy, 238

Ebers papyrus, on birth control, 93

Ecclesiastes, Book of, and VD, 170

Edda, the, and incest, 228

Eel, as phallic symbol, 139

Egypt (ancient): and divine fatherhood, 25; and evolution of bra, 42; and female circumcision, 58; and masturbation, 65; and early birth control, 93; and phallic worship, 136; and circumcision, 141, 145; and penis trophy, 153; and castration, 155; and VD, 170; and incestuous union, 228

Eichstadt, Konrad Kyeser von, and chastity belt, 24

Ejaculatio praecox, and spilling of salt, 29

Eleusis, and hymen, 15

Eli, high priest, his sons and prostitution, 159

Ellis, Havelock: on hymen, 16; on transvestism, 48

Elvira, Spain, 237

Embrun, and phallic worship at, 138

Embryo, and soul, 89
Engano, island of, and midwifery, 81
English language: and hymen, 17; and God's name, 180; and grammatical gender, 189
Ephesus, virginity test at, 20
Epistle to the Romans: and circumcision, 148; on homosexuality, 209; on Lesbianism, 213; and masochism, 222
Esau (son of Isaac), and kiss, 8
Eskimos: and kiss, 8; and polyandry, 111; and divorce, 116; and adultery, 127; and wife exchange, 133
Essay on the Principle of Population as it Affects the Future Improvement of Society, An (Malthus), 99–100
Essenes, sect of, and celibacy, 236
Etymology of: sex, 1; fascination, 4–5; necking, 13; hymen, 15; hymn, 16; vestal, 19; infibulation, 22; parthenogenesis, 26; Virgin Islands, 27; pudenda, 41; brassiere, 42; transvestism, 47; puberty, 53; menstruation, 59; masturbation, 65; wedding, 70; Issachar, 75; philter, 77; midwife, 80; *couvade,* 81; obstetrician, 83; Cesarean, 83–84; condom, 97–98; polygamy, 102; polyandry, 102; polygyny, 102; harem, 106–107; seraglio, 107; rape, 122; adultery, 125; circumcision, 146–47; semen, 150; testament, 152; testimonial, 152; castration, 152; eunuch, 155; prostitute, 162; harlot, 162; brothel, 164–65; venereal, 170; gonorrhea, 171; syphilis, 173; intercourse, 178; copulation, 179; coitus, 179; wedlock, 179; vulva, 179; phallus, 179–180; penis, 180; fuck, 180–81; cunt, 181; hysteria, 183; orchid, 184; fornication, 185; bugger, 185–86; bastard, 186–87; pornography, 195–96; homosexuality, 202; catamite, 207; sadism, 214–15; masochism, 219; voyeurism, 224; incest, 227; celibacy, 234
Eunuch: and harem, 107–108; sacred, 153; in Gospel, 154; as guard, 155–56; as singer, 156–57
Euphemism: of brassiere, 42; for pubic hair, 51; for menstruation, 59; for erect penis, 137; for genitals in Bible, 151; holy mackerel, 183; crikey, 183; biblical, for sexual intercourse, 203
Euphrates River, and masturbation, 66
Evans-Pritchard, E. E., 197–98
Eve: her creation, 2; her punishment, 61; and navel, 85
Ever Green (Ramsay), 181
Evil eye, the: and penis, 5; at wedding, 35; and "fig," 38; and exchange of clothes, 49
Excrement, as love potion, 79
Exogamy, and gender in language, 188–89

Fairy tales: and kiss, 10; on power of virgin to save, 20; and masochism, 223
Fallacy: on virgin birth, 25; on apple in Paradise, 26; on immaculate conception, 26; on the 11,000 virgins, 27; on climate and clothing, 38–39; regarding menstruation, 63; on effect of masturbation, 67; on mandrake and barrenness, 75; on biblical attitude toward abortion, 89; on Dr. Condom, 97–98; on Malthus and birth control, 99; on twins, 128, 156; on circumcision and initiation, 143; on origin of syphilis, 173; of Jehovah, 180; on homosexuality, 104–105; on David and Jonathan, 205
Fallopio, Gabriello, and condom, 96
Falsies, 44
Family relations, 102–21; polygamy, 102; polygyny, 102–105; polyandry, 110–12; concubinage, 105–106; harems, 106–108; among Mormons, 108–10; and jealousy, 112–13; and mother-in-law, 113–15
Fascination, etymology of, 4–5
Fashion, and nudity, 232–33
Fasting, and puberty, 57
Fellatio, 199
Feminism: and creation of woman, 2; and brassiere, 43; and female circumcision, 58–59
Fertility: of field and coitus, 6; promotion of, and mistletoe, 11; proof of, 15; and virginity, 17, 18–19; spell and buttonhole, 32; and the fig leaf, 38; shielded by clothes, 39–40; and "topless," 42; and menstruation, 56;

246

INDEX

and blood, 60; and adultery, 127; promoted by circumcision, 142
Fertility rites: and phallic procession, 38; and transvestism, 48; and masturbation, 65–66; phallic, 134–40; and foreskin, 149; castration in, 153–54; and graffiti, 191; and homosexuality, 207–208; sadism in, 216; masochism in, 222; and voyeurism, 225, 226
Fetishist, and hair, 52
Fig leaf, use of, 37–39
Fingers, crossing of, 36
Fire, sacred: and virgin, 18–19; and virginity test, 20
First: surgical operation, 1; commandment of Bible, 4; night, right of, 17; sin, 26; night, and kissing the bride, 33–34; "dress," 37–38; menstruation, 57; coitus and circumcision, 58; condom, 96–97; amen, 130; time of name of syphilis, 171; first use of term "sexy," 179
Fishing: and continence, 21; and menstruation, 62
Flagellations, religious: and sadism, 218; and masochism, 222
Flower girl, 18
Folklore, on virgin birth, 25–26; see also Legends
Food: and conception, 5; and origin of kiss, 9; intake in isolation, 41; of pastry-penis, 140
Forbidden fruit, eating of, 26, 135
Foreskin: its disposal, 149; and reincarnation, 149; as dowry, 149; in Bible, 149–50; and indecent exposure, 232
Fornication, etymology of, 185
Four-letter words, 180–83; sacred, 180; obscene, 180–81; their reason, 181–83
Foutin, St., and phallic worship, 138
Fracastoro, Girolamo, and origin of syphilis, 171–73, 176
France: and invention of brassiere, 41–42, 43; and castrati, 157; and brothels, 169; and spread of syphilis, 176
Francesco II, Doge of Venice, and chastity belt, 24–25
Frazer, Sir James: on puberty rites, 54–55; on menstruation, 62; on mother-in-law aversion, 114

French: and the brassiere, 41–42; and couvade, 81; "letter," 98; and fuck, 181; and buggery, 186; of voyeurism, 224
Freud, Sigmund: on mother-in-law, 115; on circumcision, 146–47; and castration complex, 157; on sadism, 218–19; on masochism, 223
Freya (goddess), 30
Friday, its luck and misfortune, 30
Frisians, and castration, 155
Fuck: etymology of, 180–81; in literature, 181
Full of beans (phrase), 184–85

Gama, Vasco da, and spread of syphilis, 176
Gambling, and genitals, 28
Ganges River, and masturbation, 66
Ganymedes, 207
Gelding, of animal, 152
Gender, grammatical, its origin, 187–89
Genetics, and incest, 228–30
Genitals: and gambler's luck, 28; symbolized by hair, 51; and cod-piece, 45–46; and oath, 151
German: and Polterabend, 34; on woman's role, 64; name of God, 180; and fuck, 181; and bastard, 186; and Yiddish, 188
Gerson, A., on origin of menstruation, 61
Gibbons, Dr. Henry, on kiss, 10
Gilgamesh, and VD, 170
Gladiatorial shows, and sadism, 217
Glass, clinking of, 34
Gluck, Christoph Willibald, and castrati, 157
Gnosticism, 236
God: and woman, 1–2; name of, 180
Godiva, Lady, 224–25
Godwin, William, 99
Goldberg, B. Z., 207
Gonorrhea: and condom, 96; and syphilis, 170; etymology of, 171
Goodyear, Charles, and condom, 98
Gospels. See New Testament
Goths, West, and abortion, 91
Graffiti: 190–93; etymology of, 190, 192; religious, 190; purpose of, 191, 192, 193; in brothels, 191, 192; and

fertility rites, 191, 193; among primitive tribes, 192; substitute for real sex, 193

Grammar, its gender, 187–89

Greece (ancient): and virginity test, 20; and sense of shame, 41; and evolution of brassiere, 42; and bedclothes, 46; and androgynous nature of man, 47; and pubic hair, 51; and love potions, 79; and midwives, 82; and navel of the world, 86; and abortion, 89; and origin of condom, 96–97; and status of woman, 107; and divorce, 116; and penis charm, 140; and circumcision, 144; and castration, 153; and eunuchs, 156; and prostitutes, 162, 163; and brothel, 166; and legend on Sipylus, 173; and homosexuality, 207, 208–209; and lesbianism, 213–14; and nudity, 231–32

Greek and: hymen, 15; mistranslation of virgin, 25; for virgin birth, 26; phallus, 38; philter, 77; condom, 98; polygamy, 102; polygyny, 102; polyandry, 111; eunuch, 155; gonorrhea, 171; God's name, 180; uterus, 183; orchid, 184; graffiti, 192; pornography, 195; scopophilia, 224; gymnasium, 231

Green, color: for fertility, 11; for jealousy, 112–13

Grigson, Geoffrey, 191

Groom, separation from bride, 30–31

Group marriage, 105

Gymnasium, etymology of, and nudity, 231, 232

Hagar: and female circumcision, 58; and concubine, 106

Hair: and sex, 50–52; and genitals, 51; pubic, 51; clippings of, 51–52; locket of, 52, 77

Ham, curse of: and nudity, 225–26; and Apartheid policy, 226

Hammurabi, code of: on concubines, 105–106; on divorce, 118; on adultery, 127; adultery test, 129; on incest, 228

Hancock, Thomas, and condom, 98

Hand, kissing of, 12

Harems, 106–108

Harlot, etymology of, 162

Hebrew for: rib, 2; chastity belt, 23; virgin, 25; bride, 31; fig leaf apron, 37; mandrake, 75; circumcision, 143; bridegroom, 143; circumciser, 148; genitals, 151; eunuch, 155; prostitute, 160; and gonorrhea, 171; name of God, 180; womb, 183; intercourse, 203; Adam, 203; Isaac, 203; Sarah, 203

Hebrides, Outer, and bundling, 13

Hector, 25

Hedonism, and circumcision, 145

Helena, Queen, and adultery test, 130

Hellenism, and nudity, 231–32

Hemorrhoids, 209

Henry II, King, and sanctioning of brothels, 169

Henry VIII, King, closes English brothels, 169

Hera (goddess): her jealousy, 78; and Zeus, 228

Hermaphrodite: origin, 2, 209–10; etymology of, 47–48; first gods as, 207–208

Hermaphroditus, 47–48

Hermes: and Hermaphroditus, 48; and cesarean, 83

Herodotus: on circumcision, 145; on penis trophy, 153; on prostitution, 160; on homosexuality, 206

Herrera Museum, Lima, 199–200

Hieroglyphic, for phallus, 141

Hillel (rabbi), on divorce, 119

Himalayan region, and polyandry, 111

Himes, Dr. Norman E., and birth control, 95

Hindus: and cesarean, 83; and divorce, 118; Shiva and VD, 170; and incest, 228

Hippocrates, and VD, 170

Hittites, and incest, 228

Homer: and chastity belt, 24; on incest, 228

Homosexuality, 202–10; and transvestism, 47; in Roman brothels, 166, 169; etymology of, 202; and Bible, 202–205; as abomination, 204–205; David and Jonathan, 205; in animals, 205–206; in primitive society, 206; and civilization, 207–208; and Jesus, 207; in primitive religion, 207–208;

and Judeo-Christian tradition, 208; psychology on, 208; and Greeks, 208–209; and Plato, 209; and Christianity, 209; origin of, 209–10; female. *See* Lesbianism

Honey, as aphrodisiac, 77

Honeymoon, 77

Horace, as homosexual, 209

Hospitality: Abraham's, 132; Arabs', 132; sexual, 132–33

Hot cross buns, and phallic worship, 139

Hottentots, and twins, 156

Hsuan Tsung, Emperor, 44

Hunting: and continence, 21; and menstruation, 62

Hupa Indians, and umbilical cord, 86

Hygiene, and circumcision, 145

Hymen, 15–17; and pregnancy, 5; its name, 15; of animals, 16; purpose, 16; and blood, 16; ritual of defloration, 17; and puberty, 57; and right of first night, 71

Hysterectomy, 183

Hysteria, etymology of, 183

Idolatry: and polygamy, 102; and prostitution, 159; and homosexuality, 208

Iliad, on blood, 60

Illegitimacy: and fertility, 15; and the bastard, 186–87

Illicit relations, 122–33; rape, 122–25; adultery, 125–32; wife-swapping, 132–33

Illustration, of cesarean, 84

Immaculate conception of Mary, doctrine of, 26

Incas: and virgin, 19, 20; and umbilical cord, 86; and incest, 228

Incest, 227–30; in Bible, 115, 228; the term, 227; as crime, 227; in ancient myth and primitive society, 228; reason for taboo, 229–30

Indecent exposure, 231–33

India: and fig, 38; and masturbation, 65; and love charm, 79; and abortion, 91; and phallic worship, 140; and eunuchs, 156

Infanticide, 111

Infibulation, 22

Initiation rites: and hymen, 17; and circumcision, 143; *see also* Puberty rites

Inquisition, Holy, 218

Instinct, and incest taboo, 229

Intercourse: magic of, 5–6; with virgin and VD, 20; during menstruation, 63; with mother-in-law, 115; terms for, 178–79; 203

Intermediate Types Among Primitive Folk (Carpenter), 206–207

Invention of: chastity belt, 22–25; clothes, 38–39; brassiere, 41–45; condom, 96–98

Ireland, and love magic, 77

Isaac: and kiss, 8; and oath, 151; etymology of, 203

Isabella, Queen, 176

Isaiah (prophet): and virgin birth, 25; and pubic hair, 51

Ishtar (goddess), and prostitute, 159

Isis (goddess): and husband's penis, 136; and incest, 228; and celibacy, 234

Islam: and female circumcision, 58; and ritual slaughtering, 60; and navel of the world, 86; and birth control, 95; and harem, 106–108; and divorce, 120; and circumcision, 148; and castration, 154–55

Israelites (ancient): and chastity belt, 23; and sense of shame, 41; and hair, 51; and *coitus interruptus,* 67; and marriage of high priest, 70; and mandrake, 75; and concubinage, 106; and divorce, 119; and rape, 123–24; and phallic worship, 136, 137; and sex cult, 159; and prostitution, 160, 164; and red-light district, 164

Issachar (son of Jacob), 75

Italian: and seraglio, 107; and graffiti, 190

Italy: chastity belt in, 24, 25; and castrati, 157

Iynx, the nymph, 78

Jachin (pillar), 137

Jacob (son of Isaac): and kiss, 8; his two wives, 75; and polygyny, 103; his concubines, 106; and Mormons, 109; his daughter's rape, 123; his dowry, 149; and oath, 151

Jacob, Udney H., and polygamy, 109

Japanese: and kiss, 7; and mistletoe, 11

Jealousy, 112–13; at wedding, 35; of baby, 36; Sarah's 58; and adultery, 129–31

Jericho, and red-light district, 164

Jerome: on eating beans, 184; and celibate priests, 237

Jesus: birth of, 26; and sin, 26; and tonsure, 51; and divorce, 120; circumcised, 148; and homosexuality, 207; and celibacy, 237

Jewelry: and cowrie shell, 40; amulets into, 40; as aphrodisiac, 78; jade, and jealousy, 113; and penis, 140; for nipples, 233

Jews: and circumcision, 141, 143, 144; and Yiddish, 188; and nudity, 232; *see also* Judaism

Job, his illness, 170

Johanna, Queen, of Naples, and brothel, 168

John of Gischala, and transvestism, 49

Jokes, crude, at weddings, 35

Jonathan, and David, 205

Joseph (son of Jacob), his oath, 151

Josephus Flavius (historian): and disguise in warfare, 49; and Essenes, 236

Joyce, James, 181

Judaism: and value of woman, 2; and sex command, 4; and sense of shame, 41; and *sheitel*, 50–51; and Bar Mitzvah, 57; and ritual slaughtering, 60; and meat preparation, 60; and menstruating woman, 62; on masturbation, 66–67; on purpose of marriage, 70; and Day of Atonement, 70; and celibacy, 70; and navel of the world, 86; and birth control, 95; and divorce, 120; and phallic worship, 139; and circumcision, 143–44, 148; and castration, 154; and name of God, 180

Judeo-Christian tradition: on masturbation, 66–67; on homosexuality, 208

Juliette (Sade), 216

Junod, Henri A., 197

Jupiter (god), and mistletoe, 11

Jus primae noctis, 16–17, 71–72

Justine (Sade), 216

Justinian, Emperor, on adultery, 128

Juvenal: on mother-in-law, 113; and divorce, 121; and brothel, 167

Jynx torquilla, 78

Kahun, Egypt, 93

Kangaroo, and subincision, 56

Kiss, 7–12; and animals, 7; and touch, 7; and sense of smell, 8; and rubbing noses, 8; and taste, 8; and primitive man, 8–9; magic of, 10; on mouth of dying, 10; under mistletoe, 11; religious, 11–12; Pope's toe, 12; symbol, 12; nuptial, 34–35; and VD, 171; in Song of Songs, 196

Konkan, India, and transvestism, 49

Koran: and polygyny, 103; and harem, 107; and circumcision, 148

La Rochefoucauld, François de, on jealousy, 112

Laban (father of Leah and Rachel), demand for dowry, 149

Lady Chatterley's Lover (Lawrence), 181

Language: origin of, 182; grammatical gender of, 187–89; *see also* Etymology, Phrases

Lapdogs, 131–32

Lascaux, 191

Lateran Council, First, and priesthood marriage, 238

Latin and: sex, 1; fascination, 4–5; infibulation, 22; and the 11,000 virgins, 27; tonsure, 51; menstruation, 59; masturbation, 65; "right of first night," 71; *couvade,* 81; obstetrician, 83; condom, 98; semen, 150; castration, 152; prostitute, 162; intercourse, 178; copulation, 179; coitus, 179; vulva, 179; God's name, 180; penis, 180; fuck, 180–81; cunt, 181; fornication, 185; incest, 227; celibacy, 234

Lawrence, D. H., 181

Leah (wife of Jacob): and mandrake, 75; and polygyny, 103, 104; dowry for, 149

Legacy of Cain, The (Sacher-Masoch), 220

Legend on: creation of woman, 1–3; rib, 2; kissing Pope's toe, 12; creation of Hymen, 15; origin of chastity belt, 23, 24; 11,000 virgins, 27; in-

vention of brassiere, 44–45; queen of Sheba, 51; Sarah's circumcision, 58; Tobias nights, 72–74; wryneck, 78; cesarean, 83; rape of Sabine women, 122; rape of Lucretia, 123; Abraham's hospitality, 132; deification of phallus, 136; Arlotta and harlot, 162–63; syphilis, 172–73; peeping Tom, 224–25
Legs, and indecent exposure, 233
Leofric, Lord of Coventry, 224
Leprosy, and syphilis, 174
Les 120 Journées de Sodome (Sade), 216
Lesbianism, 210–14; etymology of, 210; in ancient Greece, 210–14; and Sappho, 212–14; and Hebrew Bible, 213; and New Testament, 213; origin of, 213–14; and Plato, 213
Lesbos, isle of, 210–11
Lex Caesarea, 84
Li Chin, and grounds for divorce, 117
Liber (god), and phallic worship, 138
Liberalia, feast of, 138
Life of a South African Tribe, The (Junod), 197
Lima, Peru: and chastity belt, 23; and obscene art, 199–200
Lingam, etymology of, 180
Lips, and kiss, 8–9
Lives of the [first] Twelve Caesars (Suetonius), 84
Locket of hair, 52, 77
Lodestones, 76–77
Lombroso, Cesare, and kiss, 9
Lot, and sodomy, 202–204
Love: and yearning, 1–2; and sense of smell, 8; and sucking, 9; its origin, 210
Love Between Women (Wolff), 214
Love-bite, the, 223
Love charms, 76–78
Love knot, and buttonhole, 32
Love philter, 77–78
Love potions, 78–79; and jade, 113
Lucian (satirist), and jealousy, 113
Luck: touching for, 28; and superstition, 36; and clothes, 49
Lucretia, rape of, 123
Lyciscus, 209

Machu Picchu, Peru, and "Virgins of the Sun," 19

McLennan, D., on rape, 123
Magic: and intercourse, 5–6; and fertility, 6; of kissing, 10; and bridal couple, 31; and buttonhole, 32; and consummation, 35–36; and fig, 38; and clothes, 39–40; 50; and hair, 51–52; and mandrake, 74–76; to fix love, 77; and birth control, 94; and adultery, 127; and penis, 140–41; semen in, 151; of the obscene, 191, 200; of celibacy, 235
Maidenhead, 17; see also Hymen
Maimonides, Moses: and transvestism, 48; on circumcision, 145; on lesbianism, 213
Malabar, and polyandry, 111
Malachi (prophet), on divorce, 120
Malayans: and bride, 30; and female circumcision, 58; and divorce, 118
Malinowski, Bronislaw, 118
Malthus, Reverend Thomas R., 99–100
Malthusianism, 99–100, 101
Man: his supremacy, 2; disguised as woman, 48; his superiority, 64–65; and adultery, 126–27
Mandrake, as aphrodisiac, 74–76
Manicheism, and the evil of the "flesh," 236
Maoris: and kiss, 8; and divorce, 116, 119; and phallus, 140
Marduk (god), and prostitution, 165
Marquesans: and masturbation, 66; and divorce, 116; and graffiti, 192; and homosexuality, 206
Marquesan Sexual Behaviour (Suggs), 192
Marriage, 69–79; trial, 14; and virginity, 15, 21; choice of date, 29–30; kissing bride, 33–34; noise at, 34; and female circumcision, 58; and male circumcision, 59; solemnization of, 69; importance of sex in, 70–71; encouragement of, 70; and right of first night, 71–72; consummation of, 71–74; and sexual quarantine, 72–74; and love fixation, 76–79; and polygyny, 102–105; monogamy, 105; group, 105; and concubinage, 105; as viewed by South American tribes, 116; by Eskimos, 116; indissoluble, 118; plural, 118; by rape,

122, 123; after death, 128; homosexual, 206; incestuous, 227–28,
229

Marriage day, selecting, 29–30

Mars (planet), 174

Mary (mother of Jesus): and virgin
birth, 25; and immaculate conception, 26

Mary Magdalene, her hair, 50

Masochism, 219–24; and sadism, 219;
its name, 219; and Von Sacher-
Masoch, 219–22; its manifestations,
222–23; St. Paul on, 222; its origin,
223

Massachusetts, bundling in, 14

Masturbation, 65–68; and transvestism, 47; and pagan worship, 65–66;
in primitive society, 66; Judeo-Christian attitude, 66–67; biblical condemnation, 67; and birth control,
95; and use of semen, 150

Matriarchy, 64

May, month of, and marriages, 29

Mayas: and umbilical cord, 86; and
mother-in-law, 114; and divorce,
116

Maypole dance, and phallic worship,
139

Mead, Margaret, on incest, 230

Measles, and menstruation, 63

Mecca, navel of the world, 86

Medical History of Contraception
(Himes), 95

Melanesia, and incest, 228

Mémoires (Casanova), 9

Menstruation, 59–63; and subincision,
55–56; and the supernatural, 56–57;
in isolation, 57; euphemism for, 59;
significance of blood, 60–61; its
causes, 61–62; its dangers, 62–63;
superstitions on, 63; and male circumcision, 147; its simulation, 206;
and celibacy, 236

Mesopotamia, and masturbation, 65

Messalina, Empress, and brothel, 167

Metamorphoses (Antoninus Liberalis),
96–97

Mexico: and virgin sacrifice, 18; and
homosexuality, 206

Michal (daughter of King Saul), her
dowry, 149–50

Michelangelo, and navel, 85

Midwives, 81–84; male, 80–83; animals and origin of, 80–81; and Bible, 82; in Greek civilization, 82

Milton, John, on fig tree, 37

Minoan culture, and brassiere, 42

Minos, king of Crete, and first condom,
96–97

Miscarriage, 89

Mistletoe, kissing under, 11

Mithra cult, and celibacy, 234

Mochica civilization: and phallus, 139;
and the obscene, 199–200

Mohammed: and veiling, 107; and castration, 154–55

Mohel (circumciser), 146, 148

Moloch worship, and masturbation,
65, 66

Monasticism, Catholic, and Buddhism,
234

Monk, and tonsure, 51

Monogamy, 105

Montefiore, Reverend Hugh, 207

Moon: and conception, 5; and menstruation, 63

Moriah, Mount, as navel of the world,
86

Mormon Church, and polygyny,
108–10

Moses: and women's offerings, 23; and
phallic worship, 136; in Song of
Songs, 195

Moses and Monotheism (Freud), 146–47

Moslems. *See* Islam

Mother-in-law aversion, 113–15; in
primitive society, 114; causes of,
114–15; rationalization of, 115

Mozart, Wolfgang Amadeus, and castrati, 157

Museum, Herrera, Lima, 199–200;
National, of Anthropology and Archaeology, Lima, 199–200

Mushroom, as phallic symbol, 135

My Fight for Birth Control (Sanger),
100–101

Mylitta (goddess), and prostitution,
160

Myths: origin of sex, 1–3; fathering a
child, 5; the hymen, 15–16; supernatural virginity test, 20; virgin
birth, 25–26; Priapus and his phallus, 38; hermaphrodite, 47–48;
female circumcision, 58; first men-

struation, 61; mandrake, 74; creation of wryneck, 78; on Iynx and love, 78; creation of midwife, 80; creation of navel, 84–85; navels of the world, 85–86; first condom, 96–97; magic phallus, 141; castration, 152; venereal disease, 170; Niobe's transformation, 173; homosexuality, 207, 209–10; and incest, 228

Naples: brothel at, 168; and syphilis, 176
Napoleon I, and Sade, 216
National Museum of Anthropology and Archaeology, Lima, 199–200
Natural History (Pliny): on mistletoe, 11; on menstrual effects, 62; on aphrodisiac, 78
Navel, the, 84–87; mythologies of, 86
Nazirite, and hair, 51
Nazis, and sadism, 218
Necking, 13
New Caledonia, and adultery, 128
New Englanders, and bundling, 13, 14
New Guinea: and engaged girls, 30; and divorce, 118
New Testament: on virgin birth, 25; on marriage, 71; and polygyny, 103; and divorce, 120; on adultery, 128; on Jesus' circumcision, 148; on castration, 154; on homosexuality, 209; on lesbianism, 213; and masochism, 222
New Zealand, and eel, 139
Nicaea, Council of, and castrates, 156
Nightshirts, 46–47
Nile River, and masturbation, 66
Nipples, 232–33
Noah, and nudity, 225–26
Noise, at wedding, 34
Noses, rubbing of, 7, 8
Nudity: and Bible, 37; in bed, 46–47; and Renoir, 200; and indecent exposure, 231
Nufer, Jacob, 84
Numa Pompilus, king of Rome, and cesarean, 84
Nuptial kiss, 34

Oath, on genitals, 151
Obscene, the, 190–201; at weddings, 34–35; and the "fig," 38; and four-

letter words, 180–81; reasons for, 182–83, 197, 198, 199–200; and graffiti, 191–93; and pornography, 193–201; in primitive groups, 197–98
Obstetrician, 83
Oedipus complex, and circumcision, 146–47
Old Testament. *See* Bible
Olympic Games (ancient), and courtesans, 160
Onan: and masturbation, 67; and birth control, 95
Onanism, 67
Orchid, etymology of, 184
Orgasm, 6
Orgiastic rituals: and mistletoe, 11; and transvestism, 48; and drinking of blood, 60; and castration, 153, 222; and sadism, 216
Origen, 237
Origin of: woman, 1–3; kiss, 7–10; yawning and covering mouth, 10, 40–41; healing kiss, 10; kissing under mistletoe, 11; X for kiss, 12; bundling, 13–14; hymn, 16; flower girl, 18; bridesmaid, 18; poltergeist, 18; white bride, 22; chastity belt, 24; naming of Virgin Islands, 27; superstition, 28; touching for luck, 28; spilling of salt superstition, 29; choice of right day, 29–30; Friday superstition, 30; separation taboo of bridal couple, 30–31; buttonhole, 32; red carpet, 32–33; kissing bride, 33–34; tin can and wedding car, 34; church bells, 34; ship bell, 34; clinking of glasses, 34; wedding songs, 34–35; crossing fingers, 36; touching wood, 36; "Breeches Bible," 37; shells on graves, 40; shell ornament, 40; brassiere, 42–43; wigs, 50; *Sheitel*, 51–52; locket of hair, 52; Bar Mitzvah and confirmation, 57; ritual slaughtering, 60; women's inferior status, 64–65; Tobias nights, 72–74; honeymoon, 77; *couvade*, 81–82; cesarean, 83–84; condom, 96–98; green-eyed monster, 112–13; carrying bride across threshold, 35, 122; lapdog, 131–32; statuary, 135; red-light district, 164; syphilis, 173–75;

swearing, 182; "full of beans," 184; gender in language, 187–89; homosexuality, 209–10; peeping Tom, 224–25
Original sin, doctrine of, 26
Orkneys, and graffiti, 191
Osiris (god): his penis, 136; and incest, 228
Othello (Shakespeare), 113
Ottoman Empire, and harem, 107–108
Ovid, on Sipylus, 173
Ozark Indians, and menstruation, 62

Pagan worship: and Friday, 30; and transvestism, 48; and masturbation, 65; and prostitution, 158–61; and syphilis, 172–73; and graffiti, 190; and homosexuality, 207–208; and sadism, 216–17; and masochism, 222
Painted Caves (Grigson), 191
Palm Sunday, and phallic worship, 139
Pan (god), and virginity test, 20
Pantomime, and transvestism, 50
Paradise, and phallic symbol, 135
Paradise Lost (Milton), 37
Parliament, British, Act of: and brothels, 169; and homosexuality, 214
Parmenides, on lesbianism, 214
Parthenogenesis, 26
Pasiphaë, wife of Minos, 96–97
Paul, St.: and woman's hair, 50; and divorce, 120; on circumcision, 148; and homosexuality, 209; on lesbianism, 213; and masochism, 222; and celibacy, 237
Peeping Tom, 224–25
Penis, 134–57; and fascination, 5; and hymen, 16; of Priapus, 17, 38, 137; and sex glove, 45–46; and subincision, 55–56; and abortion, 91; and condom, 96; worship, 134–40; magical potency of, 140–41; its circumcision, 141–48; its foreskin, 149–50; and semen, 150–51; oath by, 151–52; and castration, 152–57; in language, 178–80; and nudity, 231; *see also* Phallus
Perfume, and love, 8
Perfumed Garden, 77
Persia: and midwives, 82; and cesarean, 83; and condom, 98; and se-

raglio, 107; and penis trophy, 153; and eunuchs, 156
Peru, and the obscene, 199, 200, 206
Peruvian Indians, and female circumcision, 58
Peter (Apostle), 235
Petting, 13
Phallus: and fig, 38; symbols of, 135–40; in hieroglyphic, 141; and oath, 151; as war trophy, 153; etymology of, 179–80; *see also* Penis
Phallus worship, 17, 38, 134–35; and Bible, 135, 136–37; in Christianity, 138; in Judaism, 139
Pharaoh, of Egypt: and VD, 170; and incest, 228
Philadelphia, and polygyny, 110
Philippines, and circumcision, 141
Philistines, and foreskins, 150
Philo Judaeus: on circumcision, 145–46; on Essenes, 236
Philters, love, 77–78
Philtrum, 79
Phrases, origin of: let down hair, 52; for menstruation, 59; German on woman's role, 64; the green-eyed monster, 112–13; Holy Mackerel, 182; full of beans, 184; peeping Tom, 224–25
Pindar, on love charm, 78
Pius IX, Pope, and immaculate conception, 26
Plato: and division of sexes, 2–3; on woman's inferiority, 64; on abortion, 89; on homosexuals, 209; on origin of homosexuality, 209–10; and lesbianism, 213–14
Pleasure: sex as, 4–5; and coitus, 5–6
Pliny: on mistletoe, 11; on effects of menstruation, 62; on bracelet aphrodisiac, 78; on cesarean, 83; on orchid, 184
Plural marriages, 108–10
Plutarch: on vestal virgins, 19–20; on May marriages, 29; on Spartan marriage, 103; on divorce, 117
Politics: and beans, 184; and pornography, 200
Polterabend, 34
Poltergeist, 18
Polyandry, 102, 110–12
Polygamy, 102

Polygyny, 103–105; among Mormons, 108–10
Polynesia: and phallic symbol, 139; and graffiti, 192
Pompeii: and venereal disease, 170; and graffiti, 191–92
Pope, kissing his toe, 12
Pornography, 193–201; and brassiere, 44–45; and graffiti, 191–93; and Bible, 193–95; meaning of, 195–96; in earliest times, 197–201; and the obscene, 196–201; and African native groups, 197–98; and pre-Inca pottery, 199–200; and politics, 200
Position of Women in Primitive Societies, The (Evans-Pritchard), 197–98
Pottery, obscene, 199–200
Pox. See Venereal disease
Pregnancy: and coitus, 5–6; unwanted, 21; and women's status, 64–65; and couvade, 81–82
Prepuce. See Foreskin
Priapus: his penis, 17, 38; 137; and sadism, 216
Priests, Christian: and tonsure, 51; and marriage, 70–71, 236–38; and castration, 156
Priests, pagan, and virgin's hymen, 17
Primitive man: and sex, 4; view on intercourse, 5–6; and kiss, 9; and bundling, 13–14; and continence, 21; his fears, 41; and puberty rites, 53–57; and marriage, 59; and blood, 60; and abortion, 88–90; and birth control, 92–93; and polygyny, 103; and mother-in-law, 114–15; and semen, 150; and graffiti, 191; and pornography, 197–98; and incest, 227–28; and nudity, 231; and celibacy, 234–35
Prostitute: and priestly marriage, 70; and contraception, 93; and jealousy, 113; her abode, 159, 164–69; her names, 162–63; her trade methods, 163; Rahab, 164; her diseases in Bible, 170; and syphilis and VD, 170–77; and pornography, 195–96; male, 207
Prostitution, 158–77; prenuptial, 33; religious, 71, 158–62, 207; male, 158, 161, 207; and idolatry, 159; and Hebrews, 159–60; payment for,

160–61; its terminology, 162–63; methods of approach, 163; and red-light district, 164; and brothel, 164–69
Protestantism, and birth control, 95
Proxy, defloration by, 17
Prussian army, and circumcision, 146
Psychical effects, and puberty, 18
Psychoanalysis on: kissing, 9; smoking, 9; spilling of salt, 29; hair, 51; subincision, 55; female circumcision, 58–59; subconscious reasons for abortion, 91; male circumcision, 146–47; homosexuality, 210; lesbianism, 214; sadism, 218–19; masochism, 223; voyeurism, 226
Psychology: of superstition, 28; on right of first night, 72; and adultery test, 130; and shape of bean, 185; and condemnation of homosexual, 208; on sadism, 218
Ptolemies, and incest, 228
Puberty: and sexual energy, 18; and poltergeist, 18; and piercing hymen, 17; and bride, 31
Puberty rites, 53–56; and male circumcision, 54; and confirmation, 57; and female circumcision, 58–59; and menstruation, 61; and masturbation, 66
Pubic hair, 51
Pudenda: as life, 39; etymology of, 41; its vulgarism, 181
Punishment: of loss of chastity, 19–20, 22; capital, 60; of masturbation, 67; for staying unmarried, 70; of abortion, 91; of rape, 123–25; of adultery, 126, 127–28; of phallus worshipers, 138; by castration, 155; syphilis as, 172–74; biblical, of homosexuality, 205; differentiation of sexes as, 210; of lesbianism, 213; of incest, 217, 227–28
Puritans, and phallic worship, 139
Purpose of: sex, 3–5; male, 4; sex pleasure, 4; coitus, 5–6; hymen, 16–17; continence, 21; superstition, 28; separation of bridal couple, 30–31; songs and jokes at wedding, 34–35; brassiere, 42; bloodless death penalty, 60
Pythagoras, on beans, 184

Quetzalcoatl, the plumed penis, 139

Rabbis: on creation of woman, 2; and kissing of hand, 12; and chastity belt, 23; on masturbation, 67; on divorce, 119, 120; on circumcision, 144, 145; on Song of Songs, 195; on lesbianism, 213
Rachel (daughter of Laban): and mandrake, 75; and polygyny, 103–104; dowry for, 149
Racial discrimination, and the Bible, 226
Rahab, and red-light district, 164
Rape, 122–25; and kissing the bride, 33; and marriage, 122–23; biblical episodes, 123–24; mass, 123–24; punished by castration, 155
Rashi, on chastity belt, 23
Rationalization: of virginity value, 21; of mother-in-law aversion, 115
Red carpet, 32–33
Red-light district, 164
Reformation, and brothels, 169
Rehoboam (son of King Solomon): and concubines, 106; on Solomon's sexual prowess, 137
Relic, of prepuce, 148
Religion: and kiss, 11–12, 33–34; its hymn, 16; and piercing hymen, 17; and virgin birth, 25–26; and blessing the couple, 35–36; on menstruation, 61; and circumcision, 148; and prostitution, 158–61; and God's name, 180; and buggery, 186; and graffiti, 190
Renoir, Pierre Auguste, on his nudes, 200
Resurrection, and foreskin, 149
Reuben (son of Jacob), and mandrake, 75
Rhinoceros, and aphrodisiac, 79
Rhythm method, 95
Rib, and woman, 1–2
Ricord, Philippe, 171
Right of the first night, 17, 71–72
Roman Catholic Church: and immaculate conception, 26; and 11,000 virgins, 27; and birth control, 95
Romans: and virgin, 18, 19; and months of May, 29; and women's restricted rights, 64; and bachelors,

70; and love potions, 79; and cesarean, 84; and divorce, 120–21; and rape, 122, 123; and adultery, 128; and penis charm, 140; and use of semen, 151; on first castration, 155; and eunuchs, 156; and brothels, 166–67; and venereal disease, 170; and homosexuality, 209; and sadism, 217
Romulus, on divorce, 117
Rumanian, for mother-in-law, 114
Rustan, 83
Ruth, the Moabite, on mother-in-law, 115

Sabine women, rape of, 122
Sacher-Masoch, Leopold von, 219–22
Sacred prostitution, 158–62
Sacred Well of Sacrifice, Mexico, 18
Sacrifice: of virgins, 18–20; of semen, 150
Sade, "Marquis" de, 215–16
Sadism, 214–19; etymology of, 215; and Sade, 215–16; and fertility cults, 216; and floggings, 216; religious, 216–17; Roman, 217; manifestations in history, 218; its cause, 218–19
Salt, spilling of: and sex, 29; on meat, 60
Samson, and hair, 50
Sanger, Margaret, and birth control, 100–101
Sanskrit: and hymen, 15; and castration, 152; and Venus, 170; and phallus, 179; and lingam, 180
Santa Rosa, her chastity belt, 23
Sapphism, etymology of, 213
Sappho, and lesbianism, 211–13
Sappho of Lesbos—Her Life and Times (Weigall), 213
Sarah (wife of Abraham): and female circumcision, 58; and king of Gerar, 127; and Pharaoh, 170; and etymology of Isaac, 203; and incest, 228
Sarah, and book of Tobit, and Tobias nights, 73
Satires (Juvenal), 167
Saturn (god), and mistletoe, 11
Saturn (planet), and syphilis, 174

Saturnalia, and Christmas, 11
Saul, King, and foreskins, 149–50
Scannel, Vernon, 193
Scipio Africanus, and cesarean, 83–84
Scopophilia (scoptophilia), 224, 227
Scrotum, 150
Semen: and virgin birth, 26; and salt symbol, 29; stopped by magic, 36; fed to gods, 66; its purpose, 67; its use, 150–51
Semiramis, and castration, 155
Seneca, on purchase of prostitute, 167
Septuagint: and virgin birth, 25; and gonorrhea, 171
Seraglio, Constantinople, 107–108
Serpent, as fertility symbol, 135
Seth, 136
Sex: etymology of, 1; its origin, 1–5, 209–10; purpose of, 3–4, 67; as pleasure, 7, 44; appeal of scent, 8; and courting, 7–27; and mistletoe, 11; its dangers, 14; premarital, 14; superstitions, 28–36; of unborn child, 36; and clothing, 37–52; and fig, 38; God-given, 39; protection by shell, 40; and shame, 40–41; stimulation by brassiere, 44–45; differentiation by clothing, 46–47; glove, 45–46; camouflage of, 49; and hair, 50–51; and puberty rites, 53–68; in marriage, 70–71; and potions, 76–79; as hospitality, 132–33; in language, 187–89
Sex and Temperament in Three Primitive Societies (Mead), 230
Sex crimes, 122–25
Sex glove, and condom, 96
Sex in Religion (Goldberg), 207
Sex organs, obscene words for, 180–83; see also Penis and Phallus
Sextus, 123
Sexual Life of Savages in North-western Melanesia, The (Malinowski), 118
"Sexy," first appearance, 179
Shakespeare, William: and green-eyed monster, 113; and homosexuality, 209
Shame: idea of, and nakedness, 37, 39; sense of, 40–41; and indecent exposure, 231
Shammai (rabbi), on divorce, 119
Shawcross, Lord, 161–62

Sheath, male. See Condom
Sheba, queen of, and pubic hair, 51
Shechem, and rape of Dinah, 123
Sheitel, 50–51
Shell, and fertility, 39–40
Shiva (deity): and masturbation, 66; and venereal disease, 170; and lingam, 180
Sin, original, and immaculate conception, 26
Sistine Chapel, and navel, 85; and castrati, 157
Slavery: in American South and right of first night, 72; and harem, 108; and captured women, 123; and castration, 152; and brothels, 166; and curse of Ham, 226
Smelling, and kiss, 8
Smith, John, 37
Smith, Joseph, and polygyny, 109, 110
Smoking, 9
Snake, and menstruation, 61; see also Serpent
Socrates, and midwifery, 82
Sodom, and homosexuality, 202–203
Sodomy, 202–204; etymology of, 203; see also Homosexuality
Solomon, King: and queen of Sheba, 51; and polygyny, 103; and concubines, 106; his Temple and phalli, 136–37; and Song of Songs, 194–95
Solon, and state-licensed brothel, 166
Song of Songs: on jealousy, 112; as love poem, 193–94; its interpretation, 194–95
Soprano, male, 157
Sorcery, and penis, 5, 140–41
Soul: and kiss, 10; and spittle, 40; and blood, 60–61; and embryo, 89
South Africa, and Apartheid policy, 226
South American natives: and polyandry, 111; and marriage bond, 116; and syphilitic bones, 175
Space travel, and syphilis, 175
Spartans, and the unmarried, 70
Spencer, Herbert: on kiss, 8; on rape, 123
Spinoza, Baruch, on circumcision, 144
Spirits, evil: and spittle, 40; and yawning, 40–41
Spittle, as soul essence, 40

Statuary, and phallic worship, 135
Stews, term for brothel, 169
Stirrup vessels, and the obscene, 199–200
Strabo, on prostitution, 161
Striptease, and voyeurism, 227
Strophium, 43
Subincision, 55–56; and birth control, 95
Sucking, pleasure of, 9
Suetonius Tranquillus, 84
Suffering, and masochism, 223
Suggs, Robert, 192
Sun: conception by, 5; Virgins of the, 19
Supernatural: and bundling, 13–14; and virginity test, 20
Superstition of: kissing under mistletoe, 11; hymeneal blood, 16; virgin's power to rejuvenate, 18; venereal disease cure, 20; touching for luck, 28; spilling of salt, 29; bees, 29; right day for wedding, 29–30; May and marriage, 29; Friday, 30; separation of bridal couple, 30–31; buttonhole, 32; red carpet, 32–33; kissing bride, 33–34; tin can, 34; *Polterabend*, 34; wedding songs, 34–35; carrying bride across threshold, 35, 122; priestly blessing at wedding, 35–36; the baby, 36; crossing fingers, 36; touching wood, 36; sex of foetus, 36; nakedness, 41; on menstruation, 63; its origin, 76; and love potions, 76–79; and abortion, 88; and birth control, 94; of jade, 113; foreskin, 149; on demi-castration and twins, 156; and the obscene, 200
Supreme Court, U.S., and multiple marriage, 110
Surgery: and creation of woman, 1; to remove circumcision, 144
Swahili tribe, and umbilical cord, 86
Swearing, 185–86
Swear words, origin of, 181–82
Symbolism of: kiss, 12; fig, 38; tonsure, 51; tortoise, 107; tree, 135; cross, 135; phallus, 135–36; sexual, in King Solomon's Temple, 136–37; of eel, 139; of fish, 190
Sympathetic magic: sowing and coitus, 6; and winter solstice, 11; and stopping flow of semen, 36; and umbilical cord, 87; and contraception, 92
Symposium (Plato), 209–10, 213
Syphilis, 170–77; and menstruation, 63; and condom, 96; and gonorrhea, 171; its name, 171, 172, 173, 176; legend of origin, 173; theories on cause of, 174–75; suggested cure, 175; its spread, 175
Syphilis sive Morbus Gallicus (Fracastoro), 171–73

Tabernacles, feast of, and phallic worship, 139
Talmud, on chastity belt, 23; on birth control, 93; on divorce, 120; on adultery test, 130
Taoism, and hair, 51
Taste, sense of, and kiss, 8
Taxation: on bachelors, 70; on prostitution, 166
Temple, King Solomon's, and phallic symbols, 136–37
Temples, pagan: and virgin, 19; and prostitution, 71, 158–62, 207
Tertullian: on abortion, 89; and masochism, 222; on woman's inferior status, 228
Testament, etymology of, 152
Testicles: and oath, 151; and testimonial, 152; and birth of twins, 156; and orchid, 184; and bean, 185
Testimonials, 152
Tests: virginity, 20; bravery, 54–55, 143; adultery, 129–31
Tetragrammaton, 180
Teutons, and umbilical cord, 86–87
Threshold: its sanctity, 35; carrying bride across, 35, 122
Tiberius, Emperor, and venereal disease, 170
Tierra del Fuego, and kiss, 9
Tin can, at wedding, 34
Tobacco, 9
Tobias, son of Tobit, 73
Tobias nights, 72–74
Tobit, book of, 74
Todas, and polyandry, 111
Toltecs, and phallic worship, 139
Tonsure, origin of, 51
Topless fashion, 42, 44
Torres Strait natives, and adultery, 127

Touching: and kiss, 7; for luck, 28
"Touch wood," 36
Tractatus Theologico-Politicus (Spinoza),
    144
Transvestism, 47–50; biblical condem-
    nation of, 48; cause of, 49; and pan-
    tomime, 50; and pagan worship,
    153–54; and homosexuality, 206
Tree: as fertility symbol, 38; and phal-
    lic worship, 135
Treponematosis, 174
Trial marriage, 14
Tribades, 213
Trobriand islanders: on pregnancy, 5;
    and divorce, 118
Troilus, 25
Turkey: and harem, 107–108; steam
    baths and stews, 169
Twins: and adultery, 128; and demi-
    castration, 156

Uganda, natives, and menstruation, 62
Ugaritic, for mandrake, 75
Ulithian myth, on phallus, 141
Umbilical cord: its representation, 86;
    its severance, 86; its removal and
    use, 86–87
Ungava Eskimos, and divorce, 116
Uranus, castration of, 152
Urethra, and subincision, 55
Ursula, St., and virgins, 27
Uterine hyperemia, and menstruation,
    61
Uterus: cancer of, and circumcision,
    146; and hysteria, 183; and compas-
    sion, 183
Uthman, Caliph, and castration,
    154–55

Vagina: and hymen, 15; and chastity
    belt, 24; envy and subincision, 55;
    and man, 58
Vedas, on incest, 228
Veil: to cover head, 50; after menstrua-
    tion, 62; among Arabs, 107
Venereal disease, 170–77; cure by vir-
    gin, 20; and condom, 96, 97; and
    brothel, 169; biblical references to,
    170, 171; the term, 170; gonorrhea,
    171; syphilis, 171–77
Venice: Ducal Palace and chastity belt,
    24–25; brothel in, 169

Venus: girdle of, 24; and prostitution,
    160; and venereal disease, 170
Venus in Furs (Sacher-Masoch), 220
Vesta (goddess of virginity), 19; and
    the threshold, 35
Victoria, Queen, and lesbianism, 214
Virgil, and soul of dying, 10
Virgin: her hymen, 15, 16; defloration
    prior to marriage, 16–17; her value,
    18; and ideal of chastity, 18–22; sac-
    rifice, 18–20; and cure of venereal
    disease, 20; her supernatural power,
    21; and chastity belt, 22–25; birth,
    25–26; and bees, 29; and high priest,
    70; if raped, 124–25
Virgin Islands, naming of, 27
Virginity, 14–27; and bundling, 13;
    paradox of, 14–15; proof of, 15, 21–
    22; its dangers, 16–17; supernatural
    test of, 20; and primitive man, 21;
    and white bride, 22; and immaculate
    conception, 26; test, 29; and thresh-
    old, 35; its sanctity, 71; and right of
    first night, 71–72
Voyeurism, 224–27; etymology of,
    224; and peeping Tom, 224–25; and
    Bible, 225–26; and Apartheid, 226;
    and fertility worship, 226; among
    animals, 226; its cause, 226–27
Vulgate, and Tobias nights, 74
Vulva, etymology of, 179

Walking Wounded (Scannel), 193
Warfare: and continence, 21; and
    transvestism, 48; and menstruation,
    62; and polygyny, 103; and rape,
    123; and circumcision, 144; and
    foreskin trophies, 149–50; and cas-
    tration, 152–53; and harlots, 162;
    and origin of syphilis, 174; and
    spread of syphilis, 175–76; and ori-
    gin of grammatical gender, 188; and
    celibacy, 235
Wars of the Jews, The (Josephus), 49
Water, and adultery test, 129
Wedding: and flower girl, 18; and
    bridesmaid, 18; and white bride, 22;
    selecting day, 29–30; separation of
    bride and groom, 30; and button-
    hole, 32; and red carpet, 32–33; and
    kissing bride, 33–34; noise factor at,
    34; songs at, 34–35; jokes at, 35;

threshold obsession, 35; and blessing of bridal chamber, 35–36; and exchange of clothes, 48

Weigall, Arthur, his reconstruction of Sappho's life, 213

Weighing, of baby, and superstition, 37

Welsh, and castration, 155

Westermarck, Edward, on temple prostitution, 161; on incest, 229

White bride, 22

Wife-Swapping, 132–33

Wigs, original reason, 50; and chastity, 50–51

Wilde, Oscar, on marriage bond, 121

Witchcraft: and penis, 5, 39, 140; and flow of semen, 35–36; and dress, 39

Wolff, Charlotte, 214

Woman: her creation, 1–3; and transvestism, 48; her hair, 50–51; and puberty rites, 56–57; circumcision of, 57–59; as property, 64; degradation of, 64–65; and harem, 106–108; and adultery, 125; and man's circumcision, 147; her separate language, 187–89; and lesbianism, 210–14; shunned, 235

Wood, touching, 36

"Wooden Phallus of Ifaluk, The," 141

Woodruff, Wilford, 110

Wounds: kissing, 10; and brassiere, 44–45

Wryneck, as love charm, 78

X, for kiss, 12

Xenophon: on eunuchs, 156; on prostitution, 160

Yahveh, 180

Yawning, 10, 40–41

Yiddish: for wig, 50; its origin, 188

York Missal, on nuptial kiss, 34

Zeus: and creation of sexes, 2–3, 210; and Io, 78; and navel of world, 86; and Niobe's transformation, 173; his name, 180; and homosexuality, 207; and incest, 228

Zohar, on masturbation, 67

Zoroastrianism: and cesarean, 83; and incest, 228

Zulus: and transvestism, 49; and women's separate language, 189

Zuñis: on navel, 85–86; and umbilical cord, 86; and homosexuality, 206